developing
MANAGERS *as* PRACTITIONER RESEARCHERS

a WORK-APPLIED LEARNING APPROACH

WAL PUBLICATIONS

SELVA ABRAHAM

© WAL Publications Pty Ltd
First edition published 2025

Except as provided by the Copyright Act 1968, no part of this publication may be reproduced, stored or transmitted in any form, or by any means, without prior permission in writing from the publisher.

Enquiries concerning these terms should be addressed to WAL Publications.

WAL Publications Pty Ltd
12-14 Unley Road, Unley SA 5061
gcwal@gcwal.com.au

 A catalogue record for this book is available from the National Library of Australia

National Library of Australia Cataloguing-in-Publication entry:

Editor:	Abraham, Selva, 1945-
Title:	Developing Managers As Practitioner Researchers
	A Work-Applied Learning Approach
	Selva Abraham
ISBN:	978-0-9873721-5-4

Design and formatting by Barbara Velasco (Papel Papel)
Printed and bound by Lightning Source

CONTENTS

Forewords	VII
About the Editor	XIII
About the Contributors	XV
Acknowledgements	XVII
Preface	XIX

Chapter 1 – A Conceptual Framework For Work-Applied Learning (WAL) For Developing Managers As Practitioner Researchers   **1**

Abstract	2
Introduction	2
The WAL Model	5
Key Concepts of WAL	8
Conceptual Framework for The WAL Model	13
The WAL Paradigm	13
Theories of Knowing and Learning	14
Conclusion	21
Note	23

Chapter 2 – Work-Applied Learning (WAL) Model   **25**

The WAL Concept	25
The Extension of WBL to WAL	25
The Fused Action Research Method and Action Learning and Reflective Practice Processes	32
The Cyclical Creative Thinking and Learning Process	38
WAL Change Process and Practice	42
Planning by the AR Group	44
Acting During Work-Based Learning (WBL) Phases	46
Joint Observation and Reflection	48
Evaluation	48
Validation	48
Flow Chart of a Typical WAL Change Programme	50
Chapter Summary	53

Chapter 3 – Designing WAL Research Plans 55

Designing The WAL Research Plan	55
Stage 1 - Conceptual Stage	59
Phase 1.1	59
Phase 1.2	61
Phase 1.3	84
Stage 2 - Action Research Method Stage	96
Phase 2.1	97
Phase 2.2	112

Chapter 4 – Designing a Research Plan for an Occupational Health and Safety Management System in Trinidad and Tobago 125

Introduction	125
Purpose of the Study	125
Research Questions	126
Research Design	127
Conceptual Stage	128
AR Method Stage	154
Validity and Reliability	180
Ethical Consideration	181
Justification of the Use of Action Research	184
Chapter Summary	187

Chapter 5 – Designing a Research Plan for a Telemonitoring System in a Victorian Health Service Network 189

Introduction	189
Purpose of the Research Project	189
Research Questions	190
Research Design	192
Conceptual Stage	193
Researcher's Interest	194

Literature Review Summary	195
The Action Research Method Stage	200
Action Research Design	210
Action Research Design Major Cycle 1 - Design	214
Action Research Major Cycle 2 – Implementation	215
Action Research Major Cycle 3 – Further Refinement and Implementation	215
Research Site of the Research Project	216
Unit of Analysis	216
Ethical Considerations	218
Action Research Data Collection and Analysis Techniques	222
Participant Observation	222
Reflective Practice	223
Quantitative Data	225
Measure 1: Time Taken for Insulin Stabilisation	226
Measure 2: Number of Clinical Contacts During Insulin Stabilisation	226
Questionnaires	228
Content Analysis	230
Chain of Evidence	231
Validity and Reliability of the Research Project	232
Validation via Peer Review	235
Data Triangulation	236
Control Group as Applied in this Research Project	237
Research Protocol	241
Summary	242

Chapter 6 – Future Directions: The Ongoing Evolution of Work-Applied Learning — 243

The Development of Work-Applied Learning	243
Demonstrated Effectiveness of Work-Applied Learning Across Diverse Settings	246
Work-Applied Learning: An Adaptive Robust Change Process	247
Future Proofing with Work-Applied Learning	248
Work-Applied Learning and the Emancipatory and Participatory Paradigm	249
Future Directions for Work-Applied Learning	250

References   253

Chapter 1   253
Chapter 2   259
Chapter 3   261
Chapter 4   268
Chapter 5   279
Chapter 6   293

Appendices   295

Appendix 3A: Doctoral Research Projects   295
Appendix 3B: Master Research Projects   297
Appendix 3C: Key Research Terms   301
Appendix 4: Research Philosophy   313
Appendix 5A: Research Paradigm   327
Appendix 5B: General Action Research Characteristics   339
Appendix 5C: Details of Research Site   344
Appendix 5D: Participant Information Sheet   351

Index   353

FOREWORD

PROFESSOR ERWIN LOH
President of the Royal Australasian College of Medical Administrators and National Director of Medical Services at Calvary Health Care

I first met Professor Selva Abraham nearly 15 years ago. At that time, I had a scholarship to undertake a PhD with one of the major universities in Australia, and my topic was on mortality reviews. However, after one year of exploring this topic, I had decided I've had enough. People say that the only way to be successful in completing a doctorate is to study a topic that you have a passion for, and I have personally found this to be true. I completely changed the topic of my PhD research, to focus on something that I was very interested in – medical leadership. That was when I came to know Selva, and his wife, Param. Selva was co-supervisor for my PhD project, and was instrumental in guiding me to the completion of my thesis.

Selva is a world-renowned expert in action research and action learning. His knowledge is not just grounded on theory – he has been a practitioner, consulting and leading management projects in many countries. Not only is he a researcher and teacher in this space, he is also an author, having written multiple peer-reviewed articles and books. This latest book by Selva brings together in one place the information that will help managers develop a project plan that is based on the action research action learning (ARAL) methodology. Research students and researchers can also use this book to help them create research project plans.

I can highly recommend this book to any management practitioner who wants to learn more about how they can implement effective change in their organisations using a validated and evidence-based method.

FOREWORD

PROF. (HON) DATO' DR A. HALIM BASARI
Brigadier General (Malaysian Army) Malaysian Pharmacists Society (MPS) - Life Member & Deputy Chairman for Halal Pharmaceuticals Chapter, Academy of Pharmacy (APh Malaysia) - Life Member.

Selva Abraham is truly a great mentor to me both as my leadership and management sifu as well as my life coach. This book genuinely captures the essence of the life of a working professional as well as a solid upstanding citizen or simply a good Samaritan who wants to be better for him/herself and for his/her group units such as family, work team, community, organisation (public/private SME to MNC), state, country, region, globe, race, religion and the whole wide world if that matters a lot to him/her.

The very concept of WAL change programmes simply enhances one's career and life be it in his/her professional practice or personal endeavours, while driving his/her group units' (i.e. organisational) improvement and generating newfound knowledge. As an individual such as myself, Selva's theories apply perfectly for me as a change agent and pioneer in my military pharmacy career as the advocate for Ethnocentric Medicine, Shariah Compliant Pharmacy Practice and Halal Pharmaceuticals/Medical Devices.

There is just so much to be gained from this book not only for me but for the benefit of the many people in my group units (ummah) around me. As a trailblazer in many innovative projects (products and services) and a strategic manager/executor of transformation plans developed by the various levels of command through my superiors, I find Selva's model of planning, acting, observing, reflecting, evaluating and validating cycles is so relevant in my work because I have used it again and again as much as I could with the changing times. I read this book with a great curiosity in mind and ended with such fulfilling satisfaction to the beautiful management gems it has to offer.

Foreword (Continued)

Selva is at his best mind yet again when he meticulously explains the operational mechanics of the ultimate purpose for any organisation which is to survive the latest political, economic, social, technological, environmental and legal (PESTEL) revolution while remained competitive and relevant under the forever changing dynamic world. Any change agent seriously needs the WAL change action skills and experiences as elaborated skilfully in the book.

I totally agree with Selva that research is the basis of problem solving for any professional. I just can't imagine offering solutions without doing a thorough and proper fact finding through good research. Thus, the WAL Practitioner Researcher is the way of life for all professional managers to emulate. My final valuable take from this book is the following 8L that is, lets listen, live, love, lend, leverage, learn and lead. Thank You Selva for showing the way!

FOREWORD

COLIN BRADLEY
President, Action Learning, Action Research Association

To remain competitive, organisations must constantly seek to adapt and change. Managers leading change must do more than define and direct change, as this path can create dissent, change fatigue and non-sustainable change. There is a growing recognition that to achieve long-lasting change and an appetite for continual improvement amongst the staff of an organisation, managers must lead change though participation of their staff. They must develop their skills as well as those of their staff, develop organisational knowledge (a learning organisation), and prepare future managers who will also lead change with their staff.

This book is a timely resource for managers wanting to achieve sustained change. Managers in this case can be from a large or small enterprise, or a community or service entity. As the case studies in the book show, the Action Research and Action Learning method that grounds Work-Applied Learning (WAL) for Change has been used in many types of industries with great success. The book takes a further step in explaining how change leaders, in whichever industry they work, need to be a researcher, not of theories, but of their own practice – reflecting in and on their actions, and educating others through presentations, writings, publications and demonstrations. As Zuber-Skerritt and Abraham state, the WAL model fosters self-directed, lifelong learning and innovative thinking that maximise the organisational and personal benefits for managers, and for those included in the change initiatives.

FOREWORD

ALVIN GOH
Executive Director, Singapore Human Resources Institute

The necessity for continuous learning in organisations has deepened over the last few years, especially where multi-faceted issues are affecting how the future of work is being carried out.

The quest for higher productivity levels has been greatly intensified as organisations look towards how artificial intelligence and automation can be better leveraged to produce the necessary and expected outcomes for efficiency and effectiveness. While doing so, let us also not forget about the need to be practical and to lead with empathy. Practicality and empathy are embedded in how Prof. Selva has carefully crafted his new book. From a practitioner's standpoint, the proposed Action Research methods and Action Learning process are not just academic exercises but practical tools that drive real change and transformation whilst engaging the people on the ground, empowering them to lead change in their workplace and equipping them with the tools to implement solutions that are both action oriented and fostering a sense of team and belonging.

The insights provided underscore the transformative need to help leaders navigate the complexities of today's business environment and position them for future success.

ABOUT THE EDITOR

SELVA ABRAHAM MBA, PhD

Selva is the Founder Chairman of the Global Centre for Work-Applied Learning (GCWAL). He is also the Founder of and Emeritus Professor at the Australian Institute of Business and was a Visiting Professor at Leeds Trinity University.

He is also the Founder and Editorial Advisory Board member of the Journal of Work-Applied Management, which is Scopus-ranked. It is jointly published by WAL Publications and Emerald Publishing.

He has a PhD in Management from Flinders University in South Australia and a Master of Business Administration from Henley Business School/Brunel University in the UK.

Over the last 40 years, Selva's experience in consultancy and research using Work-Based Learning has led him to extend it into the concept of Work-Applied Learning. Selva is a Thought Leader in Work-Applied Learning and Work-Based Learning and continues to undertake research and provide advisory services in his area of expertise to Chief Executives and Senior Managers.

Selva has worked with senior executives in work-based learning and change management programmes in private, public and community organisations in South-East Asia and Australia including Motorola, Intel, Banque Nationale de Paris, Société Generale, Eastern Pretech, Australia Post, Light Regional Council, Aboriginal Sobriety Group, Epic Valley, Global Carriers Berhad, Indigenous Land and Sea Corporation Australia, Monash Health, and the Chief Minister's Department, Sarawak Malaysia.

He has also supervised senior executives who have completed their master's and doctoral research using action research, action learning and reflective practice. He has also developed academics in the supervision of professional master's and doctoral theses using this method.

Selva has written four books related to action research and change and continues to undertake research and publish in the areas of Work-based Learning and Work-Applied Learning.

Selva has previously written six books related to action research and change: Board Management Training for Indigenous Community Leaders Using Action Research (1994); Exploratory Action Research Method for Manager Development (1997), Work-Applied Learning for Change (2012, 2015), Action Research Characteristics in a Work-Applied Learning for Change Context (2016); Exploratory Action Research Method : A Case Study for Research Candidates and Supervisors (2016); and Work-Applied Learning for Change Leaders (2022, 2024). He continues to undertake research and publish in the areas of Work-Based Learning and Work-Applied Learning.

> *Selva dedicates this book to Param, Sanjay, Vinod, Vanessa, Ashvin, Maya, Sachin, Alisha and Kate.*

ABOUT THE CONTRIBUTORS

ORTRUN ZUBER-SKERRITT, MA, MEd, 2 PhDs, DLitt, D(Hon), AO
Ortrun Zuber-Skerritt is an Adjunct Professor, Griffith University, Australia; Pro Chancellor, Global University for Lifelong Learning (GULL), USA; Extraordinary Professor, North-West University, South Africa; and Honorary Citizen of the University of Innsbruck (Austria). She has four doctoral degrees and published widely.

The highlights of her career were (1) her Festschrift edited by Kearney and Todhunter (2015) and (2) the award in 2018 of AO (Officer in the General Division of the Order of Australia), in recognition for: "distinguished service to tertiary education in the field of action research and learning as an academic, author and mentor, and to professional bodies."

LISA MOHAMMED MSc, DBA
Lisa has been involved in the field of Occupational Health Safety and Environment (OHSE) as a consultant for over 15 years. She has conducted consultancy services for several companies in varying sectors and areas of operations but more so in the oil and gas sector in Trinidad and Tobago. Her doctoral research focused on change management in the field of OHSE using a Work Applied Learning approach.

DR PAUL JURMAN BBus, MBA, DBA
Dr Jurman is a senior information technology executive with extensive experience in digital transformation and technology planning, strategy, governance and operations in large national healthcare enterprises. Paul holds a Doctorate in Business Administration, and is an Associate Fellow of the Australasian College of Health Service Management and a Certified Chief Information Officer of the College of Healthcare Information Management Executives. His doctoral research focused on digital innovation adoption and action research.

ABOUT THE CONTRIBUTORS

DR. ALAN BARNES BSc(Hons) PhD
Alan is a former senior lecturer and research fellow at the University of South Australia. He has a PhD in mathematical physics from Adelaide University. He was a senior research fellow in Aboriginal Research Institute with a particular focus on research into building indigenous capacities, especially in information technology. Alan has an extensive background in the research degrees management, quantitative methods and in the development of learning technologies. He led a group of researchers investigating cognitive technologies in learning. He has published broadly and worked on many national research projects. He is currently Senior Research Fellow for the Application of Artificial Intelligence, particularly within organisational adaptation, practitioner research and research management at the Global Centre for Work Applied Learning.

ACKNOWLEDGEMENTS

I wish to acknowledge the many people who have contributed to this book:

- Prof Ortrun Zuber-Skerritt for her consent to reproduce our jointly written article as Chapter 1 of this book,
- Dr Lisa Mohammed and Dr Paul Jurman for contributing the methodology chapters of their doctoral theses as Chapters 4 and 5,
- Dr Carmel Taddeo and Dr Alan Barnes for their invaluable input to the section on Data Collection, Data Analysis, Evaluation and Validation Techniques in Chapter 3, and
- Dr Alan Barnes for providing an objective analysis on the book in the concluding chapter and raising issues for consideration in the WAL approach grounded by Action Research and Action Learning.

My thanks also go to the people who helped me behind the scenes, namely

- Deep Sherchan who project managed the publication of this book to completion,
- Ana Mrkic who coordinated the book publication in its earlier stages,
- Barbara Velasco for her design and coping with the endless formatting changes and
- my wife, Param for challenging my thinking and for supporting me at every stage of this book.

In spite of this expert help on a variety of fronts, if there are any remaining errors and omissions, the responsibility for these rests with me.

PREFACE

The term "practitioner researcher" has been defined as:
> "Managers or other professionals who conduct research in the workplace to improve the quality of their practice, to engage in organisational improvement or other change, to create knowledge and to make the results of their research public so that their work can be scrutinised, and can inform the understandings of others, e.g., through oral presentations, written company reports, in-house papers, newsletters, dissertations or theses, articles or books." (Zuber-Skerritt, O. & Abraham, S. 2017)

Several writers have linked practitioner research with action research, including the following:

Jarvis, P (1999, pg 89) stated that: "Practitioner research is increasingly becoming known as action research, a form of research that really began in education, although it has now spread to other professions."

In 2000, Scanlon wrote that:
> "Action research is usually, but not always, collaborative. Teams of researchers and practitioners work together on a project. Alternatively, a project can be undertaken by the practitioners themselves, without any involvement from outside researchers. In action research, practitioners play an active role in designing the project, collecting data and implementing change." (as cited in Wilkinson, 2000, pg 4-5)

Sheikhattari, Wright, Silver, van der Donk and van Lanen (2022, p2) wrote that:
> "Practitioner research shares many elements with action research, such as the involvement of internal stakeholders in

research and its practical approach to generate actions and practical solutions to the pressing issues."

My conceptual framework of Work-Applied Learning (WAL) is grounded not only in the action research method, but also incorporates the processes of action learning and reflective practice. The WAL model enables managers to learn how to plan, act, observe and reflect on their work-based projects. They will also learn how to collect and analyse the data arising from their projects, evaluate and validate this data as well as how to record the planning and implementation processes in a systematic manner.

This book is designed to introduce the WAL model to managers who wish to become practitioner researchers in their organisations, with special emphasis on how it can be used to develop a plan for a practitioner research project (the ARAL research plan).

I developed the WAL model when undertaking my PhD research over 30 years ago. Since then, I have tested this model and refined it while working with chief executives, senior and middle level managers in private, public and community organisations, both in Australia and overseas, including Singapore, Malaysia, Papua New Guinea and Trinidad & Tobago.

The book starts with a reproduced article co-authored by Ortrun Zuber-Skerritt and myself. It provides a conceptual framework for WAL for developing managers as practitioner researchers for positive organisational change, through reflective practice, action research, action learning and action leadership.

In Chapter 2, I explain the concept and process of the WAL model and describe the three vital components of the WAL concept: the extension of Work-Based Learning (WBL) to WAL; the fused Action Research method and the Action Learning and Reflective Practice processes; and the cyclical creative thinking and learning process.

Chapter 3 is a critical part of this book as it describes the process involved in the designing of a WAL research plan. The research plan typically consists of a Conceptual stage and an Action Research stage, and details are provided of the phases comprised in each stage. Examples of components such as the Research Problem, the Organisational Thematic

Concern, Main and Corollary Research questions from WAL research plans are provided.

Chapter 4 shows how a WAL research plan was designed to investigate the development and implementation of an improved Occupational Health and Safety Management System for a Well Workover company in the petroleum industry in Trinidad and Tobago.

Chapter 5 presents a different WAL research plan which was designed to explore the development and implementation of an action research-oriented Telemonitoring system to enable the home-based monitoring of diabetes patients in a Victorian Health Services Network.

Chapter 6 looks at the ongoing evolution of work applied learning and its relevance to the organisations dealing with rapid, complex and profound change, including that of generative artificial intelligence. The chapter draws on the considerations of Work Applied Learning in the book to demonstrate the efficacy of WAL across diverse settings, its adaptiveness as a change process and the power of its emancipatory and participatory paradigm to develop ethically sound change processes. It argues for the future proofing potential of Work Applied Learning especially in relation to artificial intelligence, suggests directions for Work Applied Learning's evolution and points to its capacity to generate workplace knowledge relevant to a humane future.

I hope that this book and especially the examples that I have given, will help guide you in developing your WAL research plan.

CHAPTER 1

ORTRUN ZUBER-SKERRITT | SELVA ABRAHAM

A conceptual framework for Work-Applied Learning for developing managers as Practitioner Researchers

This chapter is a reprint of a refereed article, reproduced here with permission of the journal and authors: Zuber-Skerritt, O., & Abraham, S. (2017). A conceptual framework for work-applied learning for developing managers as practitioner researchers. Higher Education, Skills and Work-Based Learning, 7(1), 35-50. doi: http://www.emeraldinsight.com/doi/pdfplus/10.1108/HESWBL-05-2016-0037

Ortrun Zuber-Skerritt
Griffith Institute for Educational Research, Griffith University, Brisbane, Australia and Faculty of Education Sciences, North-West University, Potchefstroom, South Africa, and
Selva Abraham
Global Centre for Work-Applied Learning, Adelaide, Australia

ABSTRACT

Purpose – The purpose of this paper is to introduce a conceptual framework for work-applied learning (WAL) that fosters the development of managers and other professionals as lifelong learners and practitioner researchers – through reflective practice, action research, action learning and action leadership, for positive organisational change.

Based on classical and recent literature and the authors' extensive experience, the WAL model presented here is an effective and practical approach to management education, research and development. It is useful for present and future requirements of business, industry, government and society at large in this twenty-first century, and in pursuit of a world of equality, social justice, sustainable development and quality of life for all. This is because of the nature of the research paradigm, particularly its collaborative and emancipatory processes.

INTRODUCTION

In the twenty-first century, increasing globalisation, complexity and turbulence across the globe provide ample evidence of the need for a new paradigm of learning and development at work (Bawden and Williams, 2017). This paradigm is needed as an alternative or complement to, and not in competition with, the formal education system (Zuber-Skerritt and Teare, 2013). It is rooted in an understanding of learning that is different from most other learning paradigms and is particularly suited for the present and future time. The difference is its epistemology, informed by various theories of learning, as we explain in this paper. This is not a research paper or case study but a conceptual paper as defined by Emerald guidelines: "These [conceptual] papers will not be based on research but will develop hypotheses. The papers are likely to be discursive and will cover philosophical discussions and comparative studies of others' work and thinking" (www.emeraldgrouppublishing.com/authors/guides/write/abstracts.htm?part=2#sthash.7LVsPLvh.dpuf). The present conceptual paper is based on our personal and professional experience of conducting, facilitating and evaluating work-applied action learning (AL) programmes and participatory action research (AR) projects. It is informed by our reflections on these experiences and by the most recent literature since the seminal work of Zuber-Skerritt (2011). Here our aim is to introduce a conceptual framework for work-applied learning (WAL) that provides a basis for the development of managers and other professionals as lifelong learners and practitioner researchers – through reflective practice, AR, AL and action leadership, for positive organisational change.

This paper proposes WAL as a model (Abraham, 2015) for developing managers as practitioner researchers (Dahlberg and McCraig, 2010; Drake and Heath, 2011; Fox et al., 2007). We define the term practitioner researchers as managers or other professionals who conduct research in the workplace to improve the quality of their practice, to engage in organisational improvement or other change, to create knowledge and to make the results of their research public so that their work can be scrutinised, and can inform the understandings of others, e.g., through oral presentations, written company reports, in-house papers, newsletters, dissertations or theses, articles or books. We explain how the phenomenological paradigm of knowledge creation and relevant supporting theories of learning and knowing can be applied, adopted or adapted to develop and facilitate leadership and management skills in students/managers. It can do so by promoting self-directed learning and publication of findings through collaborative, qualitative AR and reflective practice. Understanding this conceptual framework is vital for both understanding and most effectively using the model of WAL in organisations or other circumstances, at a systemic level (Burns, 2007) and in a sustainable way.

Abraham's (2015) model of WAL is clearly defined in the next section. However, we recognise that to maximise the concept's potential for individual learning, team learning, organisational learning, community learning, knowledge management, work-based learning (WBL) and change, it needs to be placed in a broader methodological and philosophical context, as explained in the main part of this paper ("the WAL paradigm" and "theories of knowing and learning"). Here we aim to strengthen the conceptual framework for the WAL model by placing it in terms of theory, pedagogy and methodology. Abraham designed the WAL model as an extension of WBL through fusing AL (Revans, 1971, 1982, 1991, 1998, 2006) and AR (Lewin, 1926, 1948, 1951) with reflective practice (Knott and Scragg, 2011; Moon, 2006; Taylor, 2000) and case study methodology (Yin, 2013). The utility of these four complementary approaches for enhancing the WBL model became evident through practice. However, the meaning of the "action" terms has changed over time. As Abraham (2015, p. 6) points out:

> *The original concepts first voiced by Revans and Lewin have not stood the test of time intact and inviolate. Rather, opinions about what Action Learning and Action Research mean and how to implement them are many and varied. Consequently, every group that wants to undertake an Action Learning project or an Action Research program must consider these various opinions and then decide what form of research or learning is appropriate for its needs.*

Zuber-Skerritt's (2002a, b) definitions of AL and AR also vary slightly from those of Abraham's but what they have in common are the paradigm, theories, methods and processes of learning, development, leadership and change. From this common ground, we decided to provide a conceptual framework for the WAL model since we believe this model has particular currency for knowledge creation in contemporary workplaces wherever they may be. Offering a carefully considered conceptual framework for the WAL model enhances the capacity of model users to apply, adapt and further develop its conceptual underlay – and to enhance conceptual and practical knowledge creation and learning through this process. The WAL model is used successfully in the Australian Institute of Business (AIB) and in the Global Centre for Work-Applied Learning (GCWAL) in Adelaide, both of which were founded by Selva Abraham, in partnership with other organisations. AIB is the largest private business school in Australia that is government accredited from bachelor to doctoral levels, including PhD.

In this paper we first summarise and discuss Abraham's (2015) WAL model. Second, we explain the key concepts that characterise it. Third, we offer a conceptual framework for the model drawing from related theoretical thinking that includes aspects of phenomenology (Smith, 2013; Zohavi, 2003), experiential learning theory (Biggs, 2005; Boud *et al.*, 1985; Kolb, 1984), strengths-based theory (Harvey, 2014; McCashen, 2005; Saleebey, 2005), grounded theory (Charmaz, 2006; Corbin and Strauss, 2013) and critical theory (Bhaskar, 2008; Carr and Kemmis, 1986; Kemmis *et al.*, 2014). In clarifying the conceptual framework of WAL, we provide a theoretical, educational and methodological rationalisation of the WAL model that further develops its utility for researchers' and practitioners' applications.

THE WAL MODEL

WAL incorporates WBL, while grounded in a fusion of action research method and action learning process (ARAL). WBL focusses on learning in the workplace by individuals or teams to create and apply knowledge in the workplace. The WAL model extends the process by using the ARAL approach to create, in a more systematic and conscious way, organisational learning, knowledge management and organisational change. The ARAL approach entails a cyclical process as practitioner researchers and their teams plan, act, observe, reflect, evaluate and validate their work-based projects through the AR cycles of WAL. Figure 1 shows the cyclical nature of WAL from individual learning to team learning to organisational learning and knowledge management eventuating in organisational change.

The WAL programme as explained by Abraham (2015, pp. 1-36, pp. 177-179) begins with a substantial and often complex problem, issue or concern in the workplace that has not been solved before, that is of concern to the CEO, and that is to be addressed by senior managers in collaboration with other employees. This problem-solving team learns from and with each other (i.e. AL); they proceed through several cycles of systematic inquiry using cycles of planning, acting, observing and reflecting (i.e. AR) while applying their learning, knowledge, critical thinking and other skills to their project work. They then monitor, evaluate, reflect upon and validate their findings collaboratively and in doing so they ascertain the outcomes of the WAL programme.

These are project outcomes, process outcomes, learning outcomes and sustainable transformation, all of which constitute a valuable return on investment within the organisation. The WAL programme offers an effective way of management learning at the individual, team and organisational levels because it is systematic, systemic and work/life based and leads to organisational knowledge creation. It recognises, uses and appreciates workplace learning and its utility, not just for theoretical and practical knowledge creation and organisational improvement, but also for improving the workplace/life experiences of all in the organisation as a learning organisation (Senge, 1990).

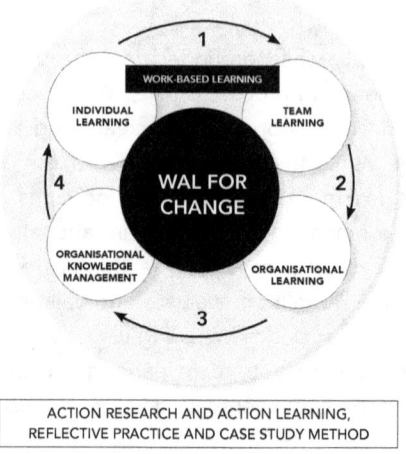

Figure 1 – Cyclical nature of work-applied learning (WAL)

Abraham (2015, pp. 7-9) identifies 12 general characteristics of AR that should emerge in WAL. It has problem focus, action orientation, cyclical process, collaboration, ethical practice, group facilitation, creative thinking, learning and re-education, and it is naturalistic (non-positivist, qualitative case studies), emancipatory, normative (but modified/changed during the AR process) and scientific (rigour).

In recent years Zuber-Skerritt has developed an approach she has called participatory action learning and action research (PALAR), which particularly highlights the participatory nature of AL and AR. She has summarised (Zuber-Skerritt, 2011) the seven C's of PALAR that somewhat overlap with the characteristics of WAL that Abraham identified independently: communication, collaboration, commitment, competence, compromise, critical reflection and coaching. All of these contribute to character building of the manager as action researcher, who is holistic, ethical, responsible, democratic, caring and loving, i.e., the global citizen required for peace and social justice in this twenty-first century.

A WAL programme is conducted by members of a workplace organisation who share an interest in collectively identifying and solving a shared workplace concern. Managers form an AR group to establish and conduct the WAL programme, which includes several AR cycles and normally six phases within each cycle. These phases constitute:

(1) AR group meetings on a regular basis as face-to-face or web-conference meetings, where managers share views, questions and experiences, discuss and reflect on the outcomes of their projects, processes and learning;
(2) knowledge workshop phase of one to four days duration, depending on managers' needs and demands of the organisation, focussing on business concepts (e.g. strategy, marketing, finance, human resources, operations, and leadership), introduced by a facilitative tutor, supplemented by distance learning and reading materials and an online library, and concluding with each manager's draft plan for a change project, including departmental projects;
(3) work-based phase where managers in their workplace are equipped as facilitative leaders to guide their departmental learning teams in planning and implementing their work-based projects;
(4) joint observations and reflections at the end of each work-based phase, with a facilitative consultant to monitor progress and to provide assistance managers might need in the next cycle;
(5) evaluation of cycles by the managers, the facilitative consultant and other AR group members, in an evaluative meeting where they analyse performance outcomes and evaluate outcomes of the projects, processes and learning; and
(6) validation of the WAL programme at the end of every two cycles by the AR group and its key stakeholders, with managers' report presentations, feedback, and possible changes to the programme if seen to be useful.

This systematic and systemic WAL model seeks to maximise the organisational and personal benefits of a cyclical WAL experience for managers at an organisational level. It is future-oriented and highly relevant for developing the skills and knowledge that Jackson (2011) and Trilling and Fadel (2009) have identified as vital for the twenty-first century. However, cultivating these skills and knowledge in the workplace requires a revised paradigm of learning and development that fosters self-directed, lifelong AL and creative and innovative thinking "outside the box". It must appreciate and generate organisational capacity to achieve the type of development essential for succeeding in this rapidly changing world, i.e., development that addresses totally new and complex problems collaboratively and effectively, and produces sustainable outcomes. In the next section we clarify the key concepts pertaining to the WAL model before offering a conceptual framework for this model.

KEY CONCEPTS OF WAL

As mentioned, Abraham's (2015) model of WAL integrates the concepts of WBL with ARAL. It includes reflective practice, lifelong learning and action leadership. It is useful to re-evaluate and re-conceptualise the WAL model's concepts, independently and in their syntheses, to maximise the model's utility for addressing twenty-first century problems. These so-called "wicked problems" (Dick, 2012) entail increasing complexity, ambiguity, turbulence and tension among different values and beliefs. Since WAL is conceived as work-applied AL/research/leadership, it is a philosophy and methodology of change and is therefore valuable for sustainable learning and change, including personal, organisational, community and environmental change. This capacity is especially pertinent in present times when changes in the global environment serve to multiply these so-called "wicked problems" across all aspects of life. From here we briefly summarise the key concepts of WAL: WBL, ARAL, reflective practice, organisational learning, lifelong learning and action leadership.

WBL
WBL refers to programmes where the learning that takes place is primarily at and through work, for the purposes of work. Gibbs and Garnett (2007, p. 411) define WBL as:

> *A learning process which focuses university level critical thinking upon work (paid or unpaid), in order to facilitate the recognition, acquisition and application of individual and collective knowledge, skills and abilities, to achieve specific outcomes of significance to the learner, their work and the university.*

Garnett (2012) explains that in the UK, WBL is often associated with lower-level learning, but it can also span all the levels of higher education from certificate through to doctoral level. WBL at higher education level can range from a component of a course unit to entire qualifications and it can be used to help young people integrate work and learning to help them enter employment or it can be the vehicle mature students choose to facilitate part of their continuing professional development. Boud and Solomon (2001, p. 1) identify a range of distinctive features of higher-level WBL:

- WBL is a partnership between an external organisation and an educational institution specifically established to foster learning;
- learners are employees or have some contractual relationship with the external organisation and negotiate learning plans approved by the educational institution and the organisation;
- the learning plans are derived from the needs of the workplace and of the learner, rather than being predetermined by a subject disciplinary curriculum;
- the starting point and level of the negotiated learning programme is established after a structured review and evaluation of the current learning of the individual;
- WBL projects that meet the needs of the learner and the organisation are a significant element of the programme; and
- assessment of the learning outcomes of the negotiated programme is carried out with reference to a transdisciplinary framework of standards and levels.

ARAL
Lewin's (1926, 1948, 1951) concept of AR and Revans' (1982) concept of AL are similar in some respects as both are problem-focussed, action-orientated and utilise group dynamics. However, they differ in a number of major respects. AR includes AL, but – like any other approach to research – AR is more rigorous, systematic and scrutinised than AL, and it is always made public in oral and/or written form. While Ortrun has integrated the two as ALAR (starting with AL and gradually developing skills for AR), Selva's focus in WAL is more on AR for project assessment and evaluation, and using AL sets for personal, professional and organisation development (OD), hence naming this integration ARAL. The effect of both ALAR and ARAL is the same.

Reflective practice
Being a "reflective practitioner" or a member of a "reflective practice" means one engages in a continuous search for knowledge – both propositional and theoretical (knowing that [...]) and knowledge derived from practice

(knowing-in-action or knowledge-in-use, i.e., tacit, spontaneous knowledge and thinking on one's feet). AL as a reflective process is iterative and continuing – it has no end point. Schön (1983, 1987) distinguishes between "reflection-in-action" (thinking while in the process of doing something) and "reflection-on-action" (reflecting after the event on what one did). The latter encourages reflective learning as well as critically reflective learning. More recently, reflective practice has been extended in theory and practice (Greenwood, 2012; Knott and Scragg, 2011; Moon, 2006; Taylor, 2000).

Organisational learning

Organisational learning is a process of creating, retaining and transferring knowledge throughout the organisation for improving practice at the individual, group/team, organisational and inter-organisational levels, and for continuous positive change and development. Like individual learning, organisational learning is about the construction and accessibility of meaning, but it is most effective in a culture that fosters collaborative work. Organisational learning occurs in "learning organisations" that Senge (1990, p. 3) explains as:

> [...] organizations where people continually expand the capacity to produce the results they truly desire, where new and expansive patterns of thinking are nurtured, where collective aspirations are set free, and where people are continually learning how to learn.

In other words, a learning organisation fosters a work environment and a culture that encourage members to draw from knowledge within the organisation and to think critically and creatively. The WAL concept understands learning as an ongoing, creative and lifelong process, one that adapts and transforms in response to the needs and aspirations of people inside and outside the organisation.

Lifelong learning

Sheehan (2001, p. xi) in his Foreword to the Kluwer *International Handbook of Lifelong Learning* offers one of the most comprehensive understandings of lifelong learning:

> Lifelong Learning is a concept that is critically important to all educators, for it expresses the importance and

> *relevance of learning at every stage of our development. The concept is equally relevant to members of our society at all stages of their life-span – as young children, maturing youth, adults, and as older persons. Further, it affects national governments, industry, information agencies and nearly every kind of institution of learning.*
>
> *So important is the concept, it should be seen by all of us as representing a new philosophy of education and training, one that aims to facilitate a coherent set of links and pathways between work, school and education, and [to] recognise the necessity for government to give incentives to industry and their employees so they can truly "invest" in lifelong learning. It is also a concept that is premised on the understanding of a learning society in which everyone, independent of race, creed or gender, is entitled to quality learning that is truly excellent.*

However, there are many different concepts and conceptions of lifelong learning (Aspin et al., 2001; Jackson, 2011; Jarvis, 2001; Zuber-Skerritt and Teare, 2013). Billet (2010) warns of the perils of confusing lifelong learning with lifelong education. Whilst the former is a personal process, the latter is an institutional process. And although school- or university- based courses may be valuable, the danger is that – as in some literature – the importance and ubiquity of learning experiences outside courses are largely ignored or marginalised, as well as the scholarship of adult learning and development across people's life courses.

In the WAL model of AR cycles explained above, we are able to integrate aspects of lifelong education (through collaborative knowledge workshops and distance education materials) with the participants' lifelong learning processes (through work-based projects, AR meetings, using joint observations, reflections, collaborative evaluation and validation).

Action leadership
Abraham's (2015) WAL model introduces four roles of facilitative leadership: facilitative training, facilitative tutoring, facilitative leading and facilitative consulting. We see that the key to all four is action leadership. WAL is the ideal model for developing action leadership among managers.

Cantwell (2015) draws from his extensive military experience in claiming that leadership in action is about emotional connections, trust and being authentic. Zuber-Skerritt (2011, p. 231) draws from her experience as an Academic Staff Developer and Consultant for over 40 years:

> *Action leadership is a new concept of leadership that involves action, concern and responsibility for others, rather than a position of power and control over them. This kind of leadership is not reserved for an elite in power or an hierarchical position, but it is possible to achieve for all who are willing and capable to develop a capacity, knowledge, skills, attitude and democratic values of freedom, equality and fraternity for all humankind. Significant action leaders know, go and show the way and take joy in helping others succeed.*

Action leadership – conceived as primus inter pares (first among equals) – can be developed through WAL. Action leaders can facilitate within their ARAL group the important knowledge and skills for vision and team building; identifying issues, strengths and weaknesses; and strategic action planning, implementation and evaluation, using critical reflection at every stage. Action leaders see the big picture, but they need to develop leaders around them (Maxwell, 1995) to achieve shared, democratic action leadership. In summary, WAL:

- is learner-centred and work-based (through project work);
- is specific to the needs of an organisation;
- uses ARAL and reflective practice;
- applies directly to managers' real life/work;
- is lifelong (pursued continuously); and
- fosters non-hierarchical action leadership.

WAL when used effectively improves the quality of life/work for all in a workplace organisation and, as a consequence, for many beyond. WAL programmes are effective for unlocking human potential and vitally, their outcomes are sustainable.

CONCEPTUAL FRAMEWORK FOR THE WAL MODEL

To explain the WAL model, we find it most useful to adapt the conceptual framework for WAL from Zuber-Skerritt et al.'s (2015) framework for PALAR. The conceptual framework of WAL, like that of its close relative PALAR, is informed by "a participatory paradigm of an engaged scholarship in higher education"[1]. Because this paper is to introduce WAL as a new concept, our discussion here includes only those aspects of epistemological theories that explain and validate use of the WAL model for workplace learning and problem solving and does not need to critically analyse these theories.

THE WAL PARADIGM

The WAL paradigm is congruent with the paradigm of PALAR explained in Zuber-Skerritt et al. (2015), and more recently in Wood and Zuber-Skerritt (2024). Traditionally, it has been assumed that scientists create theoretical knowledge in their specialist disciplines, and that practitioners then apply this knowledge in their practice. In the alternative paradigm of WAL and PALAR, we accept that there are other kinds of knowledge beyond theoretical and practical, including emotional, spiritual, local and indigenous knowledges, and so there are other sources of knowledge beyond scientific testing. WAL accepts that everyone of sound mind can learn how to identify a complex, practical problem that needs to be researched and solved urgently, plan a project collaboratively in a team of like-minded people who are passionate about inquiring into an issue, observe the action, reflect on the results of the research, think critically through the research process to identify conceptual and practical knowledge and re-plan for future improved practice or change. This process is an interaction and integration of action and research into "AR". It is not conducted by a specialist researcher, but by practitioner researchers who are involved in the action as participant observers, critical thinkers/reflectors and co-researchers who join "the tribe" (Godin, 2008), as in anthropology. This kind of research is different from traditional, disciplinary or large-scale social science research. It focusses on small groups at a time, and requires predominantly qualitative rather than quantitative research methods, and a considered understanding of phenomenological research in the participatory paradigm.

THEORIES OF KNOWING AND LEARNING

We believe the WAL model is best explained by aspects of selected epistemological theories integrated in a conceptual framework. These theories are predominantly phenomenology, experiential learning theory, strengths-based theory, grounded theory and critical theory/realism. These and theories like them are fundamental for understanding the WAL model and related practices of work-applied, lifelong learning through AL, AR and action leadership.

Phenomenology

Phenomenology is a philosophy and a research tradition that focusses on phenomena as they appear in the natural, experienced human world. Researchers study how this world actually appears to people or how people experience and conceive the world around them. We refer readers to Van Manen's (2014) comprehensive work on the "phenomenology of practice" because it presents key phenomenological ideas and methodological issues of phenomenological reflection and writing in professional contexts.

Phenomenology is the overall paradigm that guides us in WAL. According to Kuhn (1970, p. 175): "A paradigm is what the members of a scientific community share [...] it stands for the entire constellation of beliefs, values, techniques, and so on shared by the members of a given community". Here our community consists of scholars as practitioner researchers interested in improving/changing their praxis of learning, teaching, research and leadership, and their work colleagues and partners in other institutions, communities, and organisations, in business, industry and government, locally and globally.

From this paradigm we argue that the human and social sciences require methodologies and methods different from those of the natural sciences because the nature, behaviour and views of humankind constitute a complex whole that cannot be observed objectively, or in parts, by outside researchers. Observations of humankind are not neutral, objective or value free; they are subjective because choices that guided the observation and interpretations depend on the observers' theoretical framework and values. Therefore, "observers" are "participants" who are actively involved in the research process (e.g. in choosing who/what to examine, what questions to ask of whom, and in analysing and interpreting data). They seek to make the findings as objective as possible through qualitative methods and triangulation. We argue for a phenomenological approach to WAL through practitioner research into their organisational practice, in order to improve or otherwise change their organisation.

Experiential learning theory
Kolb's (1984) classic experiential learning theory is based on the premise that adults can create knowledge on the basis of their concrete experience. They can observe and reflect on that experience, formulate theoretical or abstract concepts and generalisations, and then test the implications of these concepts in new situations, which provide them with new concrete experience. This theory, envisaging an ongoing lifelong cycle of learning and of creating knowledge, was first developed by Lewin (1948, 1951) and extended by Kolb (1984, p. 21). Kolb's experiential learning theory is the cornerstone of WAL because it follows an iterative process of reflection and action. Our reflections on, in, for and through action generate new questions and insights for the next action in our learning and research, and so the cycle continues throughout our life, including in our work and other professional or organisational activities. This approach to experiential and lifelong learning can be facilitated, developed and enhanced through qualitative methods, such as keeping a reflection diary, holding reflection sessions or evaluative discussions with others who are involved and eliciting feedback from "critical friends" whose advice we trust.

Strengths-based theory
In strengths-based theory, which is informed by other theories such as positive psychology, social change theory, hope theory and motivation theory, it is assumed that every person, group or organisation has strengths and assets that can be built on and further developed in practice and research. This is opposite to the traditional deficit approach where experts observe "subjects" and identify deficits and then design interventions to solve the problem. This deficit approach often leads to a negative sense of self-confidence, self-esteem and self-efficacy. In strengths-based practice, "participants" generate strategies and solutions for themselves according to their abilities and for their contexts (McCashen, 2005; Saleebey, 2005). Harvey (2014) explains the nexus between strengths-based theory/practice and AR, and maintains that the central tenet of strengths-based theory and practice is analogous with that of AR. That is, all stakeholders in a project or activity are participants in a process of inquiry, working together as they

try to find the best solutions and to develop new knowledge.

The strengths-based approach starts with a focus upon the participants' identifiable strengths in order to achieve this critical nexus between problem solving and knowledge creation. What the strengths-based approach and AR have in common is an emphasis on action as a goal and on achieving positive change. This change is likely to be transformative because reflective practice is valued by and inherent to both. Harvey (2014) also shows how each moment of the AR cycle (plan-act-observe-reflect) can be strengthened by shared leadership, active listening, providing affirmation, positive reinforcement, acknowledgement of contributions and autonomy within agreed boundaries (e.g. ground rules and mutual expectations). This theory strongly resonates with the collaborative and positive paradigm of WAL, PALAR and action leadership.

Grounded theory

Based on the early theory by Glaser and Strauss (1967), recent reference books such as Bryant and Charmaz (2007), Charmaz (2006), Corbin and Strauss (2013) and Gibson and Hartman (2013) have developed grounded theory in the new, participatory paradigm. Grounded theory provides a theoretical framework for WAL and other methodologies within this paradigm because, as these studies reveal, it has proven that theoretical knowledge can be generated from specific contextual information and data collected within a certain context (e.g. an organisation or community). Information/data collection is an iterative process of alternating and mutually interacting the phases of discovery and subsequent testing or "sampling of grounded theory". Zuber-Skerritt (2009, pp. 108-109) explains:

> *Unlike scientific empirical research aiming to verify "grand theories" and placing little value on who and what are involved in creating these theories, "grounded theory" places value on generating meaningful theories, emphasising the process of their creation. While empirical research produces "etic" theory by an "outsider" who is seen to be "uninvolved" in the research process and "removed" from the object of enquiry, grounded theory is "emic", informed by an insider view of the people, groups, organisations or cultures being studied. The etic enquirer tries to establish*

> *generalisable (nomothetic) laws; the emic enquirer wants to provide knowledge and understanding of a particular, individual (ideographic) case. For the former, generalisations might be statistically purposeful and significant (e.g. in population audits, identifying causes of illness and health, national trends), but often they are not applicable or [are] irrelevant to the individual case and specific group. Action research is directly and exclusively relevant to an individual case and specific group.*

Grounded theory derived from data analysis is always an interpretation by researchers through their personal lenses or "windows to the world" and through their critical and self-critical reflection on the data analysis and action. This is where critical theory is helpful.

Critical theory and critical realism

Our critical theory is influenced by the Frankfurt School of Critical Theory (Adorno, 2008; Habermas, 1974, 1978) and by Carr and Kemmis' (1986) seminal work: Becoming Critical: Education, Knowledge and Action Research. In WAL programmes or projects, it is important for participants to "become critical" and self-critical because we aim at sustainable transformational change, whether personal, professional, organisational or community learning and change. As Zuber-Skerritt (2009, p. 111) points out:

> *This means critique is never taken as a personal attack (destructive), but [is] accepted as a necessary move to bring about organisational improvement, innovation or re-creation (constructive). In action learning programs, participants submit thoughts and ideas about actions to the constructive scrutiny of supportive colleagues as "critical friends". We learn from our mistakes and failures as well as from successes. We are not interested merely in changing people and organisations; we want them to grow and learn, and we want to learn ourselves within this process.*

Another important principle of critical theory is "symmetrical communication", grounded in the understanding that everyone in the WAL team regards each other as their equal, no matter what their rank or position. Each member therefore contributes equally, although differently, according to their personal strengths, individual gifts and interests, as in strengths-based theory. Each treats all others with respect, inclusion and having a right of opinion. The shared assumption is that each individual has knowledge, skills and talents in a particular area, which can be identified and used effectively for the common good.

In the English-speaking world, Bhaskar's (2008) critical realism has been influential as a philosophical approach to social and human sciences, especially in regard to social change and to the promotion of human agency and freedom. His work originated from the German tradition of critical theory and dialectics, but developed a special philosophy of critical naturalism that recognises the similarities and differences between natural sciences and social sciences and that the human and social worlds are in a much greater state of flux than those of the physical world. Human and social structures change much more readily than those of organic plants, for example or non-organic matter. Human agency is made possible by social structures, and individuals who inhabit these social structures are capable of consciously reflecting upon and changing practices that in part are facilitated by social scientific research.

Table 1 is a summary of how each of the theories discussed above impacts on practitioner researchers' actions in WAL at the individual, group and organisational levels. There is some overlap and some integration of theoretical conceptualisation and practical application, but these theories all inform the participatory paradigms of WAL and action leadership. Through WAL, practitioner researchers use participatory AR and collaborative lifelong AL in team projects aimed at practical improvement, positive social change and justice, for the common good of the organisation. Through action leadership, practitioner researchers share leadership assumed by whoever in the team is the best and first among equals for each particular task, purpose and responsibility, to achieve the best outcomes for all.

These theories listed in Table 1 provide a combined theoretical, pedagogical and methodological rationalisation of why the WAL model is an appropriate and effective approach to developing managers as professional, lifelong learners and practitioner researchers. Developed as such, they are best positioned to meet current and future requirements of the twenty-first century.

Figure 2 presents a summary of the WAL conceptual framework within the participatory paradigm. It requires participatory pathways and the integration of the three core WAL activities of managers: AL, AR and OD/change. This can be achieved through the seven C's (critical reflection, competence, coaching/ mentoring, communication, collaboration, compromise and commitment) and the three R's (relationships, reflection and recognition/ award) of WAL and PALAR. One of the important outcomes is action leadership, which enhances and strengthens praxis (i.e. integrated theory and practice).

Table 1 – Some theories embedded in practitioner researchers' actions

THEORY	PRACTITIONER RESEARCHERS' ACTIONS
Phenomenology	Practitioner researchers conduct research into phenomena/issues in their workplace/ organisation from their own experience and perspectives.
Experiential learning theory	They gain understanding of work/life/change processes and create knowledge based on reflecting critically on their projects and experiences.
Strengths-based theory	They identify and build on each team member's strengths for maximum effectiveness and results at the personal, professional, community or organisational levels.
Grounded theory	They collect, analyse and interpret action research data to elicit the main categories, constructs, concepts and principles from which grounded theory can emerge, related to the issue(s)/theme of the research project.
Critical theory	They use dialogue, dialectics, critical reflection, self-reflection and meta-reflection to change their praxis, their understanding of praxis, and if necessary, the conditions/ boundaries that constrain, inhibit or prevent any improvement or change.

Source: Adapted from Zuber-Skerritt et al. (2015, p. 19)

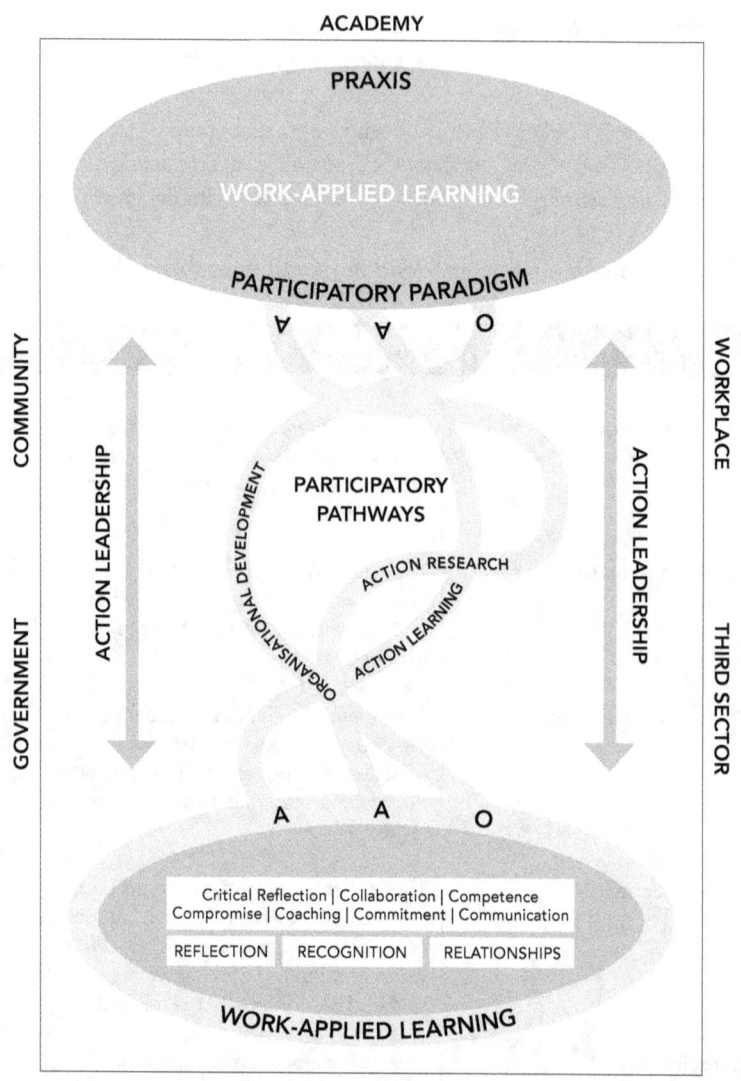

Source: Adapted from Zuber-Skerrit et al. (2015, p. 21)

FIGURE 2 – Conceptual framework of integrating action learning, action research and organisation development in the WAL model.

This framework illustrates WAL as an integrated, inclusive approach to action and learning, research, and OD/change. It makes clear that WAL is not confined within the classroom, but also takes place in the workplace (e.g. family enterprises, small, medium and large businesses and corporations, in government (i.e. at national and subnational levels), in the third sector (i.e. faith-based, non-government and other organisations), and in the wider community (including local, remote and disadvantaged communities). And of course, WAL takes place in the academy – the AIB and the GCWAL in Adelaide, both focus on this type of learning – and in other institutions of management and higher education, such as the Global University for Lifelong Learning (GULL). Many of these sites of WAL also forge close links with international networks through partnerships and other relationships across national borders.

CONCLUSION

This paper aimed to clarify and justify Abraham's (2015) WAL model (summarised in Figure 1) theoretically, pedagogically and methodologically. Therefore, we first explained the WAL model as practised in several organisations, particularly AIB (www.aib.edu.au), GCWAL *(http://gcwal.com.au)* and GULL *(www.gullonline.org)*. Second, we explained the key concepts that are integrated within WAL – WBL, ARAL, reflective practice, organisational learning, lifelong learning and action leadership – and explained why this model is especially appropriate for developing managers' knowledge and skills to cope with so-called wicked problems in the twenty-first century. Third, we offered a theoretical, pedagogical and methodological justification of the WAL model. Practical implications include that being based on this conceptual framework, managers/graduates as practitioner researchers can subsequently apply or adapt the model through empirical research and case studies in their own work contexts and by consulting Abraham's (2015) practical guidebook with case studies. Through this practical experience and the insights gained, they are likely to develop action leadership and be able to effectively steer their community or organisation into an uncertain future. The framework also helps ensure that research development is more responsive to the complex needs of our socio-cultural, economic and political contexts.

There are no fast steps or hard rules for developing action leadership through WAL. All contexts are distinctive as are all groups of practitioner researchers in their concerns, needs, interests, abilities and motivations to learn and change. That is why active participation, collaboration and critical reflection in, on, after and for action are important in the WAL paradigm. It is also why WAL, ARAL and action leadership cannot be narrowly defined and will always be emergent concepts. As demonstrated by Zuber-Skerritt (2011) in the areas of higher education, and management education for OD and community development, work-applied learners and action researchers are able to develop as ethical, entrepreneurial action leaders in all sections of society, such as the workplace in organisations, communities, government, the third sector and in the management education academy, as illustrated in Figure 2. They are able to act effectively and responsibly, observe and reflect critically and self-critically, and – on the basis of their experience and reflective practice – create new knowledge through ARAL that is contextual and relevant to their own and their organisations' development. In this way they are better positioned to work for a future world characterised by equal opportunity, social, economic and political justice, prosperity and openings for creative thinking and innovative acting. These learning and organisational outcomes have been confirmed and substantiated in the literature, for example by Coghlan and Brydon-Miller (2014) and the *Sage Handbooks on Action Research* (Reason and Bradbury, 2001, 2006, 2008, 2013; Bradbury, 2015).

Some people may see a difference between traditional, lecturer-centred and disciplinary-oriented management education and development vs a more action-, problem-, process- and future-oriented interdisciplinary approach to leadership development. The WAL model integrates both – the former approach through the "knowledge workshop phase" and the latter in the "AR group meetings", the "work-based phase", the "joint observations and reflections" and simultaneously through the "evaluation of cycles" and "validation of the WAL programme".

Our discussion here has been limited by the restrictions upon a journal article. These also preclude us from providing a practical guide for both managers as practitioner researchers and their educators on how to learn and how to become more effective WAL practitioners, action researchers and action leaders. We are considering this as the topic of a future publication and will accept readers' offerings that may contribute usefully to it. For readers seeking to deepen their understanding, here we refer to published work listed in the "References" below. Meantime the conceptual framework we have presented in the present paper outlines and concisely underscores the strengths of the WAL model as an effective, practical approach to management education, research and development for present and future requirements. It also advances an incipient literature on WAL by practitioner researchers as action leaders. Finally, we invite and encourage readers to conduct their own practitioner research to test and extend the conceptual framework we have introduced in this discussion.

NOTE

1. Here we briefly summarise the essence and adapt Table I and Figure 1 of the conceptual framework for PALAR from Zuber-Skerritt et al. (2015, pp. 13-21) in the sections on "paradigm" and "theories of knowing and learning", with permission of the authors and Sense Publishers (by e-mails of 5-6 March 2016).

2. Wood and Zuber-Skerritt (2024) have recently strengthened the WAL model's conceptual framework integrating action learning, action research and organisational development in their book, *Shaping the future of higher education*, especially in the concluding Chapter 10 on: "Frameworks for actioning positive and sustainable change in higher education" (pp. 193-217).

CHAPTER 2

SELVA ABRAHAM

Work-Applied Learning (WAL) Model

Chapter 1 provided the conceptual framework for WAL for developing managers as practitioner researchers. In this chapter, I will explain the concepts and process of the WAL model.

THE WAL CONCEPT

The three vital components in the WAL concept are:
- the extension of Work-Based Learning (WBL) to Work-Applied Learning
- the fused Action Research method and the Action Learning and Reflective Practice processes, and
- the cyclical creative thinking and learning process.

The WAL concept which is grounded in Action Research and Action Learning recognises the workplace as the crucible of learning for change. This concept has been specifically researched in the context of managers as change leaders introducing change in their divisions, departments or organisations as a whole.

THE EXTENSION OF WBL TO WAL

WAL is an extension of WBL because WAL not only incorporates the features of WBL as set out in Table 2.1 but goes beyond WBL as explained in the following pages.

Fergusson, Baker and van der Laan (2024) agree that:
> Work-applied learning (WAL) has its genesis in WBL but has been developed specifically in the context of change management for businesses and managers by extending WBL from individuals and teams to include entire

organisations. Selva Abraham introduced WAL to bring about organisational change through a fusion of action research and action learning.

Table 2.1 – Features of Work-Based Learning

Work-Based Learning:
- focuses on learning through and for work tasks
- is often a collaborative activity
- is often transdisciplinary rather than based upon the traditional subject disciplines developed and taught in business schools• is a practical yet often high level cognitive process
- is primarily learnt by working, not through reading or observing work
- is essentially learner centered and where planned often takes the form of facilitated learning through work rather than being tutor led and classroom based
- is self-directed, creative, expressive, involves feelings, is continual and reflective
- includes action projects, learning teams and other interpersonal experiences, including mentorship
- provides opportunities for professional practice, critical analysis and reflective thinking
- involves knowledge creation and utilisation as collective activities when learning becomes everyone's job
- involves thinking and developing and evaluating theory and practice
- where there is formal assessment this will link with and may contribute to work practices
- can lead to the attainment of qualifications.

Abraham (2012), Boud and Solomon (2001), Costley (2015), Garnett (2012), Helyer, Wall, Minton and Lund (2021), Raelin (2000, 2008) Roodhouse and Mumford (2010), Schon (1983), Wenger, (1999).

The similarities and differences between WBL and WAL are shown in **Figure 2.1.**

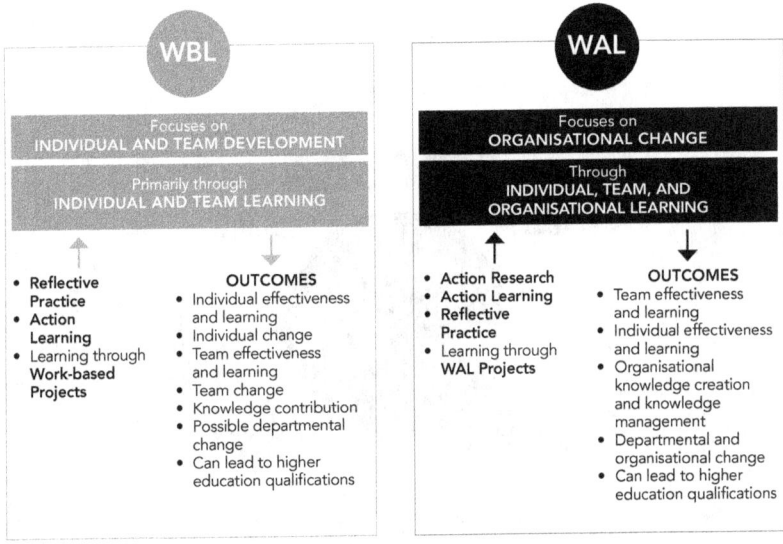

Figure 2.1 – WBL and WAL Comparison

It can be seen that:

- Both WBL and WAL focus on learning and change,

- WBL focuses on individual and team learning and change,

- In the case of individual learning, WBL uses Reflective Practice, whereas team learning involves Action Learning and Reflective Practice,

- WAL uses a fused Action Research Method and Action Learning process (ARAL). This leads to not only individual and team learning, but also to organisational learning, knowledge creation and change. These outcomes are achieved as the change leaders and their teams plan, act, observe, reflect, evaluate, and validate work-based projects through the action research (AR) cycles of WAL, and

- Reflective Practice is an essential part of both WBL and WAL.

The WAL Change Process has four distinct phases in creating change in organisations, as shown in **Figure 2.2**.

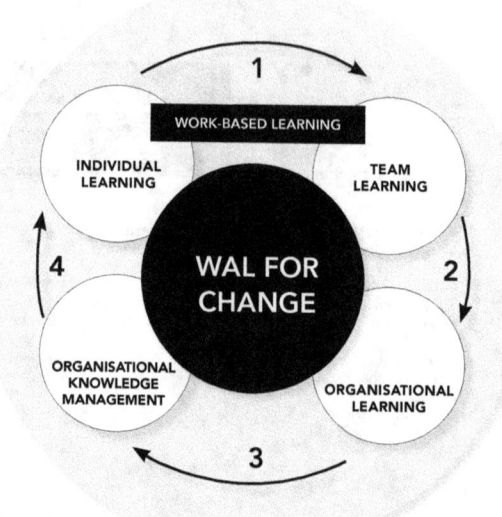

Figure 2.2 – Phases of THE WAL change process

Figure 2.2 shows how Individual Learning (Phase 1) leads to Team Learning (Phase 2), to Organisational Learning (Phase 3) and to Organisational Knowledge Management (Phase 4).

As can be seen in Figures 2.1 and 2.2, WAL is grounded in a fused action research (AR) method and the action learning (AL) and reflective practice (ARAL) processes. (Abraham S, Arnold G and Oxenberry R, 1996).

The cyclical nature of ARAL in relation to the four phases of WAL is illustrated in **Figure 2.3**.

WORK-APPLIED LEARNING (WAL) MODEL 29

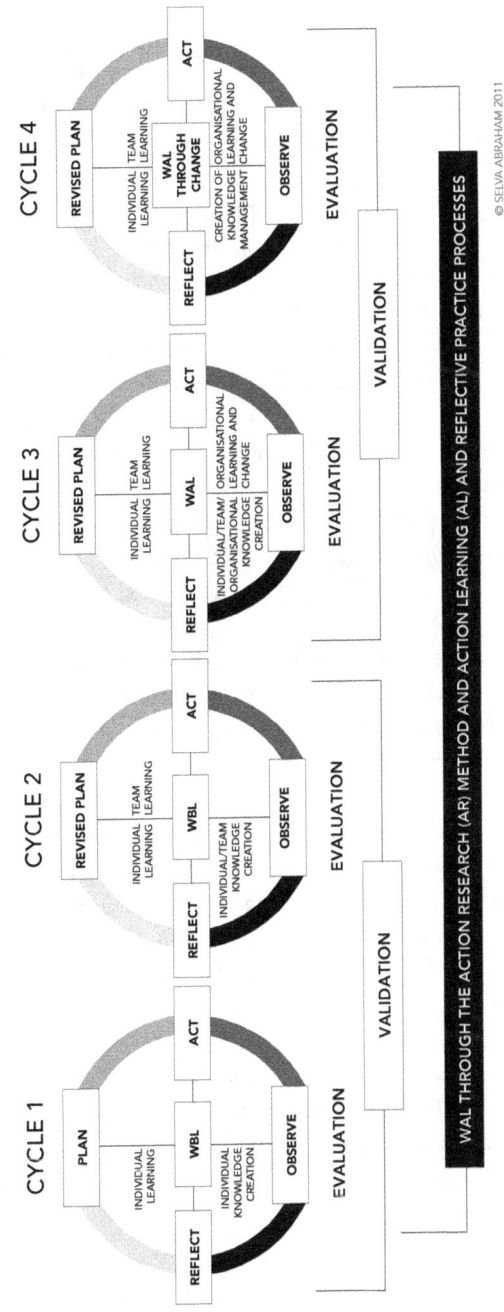

Figure 2.3 – WAL Through ARAL

While Cycles 1 and 2 in Figure 2.3 depict the emergence of individual and team learning and knowledge creation, the later cycles add organisational learning, organisational knowledge creation and knowledge management to complete the WAL change process.

Figure 2.4 illustrates a WAL programme for the Board members of Kuju CDEP, a Community Development and Employment Project. Kuju means 'fish traps' in the local Aboriginal language. Kuju CDEP was established to provide all eligible Aboriginal people in Port Lincoln with employment and on-the-job training. It commenced its operations in May 1989, and was the first urban CDEP in Australia.

The most important issue which Kuju CDEP needed to resolve was the establishment of a strong Board of Management, with Aboriginal participation, which could provide leadership and direction to the organisation. Although Kuju CDEP had achieved many good outcomes, there was still too much reliance on the staff rather than the Board for decision making. There was an urgent need for a Board which could decide on long term planning and set up broad policy structures within which the staff could work on the day to day management of Kuju CDEP. Once the broad policies were set up, the Board then would have time to spend on longer term major issues.

There was, therefore, the need for the Board members to understand the function of the Board and have the management skills and knowledge to make decisions and provide leadership to the organisation. The two solutions to this problem were to strengthen the Board by bringing in experienced people from outside Kuju CDEP and to provide management training for the existing Board members.

The WAL programme is described in my book on the Kuju CDEP Learning Experience (1994). The programme started with a WBL phase comprising an individual and team learning process for the Board members and eventually resulted in organisational change for the community organisation and the community as a whole.

WORK-APPLIED LEARNING (WAL) MODEL

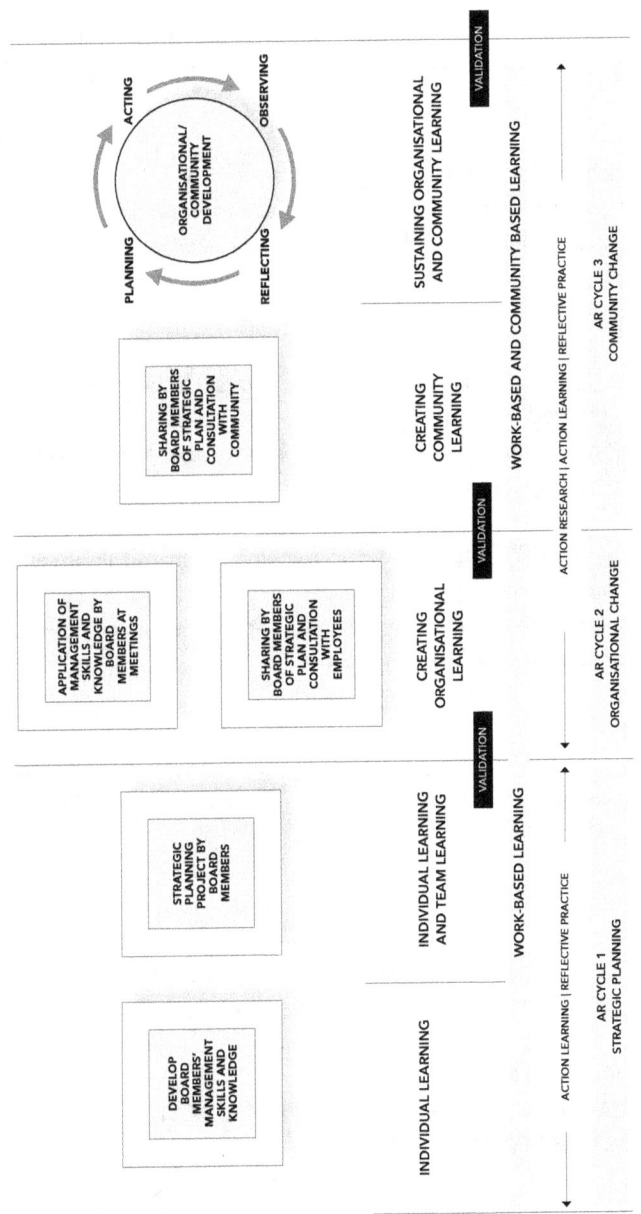

Figure 2.4 – From Individual and Team Learning to Organisational and Community Learning and Change

During AR Cycle 1, the Board members were provided with management skills in the context of their roles as Board members. Using the WBL approach, they worked as a team to develop a strategic plan for the organisation.

The Board members learned how to relate with each other and how to work as a team with the staff of the organisation, the funding agency and the community members. They also learned to reflect upon their strengths and weaknesses as Board members and to improve their practices.

In AR Cycle 2, the Board members applied such learning at Board meetings and shared their strategic plan with the staff of the organisation. In this way, organisational learning and knowledge sharing gradually developed in the organisation.

In the first part of AR Cycle 3, the Board members shared their strategic plan with the community as a whole. This involved a community consultation process where the strategic plan was presented and feedback was sought from the community.

Once there was acceptance of the strategic plan by the community members, the staff of the organisation with the assistance of the Board members implemented the strategic plan in the second half of AR Cycle 3 and beyond.

This programme is an example of how the use of the WAL model grounded by Action Research, Action Learning and Reflective Practice resulted in individual and team learning by the Board members in AR Cycle 1 and organisational and even community learning in AR Cycles 2 and 3.

THE FUSED ACTION RESEARCH METHOD AND ACTION LEARNING AND REFLECTIVE PRACTICE PROCESSES

As the Action Research method and the Action Learning and Reflective Practice processes (ARAL) ground the WAL model, it is important to understand how the fusion of the method and processes has evolved.

Action Research is a practical research method and should not be confused with the Action Learning process.

Lewin's (1946, 1947, 1951, 1952) concept of Action Research and Revans' (1982) concept of Action Learning are similar in some ways as both are problem-focused, action-oriented and utilise group dynamics; however, they differ in a number of major aspects. Revans (1983) is more interested in encouraging 'questioning insight" than in solving problems. In Revans' (1983, p.11) words:

> *Action Learning requires questions to be posed in conditions of ignorance, risk and confusion, when nobody knows what to do next; it is only marginally interested in finding the answers once those questions have been posed.*

Action Research, on the other hand, was designed as a means of introducing change in problematic situations to bring about a noticeable improvement.

Revans places more emphasis on the development of the skills and abilities of managers than Lewin, who was more concerned about making a contribution to science, and he accords outside experts a far lesser role.

Lastly, while Revans admits that Action Learning can become a cyclical process, it is not essentially cyclical in nature, unlike Lewin's concept of Action Research.

Since the time when the original concepts were first voiced by Revans and Lewin, there have been many varied opinions about what Action Learning and Action Research mean and how to implement them. Consequently, every group that wants to undertake an Action Learning project or an Action Research programme, must consider these various opinions and then decide what form of research or learning is appropriate for its needs.

Reflective Practice is common to both the Action Research method and the Action Learning process. This is because as change leaders plan and implement their Action Research and Action Learning projects, they reflect before action, reflect in action and then reflect on action either consciously or unconsciously.

In my PhD study on Board Management Development using Action Research (Abraham, 1993), I noted that Peters and Robinson (1984) had undertaken a survey of literature and had identified certain Action Research characteristics. However, 12 Action Research characteristics clearly emerged in my findings. As a result of my practice and research since 1993, I have refined my thinking on the Action Research characteristics and provide in Table 2.2 a summary of the updated 12 Action Research characteristics.

Table 2.2 – General Characteristics of Action Research

	CHARACTERISTIC	SUMMARY DESCRIPTION
1	Problem Focus	The Action Research method is problem-focused in the context of real life situations. The solving of such problems in a research sense would contribute to professional practice and the development of social science knowledge.
2	Action Orientation	The diagnosis of a problem and the development of a plan to solve the problem can only be considered to be action-oriented if the action becomes part of a process to implement the plan. This brings an action element to the solving of an immediate problem of the organisation which has strategic change implications for the said organisation.
3	Cyclical Process	The Action Research method involves cycles of planning, action, observation, and reflection (evaluation). Thus, the cycles of the Action Research method allow the group members to develop a plan, to act, to observe and to reflect on this plan, to implement the plan and then to modify the plan, based on the needs of the group members and the requirements of the organisation and situation. A record of the processes of each cycle enables its strengths and weaknesses to be reviewed so that modifications and strategies can be developed for future cycles.
4	Collaboration	Collaboration is a fundamental ingredient of the Action Research method, because without a team effort to solve problems in an environment of participation, Action Research cannot exist. Collaboration on group problems using the Action Research method can be viewed as a continuum from total dependence on the facilitator, who acts as a leader directing the group problem-solving process, through to the total management of the problem by the group members with the facilitator acting as a resource person. The position of the facilitator and the group on this continuum depends on the situation and the needs of the group.

Table 2.2 – (Continued)

	CHARACTERISTIC	SUMMARY DESCRIPTION
5	Ethical Practice	Community interests, improvements in the lives of the group members, justice, rationality, democracy and equality are some of the themes of 'ethical' behaviour. The ethical basis of Action Research is an important characteristic to consider, because the Action Research method involves, to a large extent, groups of people with limited power who are open to exploitation. It requires the researcher to concede their personal needs so that the needs of the group are given the highest priority.
6	Group Facilitation	The success of the Action Research method will depend on how well the group can operate as an effective team. An understanding of group dynamics therefore seems essential in facilitating this process and dealing with problems that arise during the Action Research cycles.
7	Creative Thinking	The Action Research Group members will experience creative thinking as they go through stages of saturation, deliberation, incubation, and illumination where the group members look for different options and seek the opinions of different relevant parties to validate those options.
8	Learning and Re-education	Action Research can be viewed as re-educative, since it contributes to a change in the knowledge base of the organisation, a change in the skills, attitudes and knowledge of the individual group members, and a change in the skills and knowledge of the researcher. It also makes a contribution to several of the social sciences.
9	Naturalistic	If one accepts that Action Research should be scientific but that there are problems in adopting a positivistic model of science and applying it to social science settings, then it follows that a naturalistic approach is appropriate for the Action Research method. The approach involves qualitative descriptions recorded as case studies rather than laws of cause and effect tested experimentally with statistical analysis of data.

Table 2.2 – (Continued)

	CHARACTERISTIC	SUMMARY DESCRIPTION
10	Emancipatory	The changes experienced by the group members during the Action Research process can contribute to some improvements in their lives and may also have wider social action and reform.
11	Normative	The normative characteristic of Action Research implies that the social 'norms' of the group are not only considered during the research, but, in order to bring about change in the group, they are modified during the Action Research process.
12	Scientific	Since the Action Research method does have a scientific basis and can provide an alternative to the positivistic view of science, it is essential that the research be conducted in such a way that it can be defended against criticisms of lack of scientific rigour.

© SELVA ABRAHAM 2015

In 1996 Graham Arnold, Rod Oxenberry and I wrote on the fusing of AR and AL in the context of organisational learning and change. We (Abraham et al, 1996) first identified the features specified by some authors as being necessary components to produce Action Research and Action Learning and expressed them in a word formula to capture the integrated nature of the Action Research method and the Action Learning process (ARAL).

The individual word formulae for Action Learning and Action Research are shown below, with the symbols used in the formulae being explained in Table 2.3:

Action Learning (AL):

$$S + P + A (+F) + RP = AL$$

Action Research (AR):

$$G + P + A + F + C + R + RP = AR$$

Table 2.3 – Symbols used in the AL and AR Word Formulae (Abraham et al, 1996, p.17)

SYMBOL	DESCRIPTION
S	The Action Learning set comprising individuals who come together to investigate solutions to shared problems and to learn from each other. There is no requirement that the set members are from the same organisation.
P	The problem to be addressed. Both Action Learning and Action Research share this problem-focused characteristic.
A	Both Action Research and Action Learning are action-oriented. The group or set takes positive action in response to the ideas and suggestions generated through questioning and discussion.
G	The nature of the Action Research Group may be rather different to the set described in Action Learning. The group comprises members of an organisation or community and could also include "Researchers" who may be seen as an integral part of the group since they work in a collaborative manner with the group for change and knowledge development.
F	The term "Facilitator" has been placed in brackets in the Action Learning word formula to indicate the disparate views amongst the authors on whether or not a facilitator should be part of the set.
C	The cyclical nature of Action Research. Lewin (1946 and 1947) indicated that the spiral nature of steps was fundamental to Action Research. His steps started with diagnosis, followed by cycles of planning, action and reflection.
R	The Researcher in Lewin's original view assisted the group. While some writers question the need for a Researcher, the role of a Researcher as a consultant to the group is widely supported by other authors.
RP	Reflective Practice
AL	Action Learning
AR	Action Research

On scrutinising of the above formulae, I noticed an overlap between some of the components of AL and AR and that in fact, AL could be considered as a subset of AR. As a result, using the definitions from above, I developed the following formula to depict the fused ARAL model:

AL + C + R = AR

Since the article was written in 1996, I have come to appreciate the importance of reflective practice in both AL and AR. As a result, I have since included Reflective Practice in the definition of ARAL.

THE CYCLICAL CREATIVE THINKING AND LEARNING PROCESS

Through my practice and research over the last 30 years with managers who have used the WAL model as change leaders, I observed that they go through a cyclical creative thinking and learning process as they work on their change projects. This process is shown diagrammatically as **Figure 2.5** below.

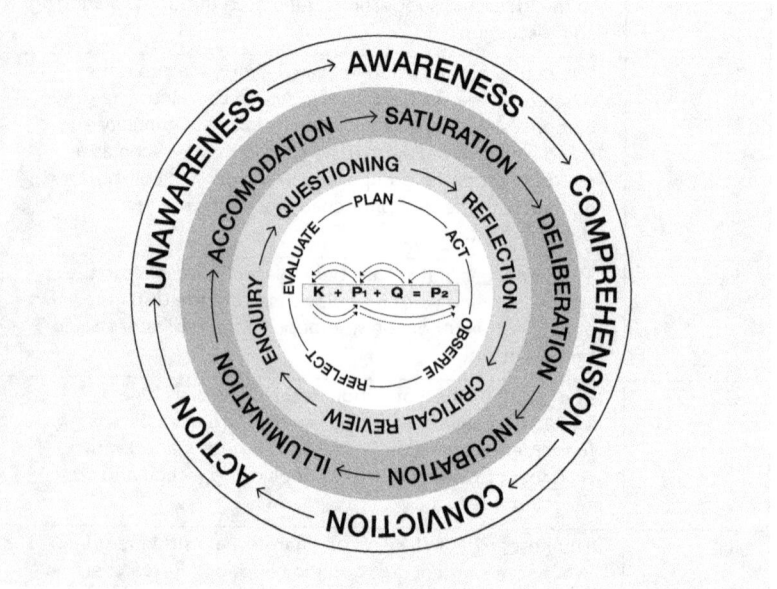

Figure 2.5 – The Cyclical Creative Thinking and Learning Process

It can be seen that there are four concentric circles with a core that contains the "Work-Applied Learning (WAL) Formula" which I developed in the course of my practice and research. This formula is repeated in Figure 2.6 and is explained in the subsequent paragraphs.

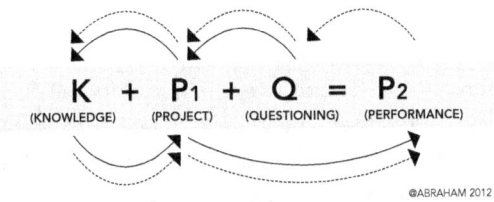

Figure 2.6 – The Work-Applied Learning (WAL) Formula

The WAL formula shows how change leaders will learn by:
- Critically reflecting on a problem in their workplace
- Questioning (Q) how to solve the problem
- Defining the project (P1)
- Reflecting and applying the relevant knowledge (K) to provide solutions
- Achieving performance (P2) outcomes including learning, project and process outcomes.

The formula shows that the natural starting point is the **Q**. The change practitioners will start by asking questions about a problem, identify a project **P1** to address the problem, then move on to read about the relevant knowledge **K** on this subject. Armed with that material, they will go back to **P1** to see if the explanations make sense, and then they can move towards achieving performance outcomes **P2**, namely project, process and learning outcomes.

But that cycle is not the end of it because, on the basis of what they have learnt, they will now want to return to the questioning stage and repeat the whole process. They can repeat the cycle again and again as each time their understanding will be refined by more practical experience. Knowledge and practice, as they will discover, go hand in hand and this formula helps to show how this is achieved.

Moving outwards from the core, the first circle shows how the WAL formula is used by managers and their teams as they plan, act, observe, reflect, evaluate and validate their work-based projects through the AR cycles.

The second circle in Figure 2.5 shows how the change practitioners critically reflect on the questions **Q** in the context of their change projects, and integrate the knowledge to their projects.

The third circle depicts the stages of the Creative Thinking and Learning process, namely saturation, deliberation, incubation, illumination and accommodation. These stages were initially formulated by Graham Wallace (1926). Since then, they have been commented upon and adapted by different writers, including Tripathi and Reddy (2007). One such adaptation by Quick, J.T (1963, pp 29-30) is provided below:

> **Saturation:** Becoming thoroughly familiar with a problem, with its setting, and more broadly, with activities and ideas akin to the problem.
>
> **Deliberation:** Mulling over these ideas, analysing them, challenging them, rearranging them, and thinking of them from several viewpoints.
>
> **Incubation:** Relaxing, turning off the conscious and purposeful search, forgetting the frustrations of unproductive labour, letting the subconscious mind work.
>
> **Illumination:** A bright idea strikes, a bit crazy perhaps, but new and fresh and full of promise; you sense that it might be the answer.
>
> **Accommodation:** Clarifying the idea, seeing whether it fits the requirements of the problem as it did on first thought, re-framing and adapting it, putting it on paper, getting other people's reaction to it.

The fourth circle depicts the Five Stages of Persuasion which were identified by Wimmer (2011). During the continuous steps of creative thinking, individuals learn as they move from a stage of Unawareness to Awareness, Comprehension, Conviction and finally, to Action. Wimmer (2011) explained that these Five Stages of Persuasion can apply to any decision a person makes from the purchase of goods and services to decisions such as marriage, careers and learning any concept. He further stated (2011, p.4):

> 1. *All people pass through these stages for every decision they make or anything they learn.*

2. All people pass through the stages at different speeds – there is no universal timing.

3. Not all people make it to the Action stage.

The only way to move people through the Five stages is through repetition of message. In most cases, people do not make decisions [or learn something] after only one exposure to a message. The process nearly always requires several exposures.

Whilst these Five stages of communication and learning were originally used in the context of marketing communications and external customers, I believe that they are equally relevant to internal customers, namely change leaders and staff of organisations.

I created this diagram because I realised there were some linkages between the various concepts depicted in the concentric circles. I noted that there was a certain degree of overlap between the third circle of the Cyclical Creative Thinking and Learning Process and the fourth circle of the Five Stages of Persuasion, especially when applied in the context of learning and change management.

The Unawareness and Awareness stages, for example, have similarities to the Saturation and Deliberation stages as they cover the process of a person becoming aware of a problem or idea and analysing it from different viewpoints with a view to finding a solution.

Also, the Incubation, Illumination and Accommodation stages of the Creative Thinking and Learning Process align with the Comprehension and Conviction stages where the person identifies a solution, obtains opinions from others and perhaps re-frames and adapts the solution.

Similarly, I saw that the second circle comprising Critical Review, Enquiry, Questioning and Reflection is closely related to the first circle which is the AR process of Plan, Act, Observe, Reflect and Evaluate. At the core of this thinking and learning process is the WAL formula $K+P1+Q=P2$, which has been explained earlier.

WAL CHANGE PROCESS AND PRACTICE

Over the last 30 years, I have worked with change leaders in various organisations who have successfully used the WAL model in change programmes as it provides a systematic approach for undertaking change in their organisations.

The WAL change programme is designed to address an organisational problem and is led by one or more change leaders within the organisation, depending on its size. The change leader may either be the Chief Executive Officer (CEO) or a person nominated for the role. The change leader will work with a team of change facilitators to plan and implement a change programme which addresses a specific aspect of the organisational problem. Each change facilitator, in turn, will work with their teams to plan and implement a change project which contributes to solving the organisational problem.

While undertaking the change programme, the change leader needs to acquire knowledge in the areas of Organisational Change using Action Research and Action Learning and Reflective Practice (ALRP). The change facilitators need to understand the concepts and practice of Work-Based Learning (WBL) and ALRP as well as the knowledge relevant to their change projects.

The change leader and change facilitators will acquire the above-mentioned knowledge through intensive face-to-face sessions or webinars supplemented by online learning materials, depending on their needs and the specific requests of their organisations. In addition, an external Programme Advisor will work closely with the change leader and change facilitators as they plan and implement their change projects.

Each WAL Change Programme comprises a number of AR cycles of planning, acting, observing, reflection, evaluation and validation. **Figure 2.7** shows the AR cycles in the WAL planning and implementation process.

WORK-APPLIED LEARNING (WAL) MODEL

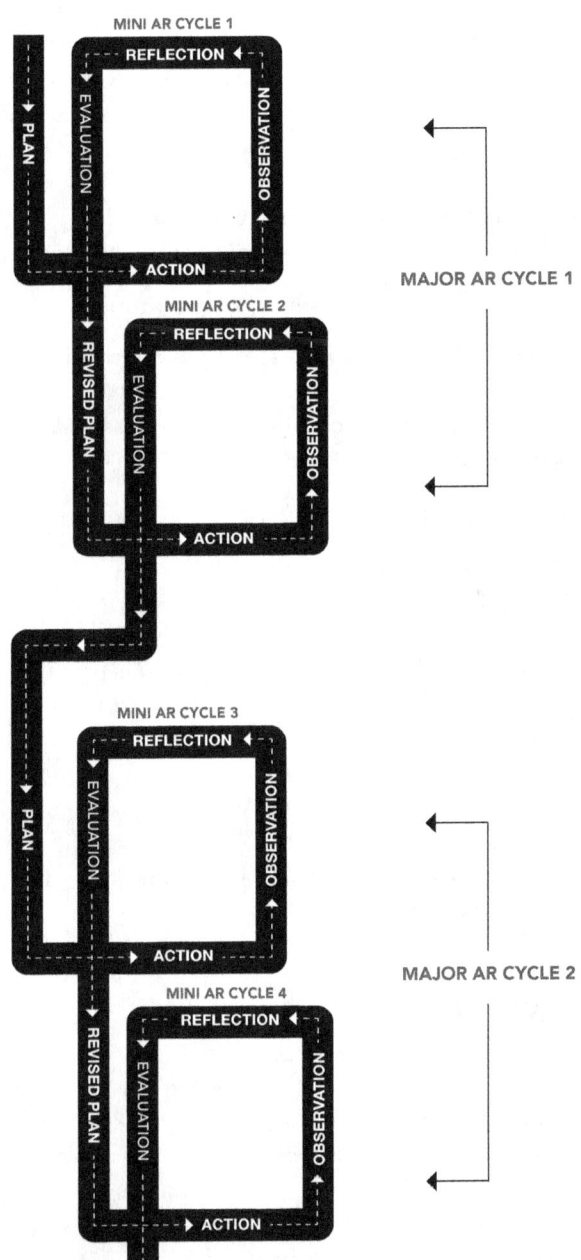

Figure 2.7 – AR Cycles within the WAL Programme

The normal duration of an AR cycle is four months. However, if an AR cycle is anticipated to take six or more months to complete, it is possible to have several AR mini-cycles within the major AR cycle. Each mini-cycle would have the same phases as the major AR cycle but compressed in a shorter timeframe.

The main players in a WAL Change Programme are:
- the AR Group made up of the change leader, the change facilitators, and the Programme Advisor,

- the change facilitators and their respective teams, and

- a Validation Committee comprising the CEO as well as external and internal stakeholders recommended by the CEO.

The following phases are embedded within each AR cycle and are elaborated upon below:
- Planning by the AR Group

- Acting during Work-Based Learning Phases

- Joint Observations and Reflections

- Monitoring and Evaluation by the AR Group, and

- Validation by an independent Validation Committee usually after every two AR Major Cycles.

PLANNING BY THE AR GROUP

The planning phase of the AR cycle is undertaken at AR Group meetings, which is to be undertaken by the change leader working with the change facilitators and their teams.

The first AR Group meeting is very important as it is the start of the WAL Change Programme. It is essential for the CEO to officially launch the WAL Change Programme and reinforce management support for it.

During the first meeting, the AR Group will:

- Clarify the organisational problem to be addressed,

- Establish the purpose of the WAL Change Programme and the goals of the change projects to address the organisational problem,

- Discuss and reflect on the potential change projects which the change facilitators could undertake in the context of the organisational problem,

- Agree on the design of the WAL Change Programme, including the number and duration of AR Group meetings, Work-Based Learning Phases, feedback and reflective sessions with the Programme Advisor, and scheduling of dates, taking into account job demands and organisational requirements, and

- Determine the obligations and commitments of the AR Group members, namely, the change leader, the change facilitators and the Programme Advisor.

As part of the planning process, the AR Group will agree on the timeline for the change facilitators to present their draft change project plans for the approval of the change leader and/or CEO. This process will help consolidate all individual change project plans into the organisational change plan for implementation.

During subsequent AR Group meetings, the change facilitators will share their experiences and lessons learned during their Work-Based Learning Phases. They will also discuss the project, process and learning outcomes that they have achieved so far and issues and challenges that have arisen and how they have addressed these. They will reflect on these issues and challenges with the other members of the AR Group who may make suggestions to overcome the problems.

Furthermore, the change facilitators are encouraged by the change leader and/or CEO and the Programme Advisor to provide assistance to their peers when they face issues and challenges with their change projects.

ACTING DURING WORK-BASED LEARNING (WBL) PHASES

Each AR Group meeting is followed by a WBL Phase where each change facilitator works with their respective team members on their change project.

During the first WBL Phase, each change facilitator will have to explain to their team members the purpose of the WAL Change Programme and of their change project. Each change facilitator, and where appropriate, their team members will:

- help refine their change project

- break down the change project into individual projects for each team member

- agree and establish
    - project outcomes for the change project and each individual project,
    - learning outcomes for the change facilitator and each team member, and
    - process outcomes

- obtain management support and, if necessary, further refine the change project as agreed with the AR Group

- implement the change project as a team using the AL process

- undertake directed reading on the relevant knowledge area

- create opportunities for effective reflection and review with the team members

- keep detailed notes of the process, project and learning outcomes

- establish and continually encourage a working relationship between the team members, and

- consult and reflect with AR Group members and other relevant stakeholders and resource experts, when required.

A template for a Change Project Plan is provided in Table 2.4. The change facilitators are encouraged to add additional dimensions as they see fit. The templates can also be adapted by the team members for the plan of their individual projects.

Table 2.4 – Template for a Change Project Plan

The need for the Change Project:
- Describe the background of the issue or problem that led to this type of project being chosen.
- Provide evidence that there is a need to resolve this problem or issue.

The purpose and outcomes of the Change Project:
- Establish the purpose of the project in a precise and concise manner.
- What are the expected project outcomes?
- What are the expected process outcomes?

The team:
- Who are the members of the team?
- Justify why they qualify as members of the team.
- What are the expected learning outcomes for each of these members?
- What activities are to be put in place to achieve the expected project outcomes?
- What type of budget is needed to achieve the project objective?
- What is the timeframe to achieve the project and learning outcomes?
- Consider other aspects of project planning and implementation.

The justification:
- Justify why the Change Project Plan is work-based learning and action learning oriented.

JOINT OBSERVATION AND REFLECTION

Typically, at the end of each WBL phase, the change facilitators will seek and collate feedback from their team members on their observations of how the change project is progressing and whether any further amendment is needed in the next WBL phase to make their change project more effective.

EVALUATION

After the Joint Observation and Reflection session, the AR Group members will come together for an Evaluation meeting. The change facilitators will report on their change projects and the feedback and observations of their team members. The AR Group members will analyse and evaluate the project and process outcomes as well as the learning outcomes of the change facilitators and their team members.

Observations by the CEO and other AR Group members will be reflected upon and discussed, triangulated, evaluated and re-planning for the next AR cycle would take place.

VALIDATION

Usually, the WAL Change Programme is validated at the end of every two Major AR Cycles by the Validation Committee. However, the frequency of the Validation meetings can vary depending upon the dictates of the situation and challenges arising during the AR cycles.

During each Validation Committee meeting, the change leader will present the project, process and learning outcomes of the WAL Change Programme to date, including the issues and challenges faced during the implementation. The change facilitators will present the findings of their own change reports and seek feedback from those present. They will then make the necessary adjustments to the WAL Change Programme and their change projects, as advised by the Validation Committee. The Evaluation and Validation phases of the various AR cycles are depicted in Figure 2.8.

WORK-APPLIED LEARNING (WAL) MODEL   49

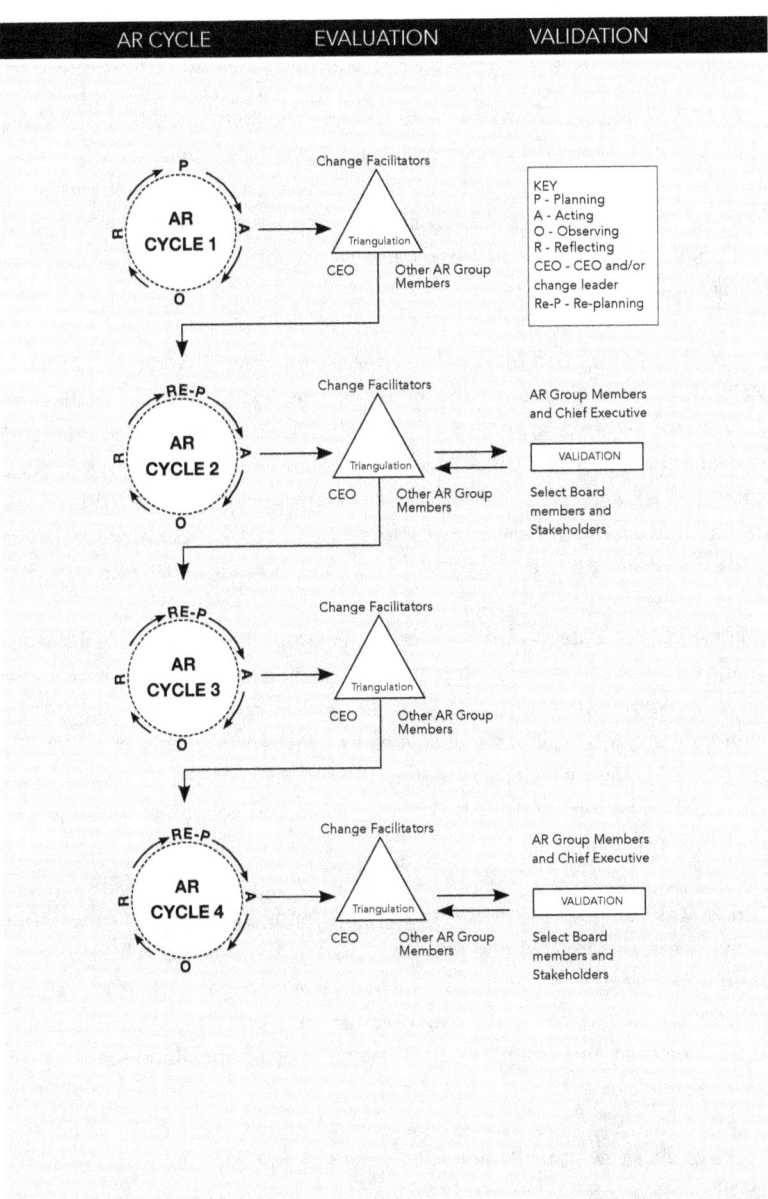

Figure 2.8 – Evaluation and Validation Process in WAL Change Programmes

FLOW CHART OF A TYPICAL WAL CHANGE PROGRAMME

Now that I have explained the WAL Change process including the various phases of the Major AR Cycles that make up a WAL Change Programme, it is useful to review the process in a diagrammatic form. Accordingly, Figures 2.9a and 2.9b are flow charts which illustrate the planning and implementation process of a typical WAL Change Programme over four Major AR Cycles.

Figure 2.9a shows two Major AR Cycles of the WAL Change Programme. Major AR Cycle 1 captures the planning process. It starts with the first AR Group Meeting attended by the CEO and/or change leader and four change facilitators and then shows the development of the WAL Change Plan and WBL Project plans. Next comes the first WBL Phase where the change facilitators select their teams, develop detailed plans for their WBL projects and obtain CEO approval and support.

Major AR Cycle 2 starts with the second AR Group Meeting where the WAL Change Plan and the WBL Project Plans are approved. It then shows the initial implementation of the WAL Change Plan over two AR Mini-Cycles where the change facilitators work with their respective teams on their WBL projects. The third AR Group meeting is held after AR Mini-Cycle 1 and an evaluation meeting by the AR Group as well as a Validation meeting are held after AR Mini-Cycle 2.

During Major AR Cycles 1 and 2, the change leaders will acquire knowledge in the areas of Organisational Change using Action Research as well as Action Learning and Reflective Practice. The change facilitators will be introduced to the concepts and practice of Work Based Learning and Action Learning and Reflective Practice and specific knowledge relevant to their change projects..

Figure 2.9b shows that Major AR Cycle 3 and 4 functions on the same basis as Major AR Cycles 1 and 2 with AR Group meetings, Mini-Cycles, Evaluation and Validation. The relevant knowledge required for these change projects include Work-based Learning, Organisational Learning and Knowledge Management and additional project-based knowledge.

WORK-APPLIED LEARNING (WAL) MODEL 51

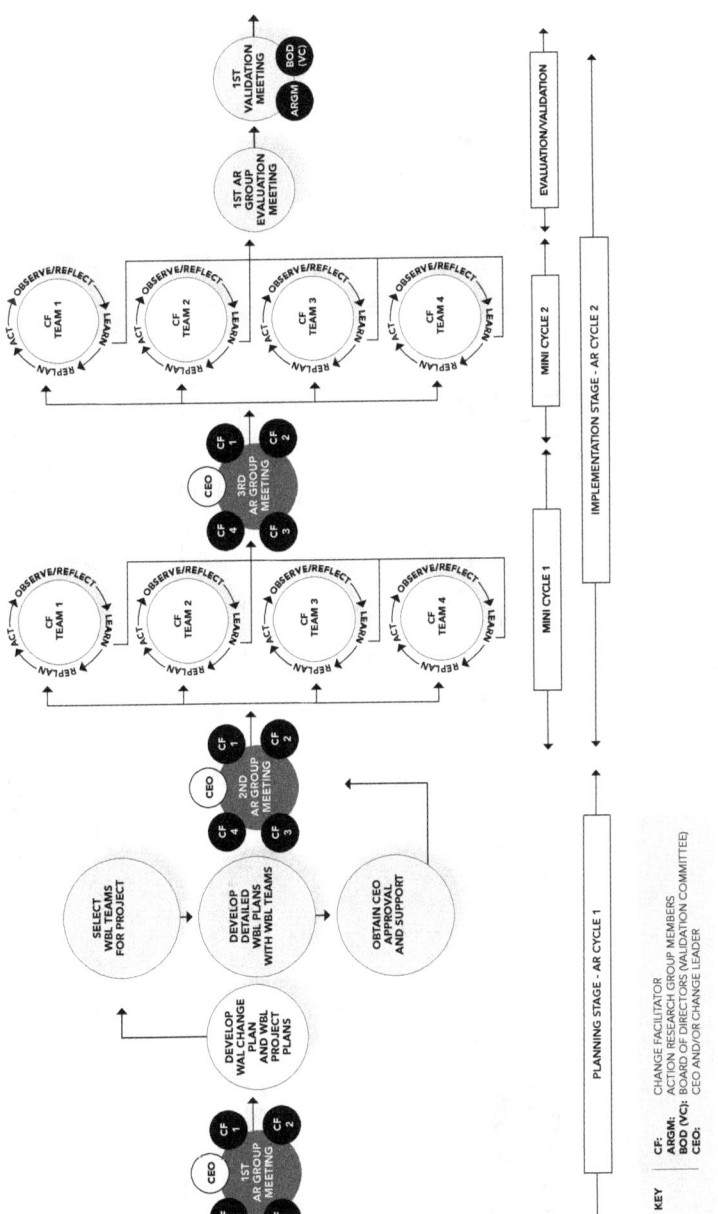

Figure 2.9A – Planning and Implementing AR Major Cycles 1 and 2

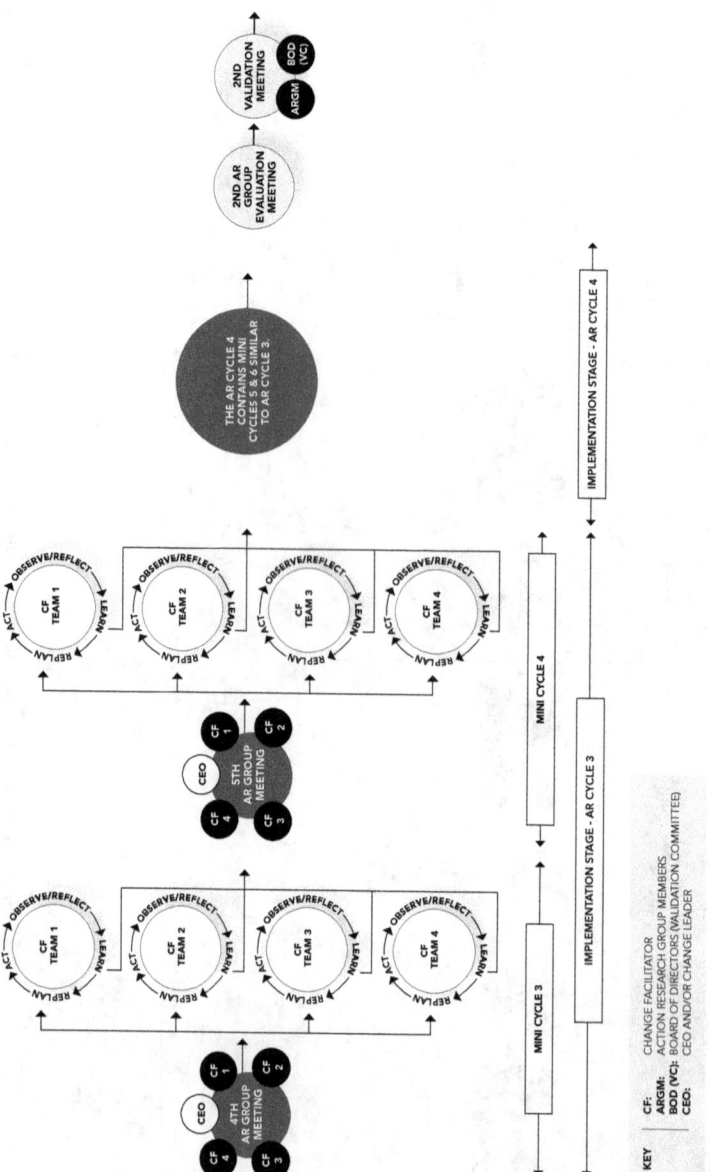

Figure 2.9B – Re-planning and Implementing AR Major Cycle 3

CHAPTER SUMMARY

This chapter has described how I developed the WAL model in the context of the concept, the practice, and the process for the planning and implementation of WAL Change Programmes.

In the next chapter, I explain how managers can develop plans for their WAL practitioner research projects using the fused Action Research method and Action Learning and Reflective Practice processes (ARAL).

CHAPTER 3

SELVA ABRAHAM

Designing WAL Research Plans

Chapter 1 introduced the conceptual framework for Work-Applied Learning (WAL) that fosters the development of managers and other professionals as lifelong learners and practitioner researchers – through reflective practice, action research, action learning and action leadership, for positive organisational change.

In Chapter 2, the concept, the process and the practice of WAL were explained, with more details provided on the fused Action Research method and Action Learning and reflective practice processes (ARAL) that is at the heart of WAL.

As stated in Chapter 1, the WAL model can also be used in undertaking practitioner research projects in the workplace. Thus, in this Chapter 3, I discuss how managers who conduct research within their workplace can use the ARAL approach within the WAL model to develop their research plans for implementation in a systematic way, to drive organisational improvement, generate new knowledge and enhance their practice.

It focuses on small groups and predominantly employs qualitative research methods, requiring a deep understanding of phenomenological research within the participatory paradigm (Zuber-Skerritt and Abraham, 2017).

DESIGNING THE WAL RESEARCH PLAN

My journey with WAL as a research approach started when I embarked on my Phd in the early 1990s. I wanted to investigate how the Action Research method can be used in the designing and implementation of a management training and development programme for a group of indigenous community leaders in South Australia. During my search for an appropriate research method, I was drawn to the exploratory case study research design, inspired by Yin's work (1989). Thus, the research plan that I developed for my doctoral thesis was based on the exploratory case study research design, grounded by an action research method. Recognizing the novelty of this research design in the field of business and management studies at the doctoral level, my supervisor provided encouragement and support.

My research plan consisted of a Conceptual stage and an Action Research method stage, as depicted in Table 3.1.

Table 3.1 – The Exploratory Case Study Research Design In My Doctoral Thesis

CONCEPTUAL STAGE	ACTION RESEARCH METHOD STAGE
• experiences and past interest of researcher • literature review (on the designing and implementation of management training and development programmes)	• data collection by participant observation at site • data analysis by content analysis • evaluation by triangulation

The separation into 'Conceptual' and 'Action Research Method' stages was critical to the success of my project. The conceptual stage enabled me to identify the gap in the literature on the use of an action research method in designing and implementing management training and development programmes that addressed the needs of indigenous community leaders. The action research method stage involved action research cycles of planning, action, observation, reflection and evaluation that took place during the planning and implementation of the management training and development programme. The research techniques used for data gathering during the cycles included participant observation, data evaluation using triangulation and data analysis using content analysis, and quantitative analysis for validity.

Over the past three decades since earning my doctorate, I have developed the WAL model, as explained in Chapter 2 of this book. During this time, I also collaborated with numerous Chief Executives and senior managers where they customised my WAL research plan for their practitioner research projects and have achieved substantial impact for their organisations, their teams, and themselves, in terms of project outcomes, process outcomes and learning outcomes. Twenty six of these Chief Executives and senior managers completed their research studies at master's level and 10 at doctoral level under my supervision or advice at Australian Institute of Business, the University of South Australia, Southern Cross University and University of Malaysia Sarawak.

In the process of supervising or advising the above-mentioned candidates in their research as well as undertaking my own research, I have continually refined the WAL research plan for practitioner research projects. The current version of the WAL research plan is shown in Figure 3.1.

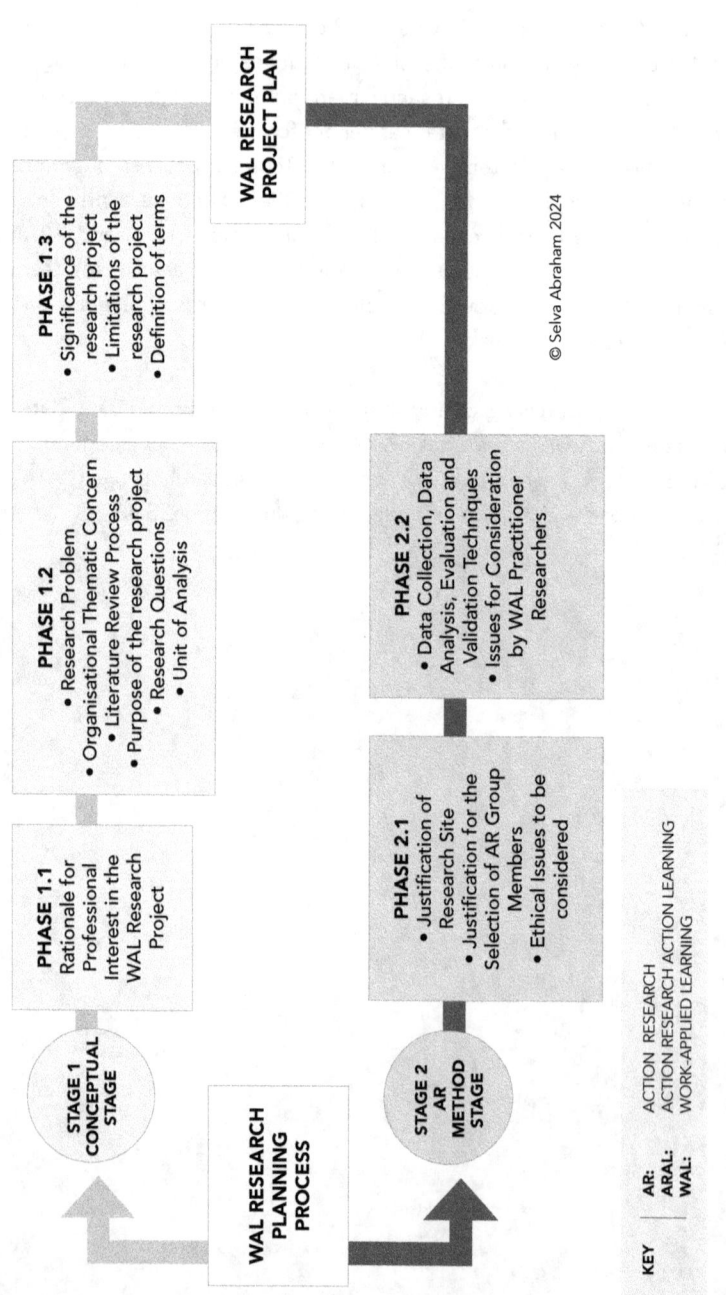

Figure 3.1 – Process Of Designing The WAL Research Plan

While the Conceptual Stage and the Action Research Method Stage of a typical WAL research plan are further segmented into phases, it is important to note that these phases may not always follow a linear progression; some may occur at the same time.

Each of these stages is explained in detail, with examples provided from three different research projects, all undertaken at doctoral level. The first example is my own research project where I used an Action Research method. The two other examples were research projects undertaken later when my WAL model had evolved further.

STAGE 1 CONCEPTUAL STAGE

The Conceptual Stage of the WAL research planning design process is divided into three phases:

Phase 1.1: This phase involves establishing the rationale for your professional interest in the WAL research project.

Phase 1.2: This phase includes defining the research problem, identifying the organisational thematic concern, conducting a literature review, establishing the purpose of the research project, formulating research questions, and determining the unit of analysis.

Phase 1.3: This phase focuses on outlining the significance of the research project, acknowledging its limitations, and providing relevant definitions.

Each phase plays a crucial role in setting the foundation for the research project and ensuring its relevance and feasibility.

Details of these phases are discussed below.

PHASE 1.1
In this Phase, you will rationalize your professional interest in undertaking the research project using the WAL model. This involves asking yourself several key questions:

1. Need for the research project:
    - What is the main problem affecting my organisation?

- Does this organisational problem align with my professional interest?
- Would addressing this problem benefit my organisation and my professional development?
- Do I understand the concept, practice, and process of the WAL model?
- Have I reviewed the relevant literature in the management or business discipline area of the problem?
- Can the WAL model used in this project be replicated in other projects within the organisation?
- Could the findings and lessons learned from the use of the WAL model in this project be replicated in other projects within the organisation?
- Will the WAL research project make a significant contribution to other organisations in the same industry, such as influencing policymaking, improving practices, or contributing to the professional development of managers and their team members?

2. Scoping the WAL research project in the organisation:
   - What is the proposed design of the WAL research project to address the organisational problem?
   - Who will be involved in the WAL research project?
   - When, how, and where will the WAL research project be planned and implemented?

3. Other issues for consideration:
   - Will the management support the WAL research project and remain committed to the project for a minimum period of at least 18 months, despite internal or external changes in the organisation?
   - Is the organisation a private, public, community, or family-owned organisation? Each type of organisation will have unique cultural issues and management styles that need to be understood while developing the WAL research project, as each will pose different types of challenges when undertaking an intervention in the organisation.

- If you intent to use the findings from the WAL research project in a master's dissertation or a doctoral thesis, have you made a full declaration to your management? Written consent for such use needs to be obtained from management prior to the initiation of the WAL research project.

PHASE 1.2

During this Phase, you will focus on several key aspects of the WAL research project:

Organisational Thematic Concern: This involves identifying and defining the specific organisational problem that the research project aims to address. This problem should align with your professional interests.

Research Problem: This refers to the broader organisational issues or themes that the research problem falls under. For example, do other organisations in the region face a similar issue, or is it an industry-wide problem? Understanding this context can help in formulating effective solutions and strategies.

Literature Review: This is about reviewing existing literature and research related to the research problem and organizational thematic concern. The aim is to understand the current state of knowledge and identify gaps that the WAL research project can fill.

Purpose of the Research Project: This involves clearly stating the overall aim or objective of the WAL research project. What does the project hope to achieve or discover?

Research Questions: These are specific questions that the WAL research project aims to answer. They should be directly related to the research problem and purpose of the research project.

Unit of Analysis: This refers to the main entity that is being analysed in the WAL research project. This could be individuals, groups, organisations, or other units, depending on the nature of the research problem and purpose of the research project.

These aspects are crucial in setting the direction and scope of the WAL research project, ensuring that it is focused, relevant, and feasible. The linkage between these various aspects is illustrated in **Figure 3.2**.

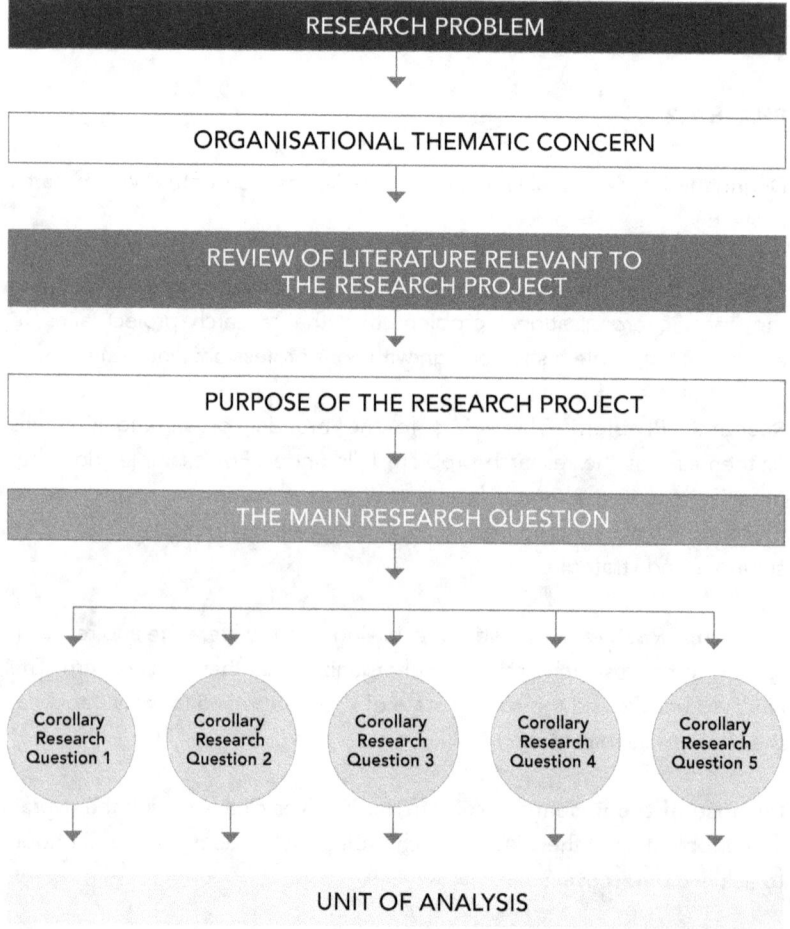

Figure 3.2 – Linkage between the Research Problem, the Organisational Thematic concern, Literature Review, Purpose of the Research Project, Research Questions and Unit of Analysis

1.2.1 Establishing the Organisational Thematic Concern

In order to establish the Organisational Thematic Concern of an organisation, you need to first have in-depth discussions with the Chief Executive Officer (CEO) to understand their perception of the organisational problem and related issues, and then validate these perspectives with other Senior Managers.

The data collection technique used here involves conversational interviews with the CEO and each Senior Manager. Following these interviews, you could invite the CEO and the Senior Managers to form an Action Research (AR) Group. The first AR Group meeting would be a focus group discussion to validate the organisational problem and thematic concern.

1.2.2 Research Problem

After identifying the Organisational Thematic Concern, you should investigate whether similar problems exist in other organisations within the same industry and located in the same country or region. This information is obtained through reviewing published secondary data, such as ministerial speeches, industry leaders' comments, discussions with experienced managers in similar industries, attending industry-specific workshops, and reviewing industry-based publications. This secondary data can also be cross-validated by meeting with executives in similar industries or organisations in the same location as your organisation.

In practice, the Organisational Thematic Concern is identified first, and then a search is undertaken to determine whether this concern is industry- wide. However, you should be aware that when you write up the WAL project report, it is helpful to the readers to start with the industry-wide Research Problem to help them understand how the Research Problem relates to the Organisational Thematic Concern.

Three examples of the link between the Research Problem and the Organisational Thematic Concern in WAL research projects are shown below:

Example 1: Kuju CDEP, South Australia

The Kuju CDEP research project was a management development programme designed to enhance the skills of the Aboriginal Board members of Kuju Community Development Employment Programme Inc (Kuju CDEP) in Port Lincoln, South Australia. Kuju CDEP was founded to offer employment and on-the-job training to all eligible Aboriginal individuals in Port Lincoln, a region where employment opportunities for Aboriginal people had been scarce for several years. The term "Kuju" translates to 'fish traps' in the local Aboriginal language, symbolizing the organisation's mission to provide resources and opportunities. Initiated in May 1989, Kuju CDEP holds the distinction of being the first urban CDEP in Australia.

The Research Problem and the Organisational Thematic Concern of Kuju CDEP are shown in Table 3.2.

Table 3.2 – Research Problem and the Organisational Thematic Concern in the Kuju CDEP Research Project

Research problem
In many countries the indigenous people are a disadvantaged minority group. In order to achieve economic independence and self-management, they must be provided with appropriate education and training including management training for their community leaders.

There are many such schemes in existence in countries, including Australia, where indigenous people are a disadvantaged group. In Australia, development programmes are designed to teach Aboriginal community leaders a wide range of management and administrative skills in a way that is in harmony with traditional Aboriginal ways of learning and adapted to meet the differing needs and requirements of the indigenous community leaders.

The Report of the Committee of Review of Aboriginal Employment and Training Programmes, 1985 (the Miller Report) recommended that the Australian government should increase its support for community enterprise development in order to improve the unemployment situation of Aboriginal people. The expansion of the Community Development and Employment Programme (CDEP) was a response to this recommendation. For such schemes to be successful, management training is needed in Aboriginal communities. The lack of adequate and appropriate management training in Aboriginal communities was noted in the Miller Report and reiterated in the Aboriginal Employment Development Policy (AEDP) Papers (1987) and *A Chance for the Future* (1989) which was the Report of the Australian House of Representatives Standing Committee on Aboriginal Affairs.

In *A Chance for the Future* (1989) it was suggested that management training was needed that would develop the confidence and self-esteem of Aboriginal people and improve their basic literacy and numeracy skills. Training programmes should be developed on site, in consultation with Aboriginal people, who should be given the opportunity to provide input on the design, delivery and evaluation of such programmes. Training should also be provided for existing non-Aboriginal personnel, so that they could become resource people, co-ordinating the performance of community organisations and providing training. The importance of monitoring the evaluation of these programmes was also stressed.

As a result of the concerns raised by these reports and policies, the Australian Commonwealth Department of Aboriginal Affairs (DAA) sought the services of management consultants to conduct management training programmes for Aboriginal community leaders.

Organisational Thematic Concern

Commenting on the issues related to Aboriginal unemployment in Port Lincoln, the chairperson of Kuju CDEP in a letter dated 8th March 1989 to the Australian Minister of Aboriginal Affairs, stated:

> *The downturn in local industry such as the South Australian Meat Corporation–Abattoirs, Freezepack, Australian National Railways, Safcol Fish Processor and various other*

> *seasonal industries in Port Lincoln left the Aboriginal people who were employed in those industries unemployed.*

In addition there have been very little employment opportunities for school leavers in the last 8 to 10 years. This had left the skill levels of the younger generation at a zero level with no role models to look up to. It was hoped Kuju filled the gap to help the Aborigines of Port Lincoln cope with the unemployment problem.

The officer of the Department of Aboriginal Affairs identified the following needs in a letter dated 15th September 1989 to the chairperson of Kuju CDEP:

> *Whilst Kuju was set up to fill the Aboriginal unemployment gap in Port Lincoln, there was a need for: 1) management structure and planning skills for its Board members; 2) training and development for its Board members, staff and the Kuju CDEP participants; and 3) the establishment of systems within the organisation.*

A report dated 22 November 1989 on the overview of the operations of Kuju CDEP stated:

> *The most important issue which Kuju needs to resolve at the present time is the establishment of a strong Board of Management. This would give leadership and direction to Kuju with Aboriginal participation. Kuju has achieved many good things in the past six months but there is still too much reliance on staff in decision-making. A Board comprised of inexperienced members only is unrealistic. Unless the Board is strengthened, ... there will continue to be a crisis management situation with little Board input into longer term planning and the setting up of broad policy structures within which staff would be required to work in the day-to-day management of Kuju.*

The researcher was one of the management consultants appointed to undertake a 12 to 18 month management training programme for Aboriginal community leaders in South Australia.

This appointment provided the researcher with the opportunity to investigate the use of the Action Research method in the design and implementation of a management training and development programme with the Aboriginal Board members of Kuju CDEP..
Source: Candidate 27 (1993)

Example 2: Well Workover company (WWC), Trinidad & Tobago

Well Workover refers to the process of performing maintenance and remedial actions to ensure the efficiency of oil wells. The WAL research project for WWC, a company engaged in Well Workover services in Trinidad and Tobago was initiated to explore the development and implementation of a Work Applied Learning – Occupational Health and Safety Management System (WAL-OHSMS) for this company. This system is designed to enhance safety measures and protocols within the context of well workover operations.

The Research Problem and the Organisational Thematic Concern of WWC are set out in Table 3.3.

Table 3.3 – Research Problem and the Organisational Thematic Concern in the WWC WAL Research Project

Research Problem
In 2011, the International Labour Organisation sponsored a "World Day for Safety and Health" and Trinidad and Tobago (T&T)held a conference in conjunction with that day with a theme of 'Occupational safety and health management systems: A tool for continuous improvement'. According to the keynote speaker, the Honourable Errol McLeod, Minister of Labour and Small and Micro Enterprise Development in T&T:
> The statistics for Trinidad and Tobago on industrial accidents and fatalities are quite alarming. Our records at the Ministry reveal that in 2010 there were 843 industrial accidents and nine fatalities. While these figures appear quite small in comparison to other countries and we may consider that we are progressing well, I refuse to accept

this as being the 'best we can do.' I have said before that one industrial accident or fatality is one too many. I agree with the human rights activists when they say that there is nothing more important than life and there is nothing more evident and compelling for a human than the right to life. (Ministry of Labour and Small and Micro Enterprise Development, 2011, pp. 6-7)

The Minister added (2011, p. 13):
At the enterprise level, the following basic principles are integral to an effective Occupational Safety and Health Management System: management commitment; planning; consultation; risk management and training. This requires a cyclical process approach of Plan-Do-Check-Act. I wish to point out that the main critical success factor in ensuring a functional and effective Occupational Safety and Health Management System is the commitment from the top management.

The same Minister, in his address at the launch of National Occupational Safety and Health Week in 2014 continued to highlight the importance of employers providing a safe place of work in an attempt to reduce workplace incidents and accidents. He noted that it has to be a collaborative effort between government, employers and employees, to improve the trend of underreporting of accidents in the workplace and effect a reduction of the losses that result from workplace accidents and incidents. (Ministry of Labour and Small and Micro Enterprise Development 2014, p.3).

The President of the Industrial Court of T&T, Deborah Thomas-Felix, in commenting on OHS at work during the opening of the Industrial Court on 19 September 2016, noted that the importance of OHS in relation to the world of work did not always receive the recognition it deserves. She further expressed concern with the 102 fatal accidents that occurred over the period 2006 to 2015. In her address (2016, pp. 7-8) she said:
One death in the workplace was one too many. These accidents and incidents in my view are to a large measure due to failures and deficiency in the policy and management

of occupational health and safety in several businesses in this country. As a nation the concept of increased productivity and increased economic activity cannot be promoted without simultaneously insisting on effective policies for occupational safety and health in all business enterprise. (Industrial Court of T&T, 2016, pp. 7-8)

At the opening of a special sitting of the Industrial Court of T&T for 2016-2017, she presented data that highlighted that apart from the 109 workplace fatalities occurring across several industries during the period 2006 to 2016, there was a significant number of non-fatal accidents. She indicated that she felt the need to present this data so that the enormity of the OHS problem could be understood.

Organisational Thematic Concern
WWC is one of approximately 15 Well Workover organisations which provide well services Company in T&T.

The prime objective of WWC is to provide the petroleum industry with high quality mechanical maintenance and well servicing and workover services. Its operations are based in the energy sector, with a staff of approximately 150 employees.

WWC currently operates three Well Workover drilling rigs on land in the execution of its services. WWC has had in the past and continues to have an accident/incident rate which is seen as unacceptable. This ranges from near misses to actual loss time accidents.

There have been many safety initiatives implemented to address these problems, including an OHS management system (OHSMS) aligned to Occupational Health and Safety Assessment Series (OHSAS) 18001 and the Plan-Do-Check-Act model.

However, WWC's OHS performance is one that has continued to cost the organisation significant financial loss both directly from the occurrences of accidents and indirectly from loss of contracts. Additionally, the loss of human resource and its reputation as an organisation that operates in a safe manner in the high-risk petroleum industry, has been severely compromised. Despite continued OHS

management efforts and initiatives, the accident/incident rate has not shown any reversal in trend which indicates that the desired objective was not being realised. Herein lies the thematic concern, and the problem that has the potential to adversely affect the organisation's sustainability and its ability to provide the necessary Well Workover services that are required in the petroleum industry.
Source: Candidate 30 (2021)

Example 3: Monash Health, Victoria, Australia

Monash Health, a comprehensive health service in the south-eastern suburbs of Melbourne, Victoria, provides a wide range of public healthcare services and operates Australia's largest diabetes service. The WAL research project was initiated with the objective of developing and implementing a Telemonitoring system within Monash Health to effectively treat and manage diabetic patients. Telemonitoring, a subset of Telehealth, is defined as a healthcare delivery method that utilizes audio, video, and other telecommunications and electronic information processing technologies to remotely monitor patient status (Institute of Medicine Committee on Evaluating Clinical Applications of Telemedicine 1996, p. 248). This system aims to enhance patient care by enabling remote monitoring and management of diabetes.

The Research Problem and the Organisational Thematic Concern in Monash Health are set out in Table 3.4.

Table 3.4 – Research Problem and the Organisational Thematic Concern in the Monash Health WAL research project

Research Problem
Diabetes is a significant national health problem in Australia. Although there is increased demand for chronic disease treatment, including of diabetes, policymakers are finding shortages in the medical workforce.....Faced with an increasing demand for healthcare delivery and a diminishing medical workforce, policymakers are looking for changes in the way in which healthcare services are provided.

Telemonitoring represents a promising technological opportunity to redefine healthcare delivery (Meystre 2005). By combining information technology and healthcare delivery mechanisms such as home-based care, more cost-effective care can be delivered while also improving patient satisfaction and quality of care (Meystre 2005; Schofield, Kline, Schmalfuss, Carver, Aranda, Pauly, Hill, Neugaard, & Chumbler 2005; Bowes & McColgan 2006). Telemonitoring can provide these benefits by redefining the existing hospital-centric delivery models of chronic disease management (Jennett, Scott, Hall, Hailey, Ohinmaa, Anderson, Thomas, Young & Lorenzetti 2004). Clearly Telehealth seems appropriate, particularly for the treatment of chronic diseases such as diabetes, yet despite increasing recognition of the benefits of Telehealth, it has not been widely adopted (Jennett, Hall, Hailey, Ohinmaa, Anderson, Thomas, Young, Lorenzetti & Scott 2003; Moffatt & Eley 2011).

A growing body of healthcare management literature supports the benefits of Telemonitoring, including improved patient outcomes and decreased costs for healthcare providers (Pare, Jaana & Sicotte 2007; Cryer, Shannon, Van Amsterdam, & Leff 2012). Despite its promise, however, low utilisation of Telehealth is a concern for both international and national healthcare management (Jennett et al. 2003; Moffatt & Eley, 2011).

The low rate of utilisation is also a concern within the Victorian healthcare sector, as evidenced by the ministerial Health Innovation and Reform Council noting that there was "significant potential to improve the rate of Telehealth adoption across the system" (Department of Health 2013, p.5). One of the measures adopted to rectify this problem is the financial incentive provided by the Australian Government Department of Health to encourage the establishment and use of Telehealth (Department of Human Services 2014).

Reasons for the low utilisation of Telehealth may include concerns raised over the accuracy of its purported benefits, legal and regulatory issues, and its impact on the quality of care. Some researchers question Telehealth's cost-effectiveness (Henderson, Knapp, Fernández, Beecham, Hirani, Cartwright, Rixon, Beynon, Rogers, Bower, Doll,

Fitzpatrick, Steventon, Bardsley, Hendy & Newman 2013) and the rigour of the benefits analysis of existing Telehealth programs (Bergmo 2009; Dávalos, French, Burdick & Simmons 2009; Jennett et al. 2003). Others argue that there still remain a number of technical and legal challenges (Kienzle 2001; May, Harrison, Macfarlane, Williams, Mair & Wallace 2003) that must be overcome, particularly in the areas of legislation and licensing, informed patient consent, and reimbursement (Baker & Bufka 2011; Mars & Jack 2010). In addition, some (e.g., Stanberry 2001) have highlighted that such a change in the care delivery model and dependency on technology may have negative consequences for the traditional patient–clinician relationship and quality of care.

Organisational Thematic Concern
Monash Health's failure to use Telehealth – and, in particular, Telemonitoring – is a concern. The Chief Medical Officer of Monash Health has stated that "[t]elemonitoring is currently not utilised within Monash Health. This emerging technology has the potential to improve outcomes for both patients and the health service" (Loh 2014, personal communication, 1 September).

This research project explores these challenges by investigating the design and implementation of a home-based Telemonitoring system for diabetes patients in a Victorian Health Service in Australia using the action research method. Specifically, the research forms an exploratory study of the development and implementation of a Telemonitoring system in Monash Health).

Thus, the research project will use an action research method to develop and implement a Telemonitoring system to treat and manage diabetic patients. The aim of the research project is to address the lack of Telemonitoring within Monash Health as a whole, and more specifically within the diabetes unit.
Source: Candidate 31 (2022)

1.2.3 Literature Review Process

As part of the process of identifying the Research Problem, it is crucial for you to simultaneously conduct an in-depth review of the relevant literature. This review should ideally follow the sequence outlined below:
1. Identify the parent and immediate literature related to the Research Problem. This involves finding and examining the broader and more specific bodies of work that are directly related to your research topic.
2. Specify the boundaries of the literature in the context of the Research Problem. This step involves defining the scope of your literature review, including the types of sources to be reviewed, the time period to be covered, and the specific topics to be included.
3. Identify the gap in the literature and the contribution to knowledge, practice, and policy. This involves determining what has not been adequately addressed or is missing from the existing literature, and how your research can contribute to filling this gap and advancing knowledge, practice, and policy.

Table 3.5 illustrates how you could undertake the literature review process to deepen your understanding of the Research Problem and identify the gap in the literature.

Table 3.5 – Literature Review Process

DIMENSION	QUESTIONS TO BE ASKED
Parent Literature	What is the broad knowledge or discipline area or the 'parent' literature of the Research Problem? If the Research Problem is in the business and management discipline area, the Parent Literature could be strategy, marketing, finance, human resource management, operations, governance, leadership, human resource development etc.

Table 3.5 (Continued)

DIMENSION	QUESTIONS TO BE ASKED
Immediate Literature relevant to the Research Problem and Organisational Thematic Concern	What is the knowledge area that is specific to the Research Problem and Organisational Thematic Concern? For example, if you have identified human resource management as the parent literature of your Research Problem and Organisational Thematic Concern, what is the specific aspect of this knowledge area which is relevant?
Boundaries of the Research	What are the boundaries of research? Here, you will determine the parts of the Research Problem that are significant for the project and which aspects can be eliminated. Examples of boundaries for a research project are a specific organisation, or sector, country or region.
Parts of the Research Problem Studied in Previous Research	What are the parts of the Research Problem which have been previously undertaken according to the literature review? The answer to this question will help identify the gap in the knowledge area.

The literature review process that was used in the Kuju CDEP, WWC and Monash Health WAL research projects is summarised in Table 3.6.

Table 3.6 – Literature Review Process in the Kuju CDEP, WWC and Monash Health WAL Research Projects

DIMENSION	KUJU CDEP PROJECT	WWC PROJECT	MONASH HEALTH PROJECT
Parent Literature	• Training & Development • Management Training & Development	Human Resource Management (HRM)	Healthcare management
Immediate Literature and Research Problem	Designing and Implementing Management Training & Development Programmes • General context • Indigenous context	Occupational Health and Safety (OHS)	Telehealth in healthcare management and diffusion of innovation
Boundaries of the Research Problem Area	Designing and Implementing Management Training & Development Programmes • In Australia • In South Australia	Occupational Health and Safety models used in the petroleum industry in T&T	Telemonitoring in Diabetes Programme in Monash Health
Parts of the Research Problem Studied in Previous Research	Designing and Implementing Management Training & Development Programmes	Occupational Health and Safety models used globally	Telehealth in diabetes management

The next steps are to identify the Purpose of the Research Project, the Research Questions and the Unit of Analysis.

1.2.4 Purpose of the Research Project

According to Marshall, Rossman and Blanco (2022), qualitative methodologists have described four major purposes for research: exploratory, explanatory, descriptive or emancipatory. Each purpose has a specific set of research questions as set out in **Table 3.7**.

Table 3.7 – Matching Research Questions To The Purpose Of The Research Project

PURPOSE OF THE RESEARCH PROJECT	GENERAL RESEARCH QUESTION
EXPLORATORY	
To investigate little-understood phenomena	What is happening in this social program?
To identify or discover important categories of meaning	What are the salient themes, patterns, or categories of meaning for the participants?
To generate hypotheses for further research	How are these patterns linked with one another?
EXPLANATORY	
To explain the patterns related to the phenomenon in questions	What events, beliefs, attitudes, or policies shape this phenomenon?
To identify plausible relationships shaping the phenomenon	How do these forces interact to result in the phenomenon?
DESCRIPTIVE	
To document and describe the phenomenon of interest	What are the salient actions, events, beliefs, attitudes and social structures and processes occurring in this phenomenon?
EMANCIPATORY	
To create opportunities and the will to engage in social action	How do participants problematize their circumstances and take positive social action?

Source: Marshall, Rossman, Blanco (2022, pg 94)

The WAL method is predominantly exploratory in nature and may at times include other purposes such as emancipatory. However any WAL research project should accurately encapsulate the following aspects in its purpose statement:
1. The subject of investigation: This refers to the specific topic or issue that the project aims to explore or understand.
2. The unit of analysis: This refers to the primary entity that is being analysed in the research project. It could be an individual, a group, an organisation, or a specific phenomenon.
3. The potential contributions of the WAL research project: This includes the possible contributions to the existing literature, the policy implications, and the practical applications for the organisation. It is important to highlight how the research project can add value or bring about improvements in these areas.
4. The potential for further studies: This refers to how the findings of the WAL research project could pave the way for additional research or studies in the future. It is crucial to identify potential areas for further exploration or investigation.

It is essential that the purpose statement is precise and remains consistent throughout the WAL research project. This ensures clarity of intent and direction, and helps you to maintain focus on the research project's primary objectives.

1.2.5 Research Questions

The Main Research Question and the Corollary Research Questions should be closely aligned with the Purpose of the Research Project. These questions are designed to gather information that will help you address the project's purpose. They serve two primary functions:
   i) To guide you throughout the WAL research project, by providing a clear direction for the research.
   ii) To provide you answers to help you achieve the project's purpose.

Therefore, Research Questions need to be clear, focused, and concise.

They should provide a central theme around which you can structure your research. Additionally, Research Questions provide a focus for the project, by guiding the research activity and later assisting in writing up your findings and conclusions of the WAL research project.

Table 3.8 below presents the Purpose of the Research Project for the Kuju CDEP research project as well as the Main and Corollary Research Questions, to show how the research questions flow from the purpose statement. At this stage, it would be beneficial to revisit the Research Problem and the Organisational Thematic Concern for Kuju CDEP (as set out in Table 3.2 to understand how the purpose statement is derived from these aspects of the research project.

Table 3.8 – Purpose Of The Kuju CDEP WAL Research Project And Research Questions

Purpose of the Research Project
The purpose of this research project was to:
1) Investigate the use of an Action Research method in the design and implementation of a management training and development programme that addressed the needs of indigenous community leaders;
2) make a contribution to the Action Research literature in the area of designing and implementing management training and development programmes for indigenous community leaders; and
3) generate hypotheses and suggestions for further studies relating to the use of an Action Research method in the design and implementation of management training and development programmes for indigenous community leaders.

Main Research Question
Could an Action Research method be used to design and implement a management training and development programme that addressed the needs of indigenous community leaders?

Corollary Research Questions
1) What were the processes that emerged within the Action Research cycles of planning, action, observation, reflection and evaluation (an important additional element in this study) during the designing and implementation of the management training and development programme for indigenous community leaders?
2) What were the characteristics of the Action Research method that were identified in this study?
3) Did the indigenous community leaders as a group perceive themselves to have increased in:
- confidence and self-esteem;
- commitment; and
- the understanding and application of management skills and knowledge?
4) Did the evaluators perceive the indigenous community leaders as a group to have increased in:
- confidence and self-esteem;
- commitment; and
- the understanding and application of management skills and knowledge?
5) Did the PR perceive the indigenous community leaders as a group to have increased in:
- confidence and self-esteem;
- commitment; and
- the understanding and application of management skills and knowledge?

Source: Candidate 27 (1993)

The Purpose Statement and Research Questions for the WAL research project conducted at WWC are outlined in Table 3.9. It will be useful to consider this Table alongside Table 3.3 which details the Research Problem and the Organisational Thematic Concern for this project.

Table 3.9 – Purpose of the WWC WAL Research Project and Research Questions

Purpose of the Research Project
The purpose of this project is to investigate the development and implementation of an improved Occupational Health and Safety Management System (WAL-OHSMS) in a Well Workover company in the petroleum industry in T&T. This project seeks to:
1. Explore the development and implementation of a WAL-OHSMS in the petroleum industry in T&T
2. Make a contribution to the literature of OHS management in relation to the development and implementation of a WAL-OHSMS in the petroleum industry
3. Make a contribution to policy and practice of OHS management using a WAL-OHSMS, specifically in Well Workover organisations in the petroleum industry in T&T; and
4. Develop hypotheses and suggestions for further studies relating to the development and implementation of a WAL-OHSMS in Well Workover organisations for the petroleum industry in T&T.

Main Research Question
Can the WAL approach be used in the development and implementation of a WAL-OHSMS in a Well Workover organisation in the petroleum industry in T&T?

Corollary Research Questions
1. What is the WAL-OHSMS that has been developed for implementation in a Well Workover organisation in the petroleum industry in T&T?
2. What were the issues and challenges faced in the development of the WAL-OHSMS for the Well Workover organisation in the petroleum industry in T&T?
3. What was the WAL-OHSMS that evolved during the implementation of the proposed WAL-OHSMS for the Well Workover organisation in the petroleum industry in T&T?

4. What were the issues and challenges faced in the implementation of the WAL-OHSMS for the Well Workover organisation in the petroleum industry in T&T?
5. What were the project, learning and process outcomes in the development and implementation of the WAL-OHSMS for the Well Workover organisation in the petroleum industry in T&T?
6. What further insights into the application of AR characteristics emerged in this project?

Source: Candidate 30 (2021)

The Purpose of the Research Project and the Research Questions for the Monash Health research project are presented in Table 3.10. Again, this table should be examined in tandem with Table 3.4 which sets out the Research Problem and the Organisational Thematic Concern related to this project.

Table 3.10 – Purpose Of The Monash Health WAL Research Project And Research Questions

Purpose of the Research Project
This research project seeks to:
1) Explore the development and implementation of an action research-oriented Telemonitoring system to enable the home-based monitoring of diabetes patients in a Victorian health services network;
2) Contribute to the policy and practice of health care management in Victoria, specifically an action research-oriented Telemonitoring system for the home-based monitoring of diabetes patients;
3) Develop hypotheses and suggestions for further studies relating to the development and implementation of an action research-oriented Telemonitoring system for home-based monitoring of diabetes patients for other health services in Australia and globally; and
4) Contribute to the literature on health care management globally.

Main Research Question
Can Telemonitoring to enable the home-based monitoring of diabetes patients in a Victorian health service (Monash Health) be developed and implemented to improve clinical diabetes management using an action research orientation?

Corollary Research Questions
The following corollary research questions have been developed to further guide the collection and analysis of data used in the research project. The corollary research questions have been categorised into four main groups.

Addressing the Development Phase
 i. What was the action research-oriented Telemonitoring system developed for use by diabetes patients at Monash Health?
 ii. What were the processes that emerged within the action research cycles during the development of the Telemonitoring system for use by diabetes patients at Monash Health?
 iii. What were the issues and problems that arose in the development of the Telemonitoring system for use by diabetes patients at Monash Health?
 iv. What were the actions taken to overcome these issues and problems during the development of the Telemonitoring system for use by diabetes patients at Monash Health?

Addressing the Implementation Phase
 i. What was the action research-oriented Telemonitoring system that was implemented for diabetes patients at Monash Health?
 ii. What were the processes that emerged within the action research cycles during the implementation of the Telemonitoring system for diabetes patients at Monash Health?
 iii. What were the issues and problems that arose in the implementation of the Telemonitoring system for diabetes patients at Monash Health?
 iv. What were the actions taken to overcome these issues and problems during the implementation of the Telemonitoring system for use by diabetes patients at Monash Health?

Addressing the Refinement Phase
  i. What were the processes that emerged within the action research cycles during the refinement of the Telemonitoring system for diabetes patients at Monash Health?
  ii. What were the issues and problems that arose in the refinement of the Telemonitoring system for diabetes patients at Monash Health?
  iii. What were the actions taken to overcome these issues and problems during the refinement of the Telemonitoring system for diabetes patients at Monash Health?

Addressing the outcomes of the research project
  i. Were improvements observed in patient insulin stabilisation?
  ii. Were improvements observed in time spent by clinical staff in obtaining and managing participant insulin data?

Source: Candidate 31 (2022)

The Unit of Analysis

The unit of analysis is essentially the 'who' or 'what' that is the focus of a research project. It is primarily dictated by the research question and is determined by the actual data analysis that you will conduct in your WAL research project.

Examples of units of analysis include:
- Individual people (for example the work satisfactions of employees)
- Groups of people (for example a work department)
- Organisations (such as businesses, colleges, associations)
- Artifacts (like photographs, newspapers, books, machines and structures)
- Geographical entities (defined by parameters such as cities or countries)
- Social phenomena (such as births, deaths, divorces)

Table 3.11 shows how the unit of analysis is determined by the research question in each of the examples being studied.

Table 3.11 – The Unit Of Analysis In The Three Example Research Projects

RESEARCH PROJECT	MAIN RESEARCH QUESTION	UNIT OF ANALYSIS
Kuju CDEP	Could an Action Research method be used to design and implement a management training and development programme that addressed the needs of indigenous community leaders?	The Board members of Kuju CDEP
WWC	Can the WAL approach be used in the development and implementation of a WAL-OHSMS in a Well Workover organisation in the petroleum industry in T&T?	The Occupational Health and Safety management system in WWC
Monash Health	Can Telemonitoring to enable the home-based monitoring of diabetes patients in a Victorian health service (Monash Health) be developed and implemented to improve clinical diabetes management using an action research orientation?	The Telemonitoring system for Diabetes patients at Monash Health

PHASE 1.3

This Phase of the WAL research project focuses on the Significance of the Research Project, Limitations and Definitions.

1.3.1 Significance of the Research Project

In this section, you will explain the importance of your research. It highlights the impact of your project on your field of research, its contributions to the existing body of knowledge, and the beneficiaries of the research findings, along with how they benefit. This section can also propose areas for future research.

Here are some examples of statements that articulate the significance of a research project:

Kuju CDEP project

This project investigated the application of an action research method in the development of a management training and development programme for the Board members of Kuju CDEP, an Aboriginal community organisation.

The significance of the project was stated as follows:

This study makes a contribution to action research in the design and implementation of management training and development programmes and specifically to the literature on management training and development programmes for indigenous community leaders.

This study has relevance for policies that relate to the provision of training for Aboriginal communities in Australia, and also to the training of indigenous community leaders in other parts of the world. It investigates a fundamentally different approach to the development of management training and development programmes for indigenous community leaders and, if successful, could act as a stimulus for policy change related to the way in which management training for indigenous communities is designed and implemented.

This study should prove useful for practitioners in management training and development, especially those working with indigenous communities, as it could provide a model for the development of other management training and development programmes using the action research method.

It should also be useful to those interested in the evaluation of management training and development programmes and could, again, provide a model for other evaluations.

WWC research project

This project explored the development and implementation of a WAL-Occupational Health and Safety Management System (WAL-OHSMS) for a Well Workover organisation in the petroleum industry in T&T.

Set out below is the significance of this project:
> Since the petroleum industry in T&T is a significant contributor to the country's revenue and Gross National Product, any changing condition in this industry would have an impact on the economy and financial stability of T&T.
>
> As indicated earlier, a significant factor in the reduction of revenue generation is accidents/incidents related to Occupational Health and Safety (OHS). These accidents/incidents result in the loss of production, down time, loss of man hours, loss of life and ultimately reduced revenue. Therefore, the management of OHS issues and challenges in the petroleum industry and the Workover organisations providing services is critical and significant for the petroleum industry.
>
> The contribution of this study is expected in two main areas: theoretical and practical. From a theoretical perspective, this would be the first comprehensive, evidence-based assessment of the use of Work-Applied Learning (WAL) in the development and implementation of an OHSMS for the petroleum industry. Considering that this study would be the first of its kind in this industry in T&T, the findings can be instrumental in changing the policies and practices that are currently being used in this industry and by extension, can be researched for use in other industries.
>
> This study is specific to a Well Workover organisation in the T&T petroleum industry. The findings may not be applicable to all other Well Workover organisations globally because the environmental and operational conditions may be different. The generation of hypothesis presented in the concluding chapter of this thesis may suggest further

research in other well workover organisations.

Monash Health research project

The purpose of this research project was to explore the development and implementation of an action research oriented Telemonitoring system to enable the home-based monitoring of diabetes patients in Monash Health.

The significance of this project was articulated as follows:
> Chronic diseases such as diabetes are a major global health issue, with chronic disease treatment being the single largest cost within global health care delivery (Johnson 2003; World Health Organization 2006). They are also the largest single source of mortality (World Health Organization 2005). Faced with the ever-increasing demand for the treatment of chronic conditions such as diabetes and a diminishing workforce, healthcare providers are seeking new and sustainable ways to provide healthcare services (Schofield et al. 2005; Bowes & McColgan 2006).
>
> Telemonitoring, combining information technology and home-based care, represents a potential solution to this problem (Meystre 2005; Schofield et al. 2005; Bowes & McColgan 2006). However, despite the potential benefits, Telemonitoring has yet to be widely adopted. The low utilisation of Telemonitoring is a concern for both international and national healthcare management (Jennett et al. 2003; Moffatt & Eley 2011).
>
> This research seeks to contribute to both theory and practice in the following ways:
> 1) Identify current issues preventing the increased utilisation of Telemonitoring for the treatment of diabetes patients within the research organisation Monash Health.
> 2) Provide evidence to assist in the successful design and implementation of action research-oriented Telemonitoring systems for the management of chronic

disease conditions within the state of Victoria, Australia, and globally.
3) Contribute to the literature on action research through evidence gained in the design and implementation of an action research-oriented Telemonitoring system for diabetes patients in a Victorian Health Service.
4) Contribute to the policy and practice of health care management in Victorian health services, and the Australian healthcare industry more widely in the area of Telemonitoring systems implementation for the management of diabetes.
5) Develop hypotheses and suggestions for further study relating to the development and implementation of an action research-oriented Telemonitoring systems for use by diabetes patients for other Victorian health services.

1.3.2 Limitations of the Research Project

Every research project has its limitations, which are often beyond the researcher's control. These limitations can include a small sample size, which may not be representative of the larger population; lack of available and/or reliable data, which can affect the validity of the research; lack of prior research studies on the topic, which can make it difficult to contextualize the findings; self-reported data, which may be biased or inaccurate and cannot be independently verified; limited access to relevant people, organisations or data, which can limit the scope of the project; and time constraints, which can limit the depth and breadth of the research. It is important for researchers to acknowledge these limitations in their studies to provide context for their findings and to guide future research. Examples of statements of limitations are provided below.

Kuju CDEP research project

This project, which investigated the application of an action research method in a management training and development programme for the Board members of an Aboriginal community organisation, Kuju CDEP, had several limitations:

Time

Time was a limiting factor in this project, because the

management training and development programme was limited to a maximum period of eighteen months, which was the time frame set by the funding agency.

Research Design
This project was limited to a particular group of indigenous community leaders, who were the Board members of a particular Aboriginal community organisation. There was no attempt in this project to carry out a comparison between several different groups using a similar approach, nor was there any attempt to compare different action research approaches.

Sample size
Due to the size of the population, the statistical analysis of data was therefore limited.

Methodological Limitation
This limitation arises from the technique of triangulation used in this project. Results emerging from the process of triangulation may be inconsistent due to inconsistencies in the actual data, or it may be that different recorders of the data have emphasised different aspects of the same phenomenon (Patton 1990). [I]t is conceivable that individuals recording their observations of the Board members may have highlighted different aspects of their development. There was also the possibility that the Board members were influenced by their relationship with the researcher, to comment favourably on the programme in their self-reports. The possibilities underline the importance of the triangulation technique by comparing data from a variety of sources. The answers to some of the research questions are based on the perceptions of a number of individuals. The nature of perceptions per se is a limiting factor in any research project and is acknowledged.

Evaluation
The evaluation of the development of the Board members was limited to a consideration of group development and

did not assess the growth of each individual Board member, due to a number of reasons as set out in the research project.

Researcher's role as the facilitator
Another limitation was the fact that the researcher was also the deliverer of the programme. Since the action research method involves collaboration between the researcher and the subjects of the research, interactions between these parties will affect the outcome of every action research programme. The researcher, acting as facilitator, would have had some influence on the group. It is impossible to know from a single case study to what extent observations made by the group were the result of characteristics of the researcher.

WWC research project

This project explored into the development and implementation of a WAL-Occupational Health & Safety Management System (WAL-OHSMS) for a Well Workover company within the petroleum sector in T&T.

The project encountered several limitations, including:

Relevant and current data
The limitation in accessing relevant, current OHS data inclusive of recorded accident statistics both for companies and the energy sector was an on-going challenge. There was very limited published data and more often than not, the data was not current. Requesting data of this nature from Government Ministries and Statutory Bodies required approvals from senior government officials and this proved difficult.

Language
The T&T language has evolved into a form of Creole dialect influenced by English, French, Spanish, Hindi, African, Arabic and Carib (Muhleisen 2001, p. 43). This language has proven to be somewhat difficult for other foreign countries to comprehend, especially when spoken at its usual pace and when documented as spoken. In this regard, the data

collected and analysed from the focus group meetings, which included the AR Groups, Validation Committee and meetings with Well Workover rigs crews and any other verbal interaction with personnel was presented in Standard English throughout this project. However, where direct quotes from some of the AR group members were in the T&T Language, these have been translated into Standard English.

Monash Health research project

This research project delved into the creation and application of an action research-oriented Telemonitoring system for home-based monitoring of diabetes patients at Monash Health. The research project encountered several limitations, two of which are outlined below:

Action Research Group Size
As an exploratory study, the research involved a small number of participants, which could be considered a limitation. This constraint has been recognised (Spalding 2009; Williamson 2012) as common in action research initiatives within healthcare settings.

The number of patients who participated in the research was 40. This number consists of a group of 20 patients utilising the Telemonitoring system and a control group of 20. The maximum number of participants undergoing Telemonitoring was fixed at 20 as it was the maximum that could be accommodated in a trial by the vendor providing the Telemonitoring system.

Number of Action Research Cycles
The research was limited to three major action research cycles which were limited to fourteen months in total duration as this was the maximum possible trial period permitted by the vendor providing the Telemonitoring system.

1.3.3 Definition of Terms

In the section on "Definitions of Terms", you will set out the terms that you will be using in your research project and their definitions. You should include and define terms that are important to your project or are used frequently throughout the report but are not common knowledge. You should also include terms that have a unique meaning within the scope of your research project. You do not need to include terms that most, if not all, of your readers will understand without having definitions provided.

Extracts from the section on Definitions of Terms in the following research projects are provided below.

Kuju CDEP research project

The purpose of this research project was to investigate the application of an action research method in the development of a management training and development programme for the Board members of Kuju CDEP, an Aboriginal community organisation.

Definitions of some of the terms used in this project are as follows:

> **Aboriginal Employment and Education Development Unit (AEEDU):** A section of the Department of Employment, Education and Training which provides funding for a range of training schemes directed specifically at Aboriginal people. It has emerged from the recent reorganisation of Commonwealth agencies involved in Aboriginal affairs having a primary responsibility for providing education and training programmes for Aboriginal people.
>
> **Community Organisation:** An organisation that is run by members of the community for the overall benefit of the community.
>
> **Community Development Employment Projects Scheme (CDEP):** First launched in 1977 and expanded under the AEDP, it provides a means by which unemployed Aboriginal people can work on projects of value to their community and receive a "wage" in lieu of unemployment benefits.
>
> **Management Training and Development (Management T/D):** Includes courses and programmes, usually designed

and conducted by external consultants or training specialists within organisations, with the aim of improving the specific management skills, knowledge, attitudes and traits needed by the trainees to perform effectively in their positions.

Triangulation: Triangulation in this project refers to the search for consistency of findings of different observers, different observing instruments, materials of observation, times, place and the use of simple events, either from different participants or observers, or from the same person at different times.

WWC research project

The research project explored the development and implementation of a WAL-Occupational Health & Safety Management System in a Well Workovers company in the petroleum industry in T&T. The following are some definitions of terms used in this project.

Drilling: A technology utilising a rotating drill pipe and bit in a cutting process. It cuts by applying pressure and rotation to the drill pipe and bit which produces cuttings from the underlying rock which are eliminated at the surface by a mud system.

Drill pipe: A drill pipe is used on drilling rigs to facilitate the drilling of a borehole/wellbore.

Occupational Health and Safety (OHS): OHS relates to health, safety and welfare issues in the workplace.

Occupational Health and Safety Management System (OHSMS): An OHSMS is a framework that allows an organisation to consistently identify and control its health and safety risks, reduce the potential for incidents, help achieve compliance with health and safety legislation and continually improve its performance. The framework also provides for supporting safe and healthy workplaces and implementing improvements.

Well Workover: Once a well has been in production for a while, it must be monitored and maintained. Quite often, mechanical alterations such as Well Workovers or interventions are required to respond to changing conditions. This is performed by inserting tools in the wellbores to effect maintenance or remedial action.

Well Workover company: A company that provides specifically Well Workover services to other companies in the petroleum industry.

Monash Health research project

The purpose of this research project was to explore the development and implementation of an action research oriented Telemonitoring system to enable the home-based monitoring of diabetes patients in Monash Health.

The following is a selection of definitions of terms used in this project:

Participants: The participants in the research project comprised patients from the diabetes outpatient clinics of Monash Health diagnosed with type 2 diabetes who were commencing insulin stabilisation treatment. Participants were assigned either to Telemonitoring insulin stabilisation or to standard insulin stabilisation treatment. The participant group provided standard insulin stabilisation treatment was clinically matched to the Telemonitoring participants and acted as a control group.

Diabetes: Diabetes is a series of metabolic disorders associated with hypoglycaemia and caused by defects in insulin secretion or action. The two main types of diabetes are type 1 diabetes (T1D) and type 2 diabetes (T2D). Diabetics have reduced life expectancy and increased incidence of micro and macrovascular complications such as myocardial infarction and stroke (Dinneen 2010).

Type 1 diabetes is an autoimmune disease characterised by the destruction of pancreatic beta cells, which produce insulin. It accounts for 5–10% of diabetes cases worldwide and is most prevalent in children and adolescents (Diabetes Australia 2014a). Type 1 diabetes is managed with insulin injections several times a day or the use of an insulin pump.

Type 2 diabetes is characterised by insulin resistance and impaired insulin secretion as a result of pancreatic beta cell dysfunction. It is caused by the interaction between genetic factors and the environment. Incidence of type 2 diabetes is increased by obesity, hypertension, poor diet and a sedentary lifestyle. Type 2 diabetes represents 80–90% of all diabetes cases (Diabetes Australia 2014b). It is managed with a combination of physical activity, diet, weight management, medication and insulin therapy.

Patient Engagement: "A set of behaviours by which patients take more responsibility for their own health care, and health care professionals take more account of patients' health needs. It implies an ethos of shifting from medical dominance within the health care environment to one of equality, that facilitates patient involvement in their health care. As a central feature it combines a patient's knowledge, skills, ability and willingness to manage his/her own health care with interventions designed to increase activation and promote positive patient behaviour." (Graham, Filippatos, Atar, Vardas, Pinto & Fitzsimons 2017 pp. 3114).

Telemonitoring: "[T]he use of audio, video, and other telecommunications and electronic information processing technologies to monitor patient status at a distance" (Institute of Medicine Committee on Evaluating Clinical Applications of Telemedicine 1996, p. 248). In the context of this research, Telemonitoring refers to the information technology system implemented to monitor patients' blood glucose levels.

Telemedicine/Telehealth: "The delivery of health care services, where distance is a critical factor, by all health care professionals using information and communication technologies for the exchange of valid information for diagnosis, treatment and prevention of disease and injuries, research and evaluation, and for the continuing education of health care providers, all in the interests of advancing the health of individuals and their communities" (World Health Organization 1998, p. 10).

Teleconsultation: "Audio, video, or other electronic consultation between two or more geographically separated clinicians" (Institute of Medicine Committee on Evaluating Clinical Applications of Telemedicine 1996, p. 248).

Telediagnosis: "The detection of disease by evaluating data transmitted to a receiving station from instruments monitoring a distant patient" (Institute of Medicine Committee on Evaluating Clinical Applications of Telemedicine 1996, p. 248).

STAGE 2 ACTION RESEARCH METHOD STAGE

The Action Research Method Stage of the WAL research planning design process is divided into two phases:

Phase 2.1: This phase involves justifying the research site, justifying the selection of Action Research Group members and considering the ethical issues involved in the research.

Phase 2.2: This phase comprises a discussion of the various data collection, data analysis, evaluation and validation techniques available for WAL research as well as some issues for consideration by WAL Practitioner Researchers when using these various techniques.

Each of these phases is discussed below.

PHASE 2.1
a) Justification of Research Site

Marshall and Rossman (1989, p.54) defined "site" as "the selection of a certain setting within an organisation or the selection of a certain group of people as subjects in the research."

In their recent work, (Marshall et al, 2022, pp. 123-124) they defined ideal sites as those where:

> a) access is possible; b) there is a high probability that a rich mix of the processes, people, programmes, interactions, and structures of interest is present; c) you are likely to be able to build trusting relations with the participants in the study; d) data quality and credibility of the study are reasonably assured. Needless to say, researchers may need to approximate one or two of these ideal criteria.

The selection of the research site in each of the three example WAL research projects is justified in Tables 3.12 to 3.14 using the criteria identified by Marshall and Rossman.

Kuju CDEP Research Project

The research site for the Kuju CDEP research project is justified as shown in Table 3.12.

Table 3.12 – Justification Of The Kuju CDEP Research Site

CRITERIA	JUSTIFICATION
Was entry possible?	The researcher was asked to propose and implement a management training programme for the Board members of Kuju CDEP, therefore entry was not a problem.

Table 3.12 – (Continued)

CRITERIA	JUSTIFICATION
Were processes, people, programmes, interactions and structures that were part of the research questions present?	The main research question asks whether action research could be used to design a management training and development programme for indigenous community leaders, while the corollary research questions refer to the action research cycles, processes and characteristics that emerged during the development of this programme, and to the evaluation of the Board members who attended the programme.
Processes?	Processes emerged during the action research cycle of planning, action, observation, reflection and evaluation of the programme.
People?	The Board members of Kuju CDEP.
Programmes?	The Board Management Development Programme (BMDP).
Interactions?	The responses and reactions of the Board members to various aspects of the programme, and the interactions that occurred between Board members during group work as part of the programme.
Structures?	The management structure and organisation of Kuju CDEP as well as the structure of the BMDP.
Was an appropriate role for the researcher possible?	The researcher's role as facilitator enabled him to become a participant observer in the action research cycles and processes as the management Training and Development programme was designed and implemented.
Did the choice of site avoid poor sampling decisions?	Sampling was not an issue in this exploratory study, since the case study involved a single organisation.

(Candidate 27, 1993)

Table 3.13 shows how the selection of the research site of the WWC research project was justified using criteria similar to the Kuju CDEP research project.

Table 3.13 – Justification Of The WWC Research Site

CRITERIA	JUSTIFICATION
Is entry possible?	Discussions with the Managing Director (MD) and other members of Senior Management revealed that entry is not a problem. The agreement between the external practitioner manager (EPS) and the MD who is also the owner of the organisation is twofold: firstly, to produce a reduction in accidents and secondly, to provide an enhanced management system for the organisation.
Were processes, people, programmes, interactions, and/or structures that were part of the research questions present?	The main research question was if a WAL approach can be used in the development and implementation of a WAL Occupational Health and Safety Management System (WAL-OHSMS) in a Well Workover company in T&T. The supporting questions refer to the project, process, and learning outcomes as well as the challenges. Since WAL uses a fused Action Research and Action Learning process, AR provides the most appropriate research method. The project relies on interactions with the AR Group, the Action Learning teams, Validation Committee and Senior Management.
Processes?	Major cycles for the processes are planned and evaluated and validation mechanisms established.
People?	The management and staff of the company.
Programmes?	The development and implementation of the WAL-OHSMS
Interactions?	The interactions between members of the AR Groups, the AL Teams are critical to the project. Additionally, the Validation Committee, which includes Senior Management interactions with AR Group members and the researcher during the evaluation and validation of the project.
Structures?	The management structure of the company included the structure of sub-committees and teams in the organisation, and the structures of the AR Group, teams, and Validation Committee..
Did the choice of site avoid poor sampling decisions?	Sampling is not an issue in the project because only one organisation is used.

Source: Candidate 30 (2021)

The justification of the Monash Health research site using similar criteria is shown in Table 3.14.

Table 3.14 – Justification Of The Monash Health WAL Research Site

DESIRABLE RESEARCH SITE CHARACTERISTICS	MONASH HEALTH RESEARCH SITE CHARACTERISTIC EVALUATION
Entry should be possible	At the time of the development of the research proposal, the manager was the Director of Information Technology at Monash Health. The employment relationship with Monash Health would allow easy entry into the organisation. The research proposal received executive support from the Chief Medical Officer and Chief Information Officer of Monash Health. This support was as a result of the low rate of Telehealth adoption being a thematic concern of the organisation (Loh 2014). Such executive support and thematic concern would facilitate easy entry to the required medical programs to conduct the research.
High probability that a large mix of people and processes, programs and interactions and structure of interest to the research are present	Monash Health is a large publicly funded healthcare network based in the state of Victoria, Australia and is a recognised leader in the implementation of new medical technologies and models of health care. Furthermore, Monash Health provides treatment for diabetic patients, the target group of the research. Monash Health provides the full spectrum of clinical services and is a full service "cradle to grave" healthcare provider. Clinical services provided range from research, allied health, all major clinical specialities, mental health, and aged and palliative care in both an inpatient and outpatient context. The organisation's size and clinical variety would provide a large mix of people, process, programs, structures and interactions that would be of interest to the research.
The ability to build trusting relations with the participants in the research project	The research project will utilise the inherent trust relationship found in the clinician-patient relationship and provider-patient level to establish and maintain trusting relations during the research project. The basis of this clinician-patient relationship is outlined well by Rowe and Calnan (2006) and is caused by information asymmetries, patient dependence on clinical competence, and the inherent vulnerability associated with suffering from an illness.

Table 3.14 (Continued)

DESIRABLE RESEARCH SITE CHARACTERISTICS	MONASH HEALTH RESEARCH SITE CHARACTERISTIC EVALUATION
The research project can be conducted and reported ethically	Ethical practice could be achieved within the research via formal means. The approval of the research by an Australian Government approved Human Research Ethics Committee (HREC) operated by Monash Health and approval from the manager's academic institution Australian Institute of Business (AIB) were required. In addition specific representation to groups of people with limited power (in this instance the patient group) could be addressed via the inclusion of a patient advisor role within the action research group.
The data quality and credibility of the research project are reasonably assured	In order to ensure data quality and credibility of the research project, the manager could utilise a number of data analysis techniques including but not limited to content analysis, and chain of evidence. In addition the research project could utilise a clinically matched control group that would not undergo home-based Telemonitoring to verify results.
The research project can be conducted and reported ethically	Ethical practice could be achieved within the research via formal means. The approval of the research by an Australian Government approved Human Research Ethics Committee (HREC) operated by Monash Health and approval from the manager's academic institution Australian Institute of Business (AIB) were required. In addition specific representation to groups of people with limited power (in this instance the patient group) could be addressed via the inclusion of a patient advisor role within the action research group.

Source: Candidate 31 (2022)

b) Justification for the selection of AR Group Members

The AR Group members are identified and their selection is justified based on the contribution that each of them will make to the research project. In respect of the Kuju CDEP research project, the management training and development programme was funded by both federal and state funding agencies, and they selected the AR Group members.

Table 3.15 shows how the AR Group members were selected for the Kuju CDEP research project.

Table 3.15 – Justification for the selection of the AR Group Members in the Kuju CDEP Research Project

ROLE	DUTIES/ RESPONSIBILITIES	RATIONALE
Board members - These were the members of the 1990 Board of Kuju CDEP and were the indigenous community leaders who were the participants in the management training and development programme that was developed during this project.	As Board members, they were responsible for the strategic direction of Kuju CDEP.	They provided feedback at regular intervals on their experiences in undertaking the management development programme and made suggestions on how changes could be made.
Administrator	He was responsible for the management and day to day running of the various programmes and reported directly to the Chairman of the Kuju Board.	He had knowledge and experience in the management of ongoing programmes.
Representative of the Department of Aboriginal Affairs (DAA	The DAA was the federal funding agency for Kuju CDEP. In January 1990, it was re-named as Aboriginal & Torres Strait Islander Commission.	As the representative of the federal funding agency, he closely monitored the management training and development programme programme.
Representative of the Department of Employment and Technical and Further Education (TAFE)	TAFE was a State Government department and was a joint funding agency to Kuju CDEP with DAA.	As the representative of the state funding agency, he too closely monitored the management training and development programme.

DESIGNING WAL RESEARCH PLANS 103

Table 3.15 (Continued)

ROLE	DUTIES/ RESPONSIBILITIES	RATIONALE
TAFE Aboriginal Community Educator	An employee of the TAFE School of Aboriginal Administration.	He had knowledge of and experience working with the Board members.
TAFE Community Management Trainer (CMT)	An employee of TAFE who worked on a long-term basis with an Aboriginal community to develop management skills.	He established the Kuju administration structure and assisted the Board to develop the Board's abilities to understand legal responsibilities and policy matters.

The selection and justification of the AR Group members in the WWC research project is shown in Table 3.16.

Table 3.16 – Justification for the selection of the AR Group Members in WWC Research Project

PERSONNEL	RATIONALE	DUTIES/RESPONSIBILITIES
Procurement Coordinator	The Procurement Coordinator plays a significant role in the sourcing and procuring of tool, materials and equipment, inclusive of Personal Protective Equipment (PPE) for the organisation. The suitability and effectiveness of these tools and equipment can impact the OHS performance of the organisation	i. Receive Material Requisition from all departments ii. Maintain records regarding suppliers and cost iii. Processing, recording and updating records iv. Interacting with vendors and negotiating prices v. Preparation of purchase orders vi. Verification of requisition orders to ensure accuracy, specifications and terminology

Table 3.16 (Continued)

PERSONNEL	RATIONALE	DUTIES/RESPONSIBILITIES
HSE Officer	This employee is responsible for all the Health, Safety and Environment (HSE) matters of the organisation. Since the HSE Officer has oversight for all the HSE matters of the organisation the knowledge, exposure and influence he has is invaluable	i. Orientation of new employees ii. Investigate and record all reported incidents, accidents and near misses iii. Document control iv. Conduct safety talks with all departments v. Internal inspection audits for all rigs vi. Certificates and authorization passes for the figs are kept current vii. Facilitate HSE training for employees viii. Conduct safety drills ix. Draft Policies and Procedures
Senior Toolpusher	He is responsible for the efficient operation of the Workover rig	i. Safe and efficient execution of the well-program (program of Well Workover jobs for respective clients).
Human Relations Officer/IT Technician	This Officer interacts both at a technological and human relations levels	i. Installation of technological hardware and software ii. Create and maintain network systems iii. Maintain electronic company employee files iv. Preparation and dissemination of pay statements to employees v. Bank transactions and Insurance matter vi. Collation and dissemination of rig status reports received from all the Toolpushers, Supervisors and Rig Mechanics to senior management.

Table 3.16 (Continued)

PERSONNEL	RATIONALE	DUTIES/RESPONSIBILITIES
Researcher	The researcher would facilitate the project and maintain accurate and complete documentation of the entire process. Additionally, the researcher can provide experience in the analysis of the problem as well as information and guidance on the research process.	i. Facilitate the research process ii. Maintain accurate records and manage research data iii. Liaise and interact with Management and all other relevant company personnel iv. Obtain necessary approvals from Management as and when required v. Schedule and make necessary arrangements for Validation Committee meetings.

Source: Candidate 30 (2021)

Table 3.17 shows the reasons for the selection of the AR Group members in the Monash Health research project.

Table 3.17 – Justification for the selection of the AR Group Members in the Monash Health Research Project

ROLE	COMPETENCE RELEVANT FOR RESEARCH PROJECT	CONTRIBUTION TO RESEARCH PROJECT
Manager	• Knowledge & experience in AR. • Knowledge and experience of IT in healthcare. • Knowledge and experience of the research organisation Monash Health.	The manager is an information technology executive with more than 15 years' experience in healthcare. Through his professional practice, the manager had identified the need to increase the adoption of emergent healthcare technologies such as Telemonitoring. This need is particularly high in the area of the management of chronic disease conditions such as diabetes where the manager believes Telemonitoring as a healthcare delivery method has the potential to not only provide increased quality of life and improved clinical outcomes for Patients, but also decrease the costs to healthcare providers.
Patient Advisor	• Knowledge and experience as an end consumer of healthcare services. • Represent the patient viewpoint and provide insights from the patient perspective.	As noted by Williamson (2012), patient involvement in healthcare-based AR has proven to have significant benefits. A Patient Advisor was included within the AR Group to ensure that "the voice of the patient" was not lost and that patient participants' perspectives was considered throughout all stages of the research. In addition, the Patient Advisor provided insights into patient behaviours. This is of importance to the research as successful patient adoption is critical to the implementation of any Telemonitoring program.

Table 3.17 (Continued)

ROLE	COMPETENCE RELEVANT FOR RESEARCH PROJECT	CONTRIBUTION TO RESEARCH PROJECT
Diabetes Unit Clinical Lead	• Clinical expertise in diabetes management. • Access to the Diabetes Unit of Monash Health. • Clinical support of the research project.	The clinical involvement of the Diabetes Unit in the research was required for a number of reasons, including: • the involvement of clinical staff ensured clinical oversight and safety of participants of the Telemonitoring program; • it provided a clinical advisory capability to the AR Group, helping to identify any potential clinical barriers to the successful implementation of the Telemonitoring program; • it increased the likelihood of success of the research by encouraging clinician engagement; and • inclusion of the Diabetes Unit Clinical Lead provided the opportunity to consolidate access to the target participant group and enable some quantitative analysis of the results.
Telemonitoring systems provider representative	• Technical expertise in the deployment and operation of Telemonitoring systems.	The systems provider was a crucial actor in ensuring the reliable provision of the Telemonitoring system to ensure success of the research project. Having a representative of the system provider as a member of the AR Group ensured accountability for systems performance, reliability and the timely delivery of requested enhancements by the AR Group.

Source: Candidate 31 (2022)

c) Ethical Issues to be considered

As your WAL research project will be conducted at a workplace (the Research Site) and will involve other human participants, there are certain ethical issues that you must consider.

The role of the researcher

The first issue is your role as a researcher. Are you a member of the organisation where you are conducting the project (an insider researcher) or are you external to the organisation, for example a consultant (an outsider researcher)?

Being internal to the organisation, insider researchers tend to have greater access to information, respondents and data but may form biases more easily (Bonner & Tolhurst, 2002). Outside researchers are likely to be more objective but they may lack the knowledge of the social context of their study (Htong Kaham, 2024).

Increasingly, the general concepts of insider/outsider research are being revisited in the context of cross-cultural educational research. A key component of this new thinking about insider-outsider positionings is that in conducting research, the researcher is neither entirely fully inside nor outside. Rather, the researcher takes on different positions depending on the situations the researcher finds themselves in, the people they interact with and familiarity of the social norms in the situation (Milligan 2016, pp. 239-240).

Whether you are an insider or outsider researcher, it is important to clearly define your role and responsibilities at the onset of the project, in a transparent manner without coercion from any individual or group.

The other participants

Sheikhattari, Wright, Silver, van der Donk and van Lanen (2022, pgs. 29-30) have identified the following three basic ethical considerations in research involving human participants:

> "(1) you need to make sure that the participants are adequately informed while respecting their privacy;

(2) you need to carefully listen to participants' concerns about the confidentiality of their data and make sure that their decision to participate is voluntary and without coercion or undue influence; and

(3) you need to make sure the participants fully understand the potential risks and benefits of (as well as the alternatives to) participating in your study."

If you are undertaking research involving human participants as part of a degree with a university or with an institution that receives public funding, your proposed research project may need to be approved by an ethics committee in your institution (Marshall et al, 2022). In such cases, the participants in your proposed project must provide their written informed consent to taking part in your project.

In cases where the research involving human participants does not receive public funding or is not undertaken as a requirement for a degree, it would not generally require the approval of an ethics committee, but it is advisable to first check with your management (Sheikhattari et al, 2022). Nevertheless, you should still obtain a signed informed consent form from each of the participants in your project where they acknowledge that they are fully informed about the purpose of the project; that their participation is voluntary; that they understand the extent of their commitment to the project; that their identities will be protected as much as possible; and that there are minimal risks associated with participating (Marshall et al, 2022 pg. 63).

Table 3.18 shows the ethical processes observed in the three example research projects we have been studying. It should be noted that all three research projects were undertaken as part of doctoral degrees, and therefore, formal approval was obtained from the Ethics Committee of the relevant educational institutions.

Table 3.18 – Ethical processes in the three example WAL research projects

RESEARCH PROJECT	PURPOSE OF THE PROJECT	ETHICAL PROCESS
Kuju CDEP	To investigate the application of an action research method in the development of a management training and development programme for the Board members of Kuju CDEP, an Aboriginal community organisation.	• Presentation by the researcher to the Kuju CDEP Board with detailed information about the purpose and process of the proposed management development programme, • Invitation to the Kuju CDEP Board members to participate in the proposed management development programme, • Written consent obtained from the Chairperson of Kuju CDEP for: • the Board members to participate in the management development programme, and • the programme to be undertaken by the researcher as part of his doctoral degree, • Approval for the research project obtained from the Ethics Committee of Flinders University.
WWC	To explore the development and implementation of a WAL Occupational Health & Safety Management System (WAL-OHSMS) for a Well Workover company within the petroleum sector in Trinidad & Tobago.	• Written consent obtained from WWC for the research project, • Presentation by the researcher to the proposed participants with detailed information about proposed study, • Invitation to the proposed participants to participate in the study, • Signed consent letter obtained from each participant, • Approval for the research project obtained from the Ethics Committee of Australian Institute of Business.

Table 3.18 (Continued)

RESEARCH PROJECT	PURPOSE OF THE PROJECT	ETHICAL PROCESS
WWC	To investigate the application of an action research method in the development of a management training and development programme for the Board members of Kuju CDEP, an Aboriginal community organisation.	• Interviews of participants conducted at random intervals by an independent WWC executive to check that the participants were satisfied with the process and were willing to continue their participation, • The privacy of the participants and employees involved in any accidents/incidents was assured by de-identifying them in all data analysis and reports, • All data to be securely stored for 5 years to prevent loss, unauthorised access or modification.
Monash Health	To explore the development and implementation of an action research oriented Telemonitoring system to enable the home-based monitoring of diabetes patients in Monash Health.	• Given the nature and context of healthcare, the researcher addressed the seven factors of clinical research (which are set out in detail in Chapter 5 of this book). In summary: • The research used a case study protocol (research protocol) to ensure that vulnerable subjects were not targeted or powerful subjects favoured, • A participant information sheet containing the details of the proposed research including but not limited to roles and responsibility, data treatment, and purpose was made available to all participants in the research, • Informed consent was obtained from participants, • Approval for the research obtained from the Ethics Committee of Australian Institute of Business,

Table 3.18 (Continued)

RESEARCH PROJECT	PURPOSE OF THE PROJECT	ETHICAL PROCESS
Monash Health	To explore the development and implementation of an action research oriented Telemonitoring system to enable the home-based monitoring of diabetes patients in Monash Health.	• Approval for the research obtained from the Monash Health Human Research Ethics Committee, • Welfare of participants was maintained at all times with clinical oversight from the clinical lead, and patient advocacy from the patient advisor, • All data collected by the research project was made non identifiable prior to being published, shared or re-used, • Ethical conduct of the research was also assured via the periodic review of the research by the Validation Committee.

PHASE 2.2
a) Data Collection, Data Analysis, Evaluation and Validation Techniques

When designing your research plans, it is useful to look at the methodologies others have used in the design of their plans. Methodology includes the research method/data collection, data analysis and validation techniques.

Each research context may lend itself to its own set of methodological approaches that might not be particularly common or relevant in other circumstances. In developing your research plan, you need to consider possible research methodologies in that context. Such a choice of research methodology is a critical aspect of research design and that choice needs to be reasoned through and justified, since that choice impacts not only the practical aspects of the research but also its intellectual basis, its verifiability, its relevance and the ethics of the research.

Table 3.19 shows the data collection, data analysis and validation techniques used in the three WAL research projects studied in this chapter. The left column lists a wide variety of techniques that could be employed, but each project ended up deploying its own subset of techniques. Thus, interviews were appropriate in the first two projects, but questionnaires were more appropriate to the Monash project. Many factors may influence the choice of technique. The shaded rows show the techniques which were used in all three projects.

Table 3.19 — Data collection, data analysis, evaluation and validation techniques used in the three WAL research projects

DATA COLLECTION, DATA ANALYSIS, EVALUATION VALIDATION TECHNIQUES	KUJU CDEP RESEARCH PROJECT	WWC RESEARCH PROJECT	MONASH HEALTH RESEARCH PROJECT
Assessment			✓
Chain of Evidence	✓	✓	✓
Clustering		✓	
Content Analysis	✓		✓
Document Analysis	✓	✓	
Document collection	✓	✓	
Focus Group	✓	✓	
Participant Observation	✓		✓
Participants' Reflection		✓	
Questionnaires			✓
Recording Non-verbal Communication	✓		✓
Reflexivity	✓	✓	
Researcher Conducting Interviews	✓	✓	
Researcher's Observation	✓	✓	✓
Researcher's Personal Diary		✓	
Researcher's Visit to Relevant Sites	✓		

Table 3.19 (Continued)

DATA COLLECTION, DATA ANALYSIS, EVALUATION VALIDATION TECHNIQUES	KUJU CDEP RESEARCH PROJECT	WWC RESEARCH PROJECT	MONASH HEALTH RESEARCH PROJECT
Researcher's Reflection		✔	✔
Tape/Video Recordings			✔
Triangulation	✔	✔	✔

A much broader review of methodological approaches can be obtained by examining 36 research projects that I supervised, 10 at doctoral level and 26 at masters level, which used the Action Research method and action learning and reflective practice processes. Table 3.20 below shows the frequency of aspects of methodology occurring across these 36 research projects, while detailed information on the techniques used by each candidate in these doctoral and masters level research projects is provided in Appendices 3A and 3B respectively.

Table 3.20 — Summary of methodological approaches including data collection, data analysis, evaluation and validation techniques used in Research projects

METHODOLOGICAL APPROACHES	OUT OF 10 DOCTORAL RESEARCH PROJECTS	OUT OF 26 MASTERS RESEARCH PROJECTS
Assessment	2	0
Brainstorming	1	4
Chain of Evidence	10	7
Clustering	7	7
Content Analysis	5	6
Discussion	2	6
Document Analysis	6	8
Document Collection	6	7

Table 3.20 (Continued)

METHODOLOGICAL APPROACHES	OUT OF 10 DOCTORAL RESEARCH PROJECTS	OUT OF 26 MASTERS RESEARCH PROJECTS
Emancipatory Method	3	19
Evaluation	1	11
Focus Group	4	8
Meetings	3	7
Mind mapping/ Flowchart	1	0
Mixed Method Approach	5	5
Open, Axial Selective Coding	1	0
Participant's Observations	6	12
Participant's Personal Diary	0	10
Participant's Visits to Relevant Sites	0	1
Participant's Written Descriptions	1	5
Participants Conducting Interviews	1	1
Participant's Reflections	4	15
Qualitative Approach	5	21
Questionnaires	2	9
Recording Non-verbal Behaviours	4	4
Reflexivity	8	5
Researcher Conducting Interviews	7	12
Researcher's Observations	10	24

Table 3.20 (Continued)

METHODOLOGICAL APPROACHES	OUT OF 10 DOCTORAL RESEARCH PROJECTS	OUT OF 26 MASTERS RESEARCH PROJECTS
Researcher's Personal Diary	5	12
Researcher's Reflections	5	14
Researcher's Visits to Relevant Sites	3	1
Root-cause Analysis	1	0
Statistics	0	2
Surveys	1	5
Tape/Video Recordings	1	7
Triangulation	10	20
Validation	1	7

Investigations revealed there were reported qualitative approaches and mixed methods approaches but no reported solely quantitative approaches. The above table shows that a common data collection approach is researcher's observations, as well as by interviews and participants' observations. This is what we should expect of research in the context of WAL research projects. Participants' reflections also provide useful information and are used in half of the projects examined. Researcher's reflections and researcher's diary are data collection "techniques" but they can also be data analysis techniques depending on the way data are recorded, for example if coding of the data occurs at the time of documenting reflections and observations.

I invited Dr Carmel Taddeo, an independent research academic, to undertake a statistical analysis of the 36 research projects. Table 3.20 is collated from selected research outputs/findings of that study. As a first step, she defined the key research terms related to the methodologies, methods, analyses, validation processes, and strategies in the research projects. Definitions of key terms are set out in Appendix 3C. Using correct and broadly agreed terms is an important aspect of research design. The next step was an inter-rater reliability analysis based on a sample size of 10 percent of the total number of research projects. That is, four of the 36 methods chapters were coded independently by the two researchers. This process was undertaken separately by two researchers to crosscheck the accuracy and reliability of the data collected and coded. The consistency and accuracy of the coding of the four methodology chapters completed by the two researchers were then analysed using a statistical software package.

In her report, Dr Taddeo found that this analysis showed a high level of agreement between the two researchers/coders, which indicated that "there could be a high level of confidence in the coding of the methodology related data in the remaining 32 research projects which had not been included in the inter- rater reliability process", but which had been coded by the second researcher.

b) Issues for Consideration for the WAL Practitioner Researcher

Set out below is Dr Taddeo's summary of the more commonly used methodological approaches such as analyses, validation processes, and strategies used in the research projects, together with some useful issues for your consideration (Taddeo, 2023, 2024):

1. An emancipatory paradigm was frequently reported in the WAL context. In an emancipatory WAL approach, power is distributed within a group. Power does not rest with any one individual but represents a shared responsibility and ownership amongst practitioners for the research process, with the aim of facilitating positive change (Grundy, 1982; Nehez, 2022).

If thinking about using an emancipatory approach, consider:
- If underpinning your WAL research project by an emancipatory approach aligns with your research aims and objectives and if an emancipatory approach may have relevance and benefits for your project and work context/setting.
- The positions and roles of those involved in the WAL research project. Are there any power imbalances that might compromise the authenticity of the research process, or conversely, are there any work setting structures that may

enrich the WAL process?
- What is the role of leadership in an emancipatory approach? Are there leadership and workplace structures that need to be considered to:
  - address any leadership challenges that may surface in a WAL project?
  - maximise the benefits of action learning and reflective practice as part of undertaking a WAL research project in the workplace?
- What, if any, implications are there for those involved in a WAL project that is underpinned by an emancipatory approach? Are there any ethical considerations? For example, do you need to consider collecting data anonymously to protect identities and allow for genuine feedback and insights?
- That if employing an emancipatory design, your research and findings are likely to be closely aligned to your workplace context/setting, and whilst skills may be transferable, the findings are unlikely to be generalisable to other work settings/contexts because of the context specific nature of the methodology/approach.

2. Predominately qualitative approaches were employed across masters and doctoral studies with some mixed method designs also reported. Qualitative research tends to produce descriptive (non- numerical) data and can include observations of behaviour or practices, or personal accounts/reflections of experiences, with a view to gaining an understanding of how individuals perceive the world/setting around them. These methods can include interviews, focus groups, and often occur in naturalistic settings (and not in laboratories).

Quantitative research methods tend to focus on measuring variables using numerical data and tend to rely on statistical analysis to help explain or predict a phenomenon or a relationship between variables of interest. These methods can include surveys and experiments. Mixed methods generally bring together more than one method/approach and often incorporate both qualitative and quantitative methods to address a research topic.

When thinking about research design in a WAL project, it may be worth

noting that:
- The research design should align with the aim of the research project question. For example, a research question such as, *'what is the experience of stax who have been involved in the employee mentoring program?'* lends itself more to a qualitative research design as it suggests an intent to gain rich insights into stax experiences. Whereas a research question such as, *'how often do stax engage in professional development training over a period of a year?'* suggests a more quantitative research design is warranted as the data is likely to be numerical.
- Whilst qualitative design frequently aligns well with the type of research challenges identified as part of action research in WAL research contexts, this does not discount the potential relevance and benefits of employing quantitative research methods and associated analyses. Methods chosen will depend on the research topic, and if required, it may be helpful to resource expertise and/or training in research methods that may be unfamiliar for a research practitioner.

3. Observations, reflections, and researchers conducting interviews featured often in data collection in WAL projects, with secondary data sources (documents) and primary sources such as personal diaries also utilised to record reflections.

Primary data are data typically sourced directly by the researcher from their own experiments or from first-hand observations and reflections and may be considered raw data. Observations, reflections, personal diaries, and researchers conducting interviews/focus groups/ workshops are examples where raw data and primary sources of data may be generated. Secondary data are not collected directly by a practitioner researcher but accessed from sources such as studies which may have been previously conducted or archived data by other researchers or data available on publicly available websites or databases.

In the context of this study, primary and secondary data are used as broad categories, acknowledging, however, that technological innovations including artificial intelligence are likely to require review of how these categories relate to praxis. This will better enable organisations to operationalise such categories in a way that best aligns with organisational practices and the purpose of the research.

When deciding data collection methods to employ in the WAL context, it may be helpful to consider:

- The suitability of researcher's observations, participants' observations, researcher's and participants' reflections, which can help generate rich insights and which can provide opportunities for participants to demonstrate agency as part of an emancipatory approach.
- The potential rich and varied sources of data that may be available and accessible to you within your work setting and as part of your WAL project.
- How to identify and collect primary sources of data- can you observe practices in your work setting/context? Can you create and disseminate an anonymous online survey to collect data about the research topic/focus? Can you conduct interviews with colleagues or other stakeholders who can provide insights for your research? Can you incorporate written reflections or complete personal diaries as part of your data collection?
- If including interviews as part of your data collection method, will you have the sole responsibility for conducting interviews to maintain a consistent approach or if you are involving others to conduct interviews, will you establish protocols to ensure consistency and to avoid compromising the integrity of the data collection process?
- Are there any biases or ethical considerations that need to be addressed in the data collection process and how will these be managed?
- Will reflexivity be incorporated, for example, through the use of recoding reflections in personal research diaries, and reflecting on one's own practices, beliefs, and biases, which also may facilitate transparency in a WAL project.
- How to identify and collect secondary sources of data (if relevant for your topic)? If needed, can you access archived documents, such as past financial or other records or perhaps

review current policy documents that may be useful for your WAL research project?

4. When considering data analysis, findings suggested clustering analysis, which appears closely related to coding, provided a way to organise qualitative data to allow manageable and meaningful themes to be identified and discussed.

Cluster analysis can be used to facilitate exploration of qualitative data to see what, if any, links/connections there may be. Whilst it may not be suitable for all qualitative projects, cluster analysis can be useful in helping to identify and organise patterns and themes across sometimes complex and large volumes of data collected, without compromising the meaning and richness of the data (Macia, 2015).

When deciding whether to utilise clustering analysis in your project, it may be helpful to consider:
- What type of data you have collected? Is it text based or numerical or both or other, such as images/photos?
- Do you need to manipulate the data so that it is suitable for clustering? For example, do you need to recode any data? Do you need to be mindful of missing data/cases?
- If this type of analysis can be useful in providing you with a framework to:
  - guide the organisation of the data you have collected?
  - underpin an approach for helping you to reduce the data and themes to a manageable and meaningful size that still captures the richness of the data?

5. Validation processes, and in particular triangulation, is a key consideration for research practitioners who conduct WAL research projects.

Validation is the process of establishing the truth or logical soundness of something, such as validating a claim or research project result or finding. Validation can help to inform/confirm if a research instrument has accurately measured what it was designed to measure. It is a process which brings together more than one approach/procedure (within or across quantitative, qualitative, or mixed methods) to collect data to generate strong/comprehensive evidence on the topic of focus, and to support the trustworthiness (qualitative) and validity and reliability (most often associated with quantitative) of findings and results presented.

When considering your approach to data collection and validation processes, it might be worth thinking about:
- The relevance, benefits and challenges associated with validating the data you intend to collect for your project.
- How you can ensure data accuracy and completeness. Will you use different types of methods to collect data so that you can crosscheck your results/findings across different methods for data accuracy and completeness?
- Will you triangulate your data? Will you use different types of qualitative data collection methods e.g., interviews or focus groups or reflections, or different types of quantitative methods such as surveys, polls, or quantitative observations (counts) or a combination of both qualitative and quantitative or data from different sources to triangulate your data and to help ensure you have comprehensively and accurately captured the data you need to address your research question?

6. Leveraging a variety of research related strategies, such as holding meetings, discussions, brainstorming session or visits to relevant sites, can align with an emancipatory and participatory research design and can enable distributed power and shared ownership of both the problem and solution to reflect context specific needs.

Research-related strategies can form part of, and/or facilitate the research process, including the data collection process. There are various research-related strategies which can be employed to empower practitioners and can be tailored to suit the needs and strengths of the workplace.

Additionally, there are various research-related strategies that may be useful for use in WAL projects. When deciding which research-related strategy/ies to employ, consider:
- What research-related strategy/ies can help you achieve what

you need for your WAL research project?
- Which research-related strategies best align with your chosen research methodology?
- What resources do you have available to you? Depending on your topic/project, resources can include human resources to support a brainstorming session, or technical support to enable the video or audio recording of workshops/focus groups/interviews or funding to support visits to other sites/ work settings.
- What workplace structures/process may already be in place that could be utilised to facilitate and enable the data collection process? For example, as part of data collection, a weekly staff meeting could be used to conduct a staff poll or could be used for conducting a focus group session.
- How a research-related strategy may help to address any power imbalances and further encourage shared ownership of the research project and outcomes.
- How you can be selective and intentional with the research-related strategy/ies you choose, and consider timeliness and efficiency so that any research-related strategy is employed to meet a specific project aim in a timely, efficient and useful way.

7. Overall, interesting patterns and findings were evident in the use of various data collection methods, analyses, validation processes, and research-related strategies reported across the doctoral and masters level methodology chapters. The findings have potential applicability and relevance for research practitioners engaging in WAL projects, however, it is important to acknowledge workplaces are unique settings/contexts and research approaches, methods, analyses, validation processes, and strategies may need to be tailored to suit the unique needs and strengths of a workplace/setting.

The nature of the WAL approach can accommodate the uniqueness of work environments. WAL projects enable opportunities to conduct practitioner research that aligns with available resourcing and the unique needs and strengths of staff and the work settings more broadly.

When thinking about engaging in WAL as a research practitioner, it may

help to consider:
- What data collection methods, analyses, validation processes, and research-related strategies are most likely to generate the data needed to address the research/project aims and objectives?
- What data collection methods, analyses, validation processes, and research-related strategies will utilise and develop the unique strengths of the organisation and in particular, the research practitioner?
- If data collection methods, analyses, validation processes, and research-related strategies need to be tailored to suit the workplace setting/context? If so, how will this occur/ be supported and who will be responsible? Is there a need for capacity building for research practitioners in the organisation to develop research skills and competencies in identified areas of need/gaps?
- Is there a need to connect with expertise beyond the organisation to support data collection methods, analyses, validation processes, and research-related strategies? If so, how will/can this be resourced?

In this Chapter, I have attempted to provide a guide on developing a plan for your WAL Research project. Chapters 4 and 5 illustrate how the WAL research plan was customised, based on the needs of the research projects undertaken for two disparate organisations.

CHAPTER 4

LISA MOHAMMED

Designing a Research Plan for an Occupational Health and Safety Management System in Trinidad and Tobago

INTRODUCTION

This chapter presents the methodology chapter of Lisa Mohammed's doctoral thesis. It begins with a description of the purpose of the study and the research questions. This is followed by an overview of the research philosophy and then the Action Research (AR) method chosen for this study. This leads to a description of the research design, the data collection and analysis techniques including evaluation and validation. In the conclusion for this chapter, there is a discussion on validity and reliability, ethical considerations and the justification for the use of AR in this study.

This chapter will provide an understanding of the research techniques within the AR method. The sections on research philosophy and research paradigm, which were included in the original work of the author, have been moved to Appendix 4 as it will be useful only if you are undertaking doctoral research.

PURPOSE OF THE STUDY

The purpose of this study is to investigate the development and implementation of an improved Occupational Health and Safety Management System (WAL-OHSMS) for a Well Workover company in the petroleum industry in Trinidad and Tobago (T&T).

This study seeks to:

1) Explore the development and implementation of a WAL-OHSMS in the petroleum industry in T&T.

2) Make a contribution to the literature of Occupational Health and Safety (OHS) management in relation to the development and implementation of a WAL-OHSMS in the petroleum industry.

3) Make a contribution to policy and practice of OHS management using a WAL-OHSMS, specifically in Well Workover organisations in the petroleum industry in T&T.

4) Develop hypotheses and suggestions for further studies relating to the development and implementation of a WAL-OHSMS in Well Workover organisations for the petroleum industry in T&T.

RESEARCH QUESTIONS

The research question and the supporting corollary questions are as follows:

Main research question
Can the WAL approach be used in the development and implementation of a WAL-OHSMS in a Well Workover organisation in the petroleum industry in T&T?

Corollary research questions
1. What is the WAL-OHSMS that has been developed for implementation in a Well Workover organisation in the petroleum industry in T&T?

2. What were the issues and challenges faced in the development of the WAL-OHSMS for the Well Workover organisation in the petroleum industry in T&T?

3. What was the WAL-OHSMS that evolved during the implementation of the proposed WAL-OHSMS for the Well Workover organisation in the petroleum industry in T&T?

4. What were the issues and challenges faced in the implementation of the WAL- OHSMS for the Well Workover organisation in the petroleum industry in T&T?

5. What were the project, learning and process outcomes in the development and implementation of the WAL-OHSMS for the Well Workover organisation in the petroleum industry in T&T?

6. What further insights into the application of AR characteristics emerged in this study?

RESEARCH DESIGN

A research design seeks to determine and justify the logical steps in the study, "to link the research questions(s) and issues to data collection, analysis and interpretation in a coherent way" (Cassell & Symon 2006, p. 326). The design must be clearly defined with a logical relationship between the research questions and methods which will result in valid and reliable data. In a practical context, there is an iterative relationship between the research design, theory, data collection and analysis with each informing and being informed by the other. As such the "research design is therefore not a discrete stage but a continuing process" (Ritchie et al. 2013, pp. 74-75). Social research always involves an element of the unknown, and qualitative research offers the particular advantage of flexibility.

The research design for this study was strongly influenced, and ultimately adapted from, the management development study using AR conducted by Abraham (1997), as well as in works by other researchers using an AR method such as Hashim (2001), Daton (2007), Khan (2015) and Hollyoake (2016).

The research design in this study is separated into two distinct stages, the conceptual stage and the AR method stage. These stages are represented in Table 4.1.

Table 4.1 – Research Design in this study

CONCEPTUAL STAGE	ACTION RESEARCH METHOD STAGE
1. Researcher's interest 　i) meetings with experts including reading in AR and OHS 　ii) attendance at workshops and seminars in AR and research methods 2. Literature review 　- Human Resource Management (HRM) 　- Occupational Health and Safety (OHS) 　- OHS models used globally 　- OHS models used in the petroleum industry in T&T 　- Literature of Action Research (AR) method and its fit into the research paradigm 　- AR and its link to Action Learning (AL) and reflective practice 　- How ARAL is linked to WAL 　- What is WAL and how its programs are designed	1. AR method and design 2. AR site and justification 3. Data collection techniques 　- Interviews 　- Focus Groups 　- Participant Observation 　- Direct Observation 　- Document Review 　- Field Notes 　- Reflexive Journals 4. Data analysis techniques 　- Chain of Evidence 　- Clustering 　- Document Analysis 5. Validation technique 　- Triangulation

Source: adapted from Abraham 1997, Hashim 2001, Daton 2007, Seng 2014, Khan 2015 and Holyoake 2016.

The conceptual stage reviews the interest of the researcher that led to the study and presents the literature summary of AR, ARAL and WAL. The AR method stage deals with the research site, AR design, data collection and analysis techniques and finally the techniques used to evaluate and validate the data collected and analysed. More details of this research design are provided in the following paragraphs.

Conceptual Stage

The conceptual stage is divided into two major parts, the first addressing the researcher's interest and the second presenting summary of the literature presented in Chapter 2 of this study, followed by a review of the literature specific to the AR methodology.

Researcher's interest

The researcher has always had a passion and keen interest in the field of OHS, in a career with academic qualifications being centred on this particular field as well as professional pursuits. One of the major driving forces of this passion is the desire to enhance consultant capabilities in the field of OHS. This would be a great benefit to petroleum companies and their performance on an individual basis, and ultimately the energy sector of T&T on the whole. Despite the fact that there are many positive drivers in the field of OHS, there is still so much that needs to be done throughout the industries and sectors in the country.

The concepts and ideas associated with AR were introduced to the researcher in contact with the Australian Institute of Business (AIB). AIB has on its faculty, an expert in the field of ARAL, WBL and WAL, Emeritus Professor Selva Abraham, and the review of publications and discussions with Professor Abraham and his team were influential factors in stimulating the interest of the researcher in this direction.

After the initial exposure to AR, the researcher attended a research methods workshop at AIB in July 2011, a research-in-progress workshop in November 2013 and also the first WAL Conference in November 2013. The workshop was attended by many experts in the field and an extensive literature of journals, books and research studies undertaken by other researchers was disseminated. Having been exposed to all this information and personal interactions with experts in this field of study, the researcher focussed in on the AR method as offering an ideal opportunity to bring a new dimension to the study of OHS.

Literature summary

The literature review conducted in the previous chapter of this study has dealt specifically with the literature on HRM, the literature on OHS and the development of the OHS programs in the petroleum industry in T&T. This is represented in Figure 4.1.

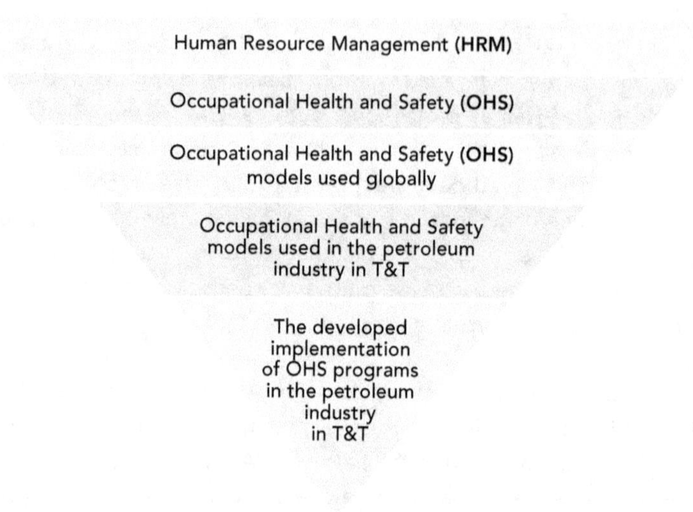

Human Resource Management (HRM)

Occupational Health and Safety (OHS)

Occupational Health and Safety (OHS) models used globally

Occupational Health and Safety models used in the petroleum industry in T&T

The developed implementation of OHS programs in the petroleum industry in T&T

Figure 4.1 – Literature review components
Source: adapted from Hofstee 2006.

The HRM literature represents the umbrella discipline under which OHS falls. HRM deals with the importance of the management of the workforce or employees of an organisation inclusive of recruitment, training and development, allocation of resources, employment security, other areas associated with them, and occupational safety.

The examination of the literature in this study primarily focuses upon the field of OHS. There is a general overview, followed by OHS models used globally in various industries. This is then narrowed down to the models used in the oil and gas industries worldwide. A further review is conducted that looks at models used in T&T and it is clear that none of the OHSMS here have been developed using a WAL change management process.

The WAL model is a change process based upon AL and the principles of AR. So, before turning to an outline of the methodology for the research, we first look at the outline of AR, AL and its key component of reflective practice. A summary of this is provided in the following sections, including details of AR, ARAL and WAL. This is illustrated in Figure 4.2.

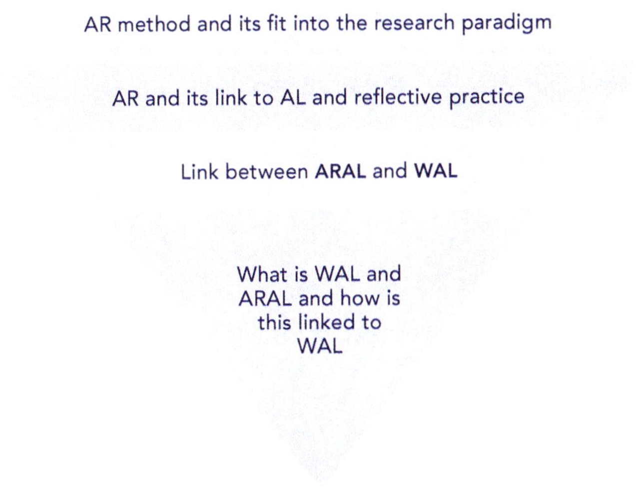

AR method and its fit into the research paradigm

AR and its link to AL and reflective practice

Link between **ARAL** and **WAL**

What is WAL and ARAL and how is this linked to WAL

Figure 4.2 – Literature review components specific to AR, ARAL and WAL
Source: adapted from Hofstee 2006.

ACTION RESEARCH (AR)

AR is a method to research that has emerged over time in many fields and is not proprietary to a single academic discipline. John Dewey, who is described as the Dean of American philosophy, showed strong elements of AR in his philosophical work and other academics (Miller, Greenwood & Maguire 2003; Reynolds 2017). There is also evidence of AR perspectives in early labour-organizing traditions and in the Catholic Action movement (Miller, Greenwood & Maguire 2003). AR encompasses two main components, action which deals with practice and the improvement thereof and research which involves description of what is being done and why it is done as action is being taken (McNiff & Whitehead 2016; McNiff 2017). As with the aim of other types of research, AR seeks to create new original knowledge (McNiff & Whitehead 2016).

The concept of AR was pioneered by Kurt Lewin in 1946 during World War II where the emphasis was to determine the link between practice and knowledge (Thompson 2003). Kurt Lewin is credited with coining the term 'action research' (Susman & Evered 1978; Greenwood & Levin 2007;

Williamson, Bellman & Webster 2012; Inbaraj 2018). During the 1940s in the US there was only one form of AR that attributed to Kurt Lewin. Despite this claim there are many historical records that show the values and concepts that underpin AR (McNiff & Whitehead 2016).

Moreover, Noffke (cited in Tromp, Beukema & Almekinders 2009) argues that the history of AR is characterised by the tension between democracy and social engineering. This tension works itself out by the changing configurations in AR practice.

The basic concept of AR is a group process that is geared towards "learning by researching" (O'Brien 1998; Daton & Abraham 2009). Having indicated this however, there is no formal definition for AR with Chandler and Tolbert (2003) noting that AR is not easily defined. One possible definition was presented by Abraham, Arnold and Oxenberry (1996, p. 4) which states:

> *Action research aims to contribute to both the practical concerns of people in an immediate problematic situation and to the goals of social science by joint collaboration within a mutually acceptable ethical framework.*

Another definition was presented by Ramos (2002) from Davydd Greenwood and Greenwood and Levin (2007, p. 3) that is focused in an organisational context. It states:

> *Action research is social research carried out by a team encompassing a professional action researcher and members of an organization or community seeking to improve their situation. Action research promotes broad participation in the research process and supports action leading to a more just or satisfying situation for the stakeholders.*

A short and somewhat straight forward definition of AR was presented by John Elliott (1991:69) whose work was cited in Altrichter et al. (2013, p. 4) as being influential in the AR movement. The definition identifies AR as "the study of a social situation with a view to improving the quality of action within it".

AR is a qualitative research method that provides a link between research and practice where there is a synergistic relationship between the two (Avison et al. 1999) linking practice and ideas (Reason & Bradbury 2013). It is a method involving a joint process between researchers and employees. The goal of the process is to achieve both research and intervention objectives (Israel, Schurman & Hugentobler 1992). This is achieved by researchers trying out theory with practitioners in real situations. As a result, the researcher gains feedback, modifies the theory and tries again. In addition, it was noted that AR is not just a single method for collecting and analysing data but a holistic approach to problem-solving (Greenwood & Levin 2007).

AR is not simply a 'tool' for practice but is the development of change management (Williamson, Bellman & Webster 2012). It has a tradition dating back to the early part of the twentieth century (Antonellis & Berry 2017). In AR, there is the evolution of action and inquiry addressing questions and issues significant to the participants; the participants that are involved as co-researchers (Reason & Bradbury 2013). Greenwood and Levin (2007) noted that AR is a research strategy that generates knowledge for the sole purpose of taking action to effect social analysis and democratic social change.

AR was conceptualized as a cyclical methodology involving discrete phases (Lewin 1946, cited in Williamson, Bellman & Webster 2012). First, a planning or fact-finding phase, beginning with a general idea following extended 'diagnosis', and next, implementation of the execution of a plan, with this 'experimental' phase followed by further fact finding to evaluate the results of the action.

The work done by Lewin on minority problems describes a four step cycle of AR with repeated turns around the cycle. The benefit of these repeats is to ensure the experience gained during the evaluation phase can be fed back into the experimental phase and is represented in Figure 4.3.

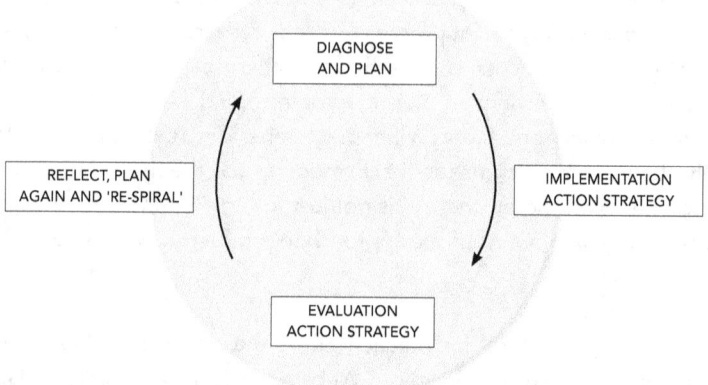

Figure 4.3 – Action research spiral framework
Source: adapted from Lewin 1946 cited in Williamson, Bellman and Webster 2012, p. 13

The cyclical concept associated with AR is supported by McNiff and Whitehead (2016). They noted that there is general consensus that the process of acting and reflecting is a continuous one. It involves taking action and reflecting on the action taken and then acting again based on the new information of data that was found which results in a cycle of action–reflection. When there is an ongoing process of action-reflection it can be seen as a cycle of cycles (McNiff & Whitehead 2016).

It was postulated by Molineaux (2018) that AR is actually an effective method to influence change in the workplace. Additionally, the emphasis placed on reflection in the process means that there is the generation of new knowledge and understanding (Winter & Munn-Giddings 2001 cited in Williamson, Bellman & Webster 2012). It was identified that the AR process does not only involve the diagnosis of the organisational issue but the development and selection of alternative actions (Antonellis & Berry 2017). An important aspect of the AR process is the evaluation of the outcome of the implemented change. This AR process is represented in the following figure, Figure 4.4 adapted from Antonellis and Berry (2017, p. 43).

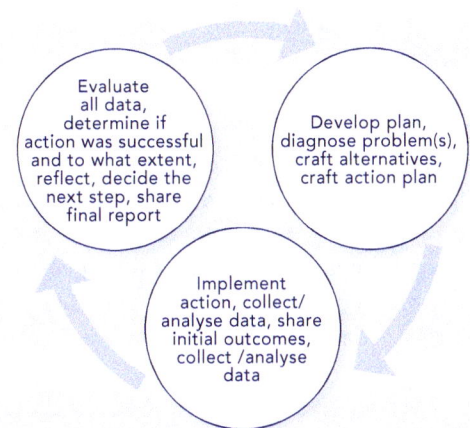

Figure 4.4 – Action research spiral process
Source: adapted from Antonellis and Berry 2017, p. 43

Following Lewin, there were a number of researchers that used this concept, extended and even shaped the model since then. Farren (2005) highlighted that Kemmis and McTaggart (1982) had developed a simple cyclical model of AR based on its iterative nature. Abraham (1997, p. 18) too had taken it further. He summarised Lewin's five fundamental features of AR:

1. AR has to be focussed on real problems in the everyday world as distinct from theoretical problems.
2. AR involves actually taking action to redress the problems.
3. AR involves a cycle of action which should be part of a cycle of steps comprised of planning, action and evaluation.
4. Professional researchers should collaborate with members of the group or organization that are the subject of the research.
5. AR is a scientific process which, in addition to solving particular problems, can provide insights into the laws which determine social behaviour.

The study presented by Abraham and Daton (2009) that AR involves systematic cycles of action and reflection was supported by Tromp, Beukema and Almekinders (2009) and Reason and Bradbury (2013). In the action phase, the practices are tested and evidence gathered by co-researchers, and the reflection stage involves making sense of the data gathered and planning for further action. In the AR process, acting and research are not separate.

AR was described by Ramos (2002, p. 2) as a process that is open to many and facilitated to promote fairness. He noted that the outcomes "support participants' interests so that the knowledge created helps participants to control their own destiny". He explained that actions are normally generated by the participants which ensure a maximum amount of self-determination. He further noted that the researcher ultimately becomes redundant as a result of capacity building in the research process.

In describing AR, Williamson, Bellman and Webster (2012) referenced Reason and Bradbury (2006), suggesting AR to be a 'new paradigm' in research, focussed on participation and change. Reason and Bradbury (2013, p. 2) highlighted five aspects of AR presented in the following Table 4.2.

Table 4.2 – Five points of description of AR

1. A set of practices in response to the desire of people to creatively act as a result of practical and pressing issues in their lives, organizations and communities.
2. A collaborative relationship with people, opening new 'communicative spaces' where dialogue and development can flourish.
3. 'Draws on many ways of knowing, both in the evidence that is generated in inquiry and its expression in diverse forms of presentation as we share learning with wider audiences.'
4. Action research is values oriented which intends to address significant issues concerned with the flourishing of persons, communities and the wider ecology where we participate.
5. A process that is living and emergent that cannot be predetermined but evolves as participants deepen their understanding of the specific issues and develop their capacity, both individually and collectively as co-inquirers.

Source: Reason and Bradbury 2013, p. 2

Holwell (2004), cited in Reason and Bradbury (2013) proposed three concepts that legitimize AR, namely, the recoverability, iteration and purposeful articulation of research themes. Greenwood and Levin (2007) proposed that AR is focused on conducting social research with the use of a set of collaborative ways to do so. It was further suggested that in conducting AR, rigorous scientific requirements and the promotion of democratic social change is achieved simultaneously.

Reason and Bradbury (2013) note that AR as with other forms of research, is committed to making a useful contribution to understanding and knowledge. AR intends to show methodologically how this contribution is achieved to those who are exposed to it whether they agreed with it or wanted to replicate the research. The ultimate outcome is both individual and collective learning.

The aim of the AR process is to create learning at two levels, namely, the persons involved with the problem and for the professional researchers. As a result, when the AR project is developed, there must not only be the selection of method but also a comprehensive plan for the social change and learning processes that will occur throughout the project (Greenwood & Levin 2007). Additionally, all the knowledge and experience of the stakeholder will be used in a structured process of cogenerated learning.

In emphasising the objective of AR to achieve change, Tromp, Beukema and Almekinders (2009, p. 211) posed the following question:

> Is the extent to which research is part of the process of change itself: does the research stop after analysis of the current situation and formulation of recommendations for improving this situation by the researcher, leaving the researched party to decide how to deal with these recommendations?

In answering this question, most action researchers according to Tromp, Beukema and Almekinders (2009) would do so in the negative because in AR, while the process of change is being effected, the research continues. Additionally, AR is associated with improved learning by the researcher which would be used to influence new action. Then, the new learning and action by the researcher is used to influence the learning of others so their new learning can in turn be used to inform new action (McNiff

& Whitehead 2016). This relationship is represented in Figure 4.5 below.

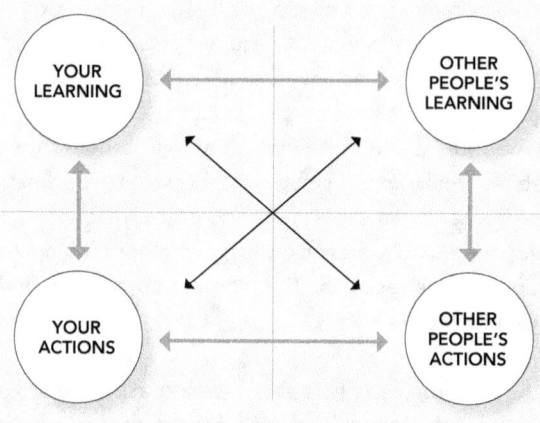

Figure 4.5 – Learning relationship
Source: adapted from McNiff and Whitehead 2016, p.144

One of the main qualities of professional AR is the researcher knowing how to be a friendly outsider. This is important because it is the external perspective that is the key to opening the local group processes for change. The researcher must be able to reflect back to the group, things about them inclusive of criticisms of their perspectives or habits in a manner that is positive and supportive instead of negative, critical or domineering (Greenwood & Levin 2007).

The balance of critique and support demonstrated by a professional AR researcher is achieved through a variety of actions. These include direct feedback, written reflections, data from comparable cases, citing cases from professional literature with similar problems, opportunities or processes. This concept of the "friendly outsider" is quite applicable in this study where the researcher is in fact an outsider to the research site. The ability to provide a different perspective as well as critical and relevant observations of the research site, operations and management, is useful in providing leadership and guidance in the research.

AR can be further described as a practice-driven approach. It begins with the practice under study, a diagnosis and then the design of an intervention, based on the practical knowledge of the action involved and the researcher's input of the theory (Tromp, Beukema & Almekinders 2009). The research is continued during implementation of the intervention, resulting in a process that leads to intended change. However, some authors (Reason & Bradbury 2001; Greenwood & Levin 1998 cited in Tromp, Beukema & Almekinders 2009) suggest that there is hardly ever the design of a whole series of cycles planned beforehand.

The importance of planning of the intervention and the intervention itself was stressed by Tromp, Beukema and Almekinders (2009, p. 211). This process involves both the researcher and the cooperation of the co-researchers. As such, AR is not "limited to the application of real scientific research, where methodological knowledge is reserved for the researcher". It was further highlighted that the intervention has both intended and unintended consequences of action. All of these have to be analysed and assigned a role in the research process and change. It is important that the action researcher is competent enough to maintain an overview of the process and design the evaluation in such a manner that a redefinition can be recognized and dealt with by those involved (Tromp, Beukema & Almekinders 2009).

The concept that AR is a process which results in change and the generation of new knowledge about the situation, was supported by Williamson, Bellman and Webster (2012). In most AR studies, the two objectives are interrelated to a greater or lesser degree. This is justified by the authors in that it is difficult to change a situation without working to understand it more fully and in so doing the possibilities for change often emerge (Williamson, Bellman & Webster 2012).

Many researchers discussed key attributes of AR and broad characteristics. A summary of three of the main contributions is provided in Table 4.3.

Table 4.3 – Summary of Characteristics of AR

Coghlan & Brannick (2010 cited in Tromp, Beukema & Almekinders 2009) and Williamson, Bellman & Webster (2012, p. 73)	Cassell and Symon (2006, p. 350)	McNiff & Whitehead (2016, p. 17)
• AR is educative • Deals with individuals as members of social groups • Is problem-focused, contextspecific and future oriented • Involves a change intervention • Aims at improvement and involvement • Involves a cyclic process in which research, action and evaluation are interlinked • Is founded on a research relationship in which those involved are participants in the change process • AR is about research in action rather than about action. This means a 'scientific' process of inquiry is used in social settings to link important issues with those who experience them	• A close relationship between knowledge acquisition and action • Knowledge acquisition and implementation is for the benefit of the client and participants as much or more than for the researcher and her/his community • Validation is through the learning-action process itself and whenever possible, through co-interpretation of outcomes with the participants. • The knowledge-action or the action-knowledge process may be contingent on specific circumstances but must not exclude a degree of generalizability within similar contingencies • The results of the process must be available and widely shared between clients and researchers. This differentiates it from many forms of consultancy.	• AR is practice based, and practice is understood as action and research; • AR is about improving practice (both action and research), creating knowledge, and generating living theories of practice; • AR focuses on improving learning, not on improving behaviours; • AR emphasises the values base of practice; • AR is about research and knowledge creation, and is more than just professional practice; • AR is collaborative, and focuses on the co-creation of knowledge of practices; • AR involves interrogation, deconstruction and decentring; • AR demands higher-order questioning; • AR is intentionally political;

Table 4.3 – (Continued)

• It is a collaborative, democratic process, meaning that there is active participation of those who experience the situation in working towards solutions. This is distinct from traditional research approaches both quantitative and qualitative, where research participants are subjects rather than collaborators. • Action and knowledge are joined so that change occurs while there is a simultaneous process of knowledge generation • It is a sequence of events and an approach to problem solving which contributes to knowledge and understanding.	• There is always an ethical dimension to the process with a degree of shared values and reflexivity between client and researcher. • AR tends to call on more than one scientific discipline and more than one knowledge acquisition method.	• AR requires people to hold themselves accountable for what they are doing and accept responsibility for their own actions; • AR can contribute to social and cultural transformation.

Source: Summary of Characteristics of AR

Reason and Bradbury (2013) provide a diagrammatic summary of these characteristics captured in Figure 4.6. One key characteristic worth noting is that AR is emancipatory, in that it leads to both new practical knowledge and new abilities to create knowledge. One criticism has emerged to AR being described and presented as emancipatory (Romme 2004 cited in Tromp, Beukema & Almekinders 2009).

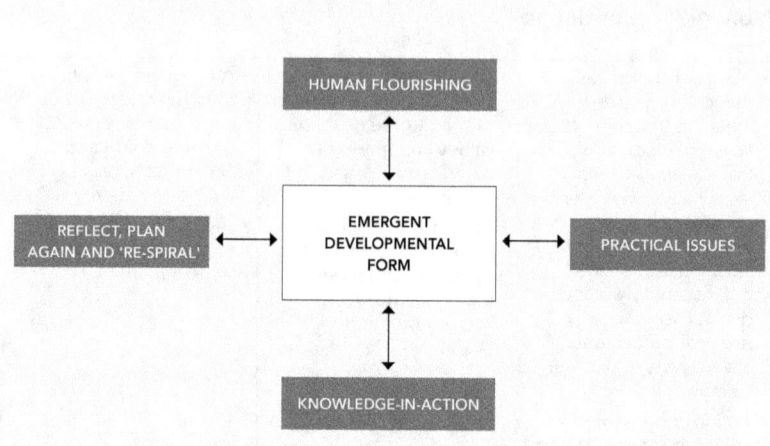

Figure 4.6 – Characteristics of action research
Source: adapted from McNiff and Whitehead 2016, p.144

The emancipatory characteristic of AR (Reason & Bradbury 2013) as well as other characteristics noted above are included in the list of AR characteristics presented by Abraham (2012; 2016). The list presented consists of twelve characteristics and include Problem Focus, Action Orientation, Cyclical Process, Collaboration, Ethical Practice, Group Facilitation, Creative Thinking, Learning and Re-education, Naturalistic, Emancipatory, Normative and Scientific. The list of characteristics presented by Abraham (2016, pp. 56-62), was a result of extensive reading and consideration of the various views of several authors.

In a comparison of Abraham's characteristics to those of other authors highlighted in Table 4.8, there is consistence and the recognition of 10 of the characteristics. However, the characteristics of AR being naturalistic and allowing for creative thinking were not identified.

Although the learning characteristic was recognized by other authors, it was categorised as change intervention and an improved practice. It was highlighted that more than one scientific discipline and more than one knowledge acquisition method are required. Further, it was noted that the process allows for improved learning but not the improved behaviours of individuals. However, in Abraham's description of the learning characteristic, it caters for change in the skills, attitudes and knowledge of the individual group members, and a change in the skills and knowledge of the researcher. This suggests that with this level of re-education, the bahaviours of individuals would also change.

An opposing characteristic to those by Abraham was presented as AR being intentionally political. It is based on the notion that challenging an existing situation and taking action is in itself a political act since the action would present consequences to people. Additionally, when the injustices are revealed, the researcher is faced with the dilemma of following their values and trying to influence the situation, or go along with the status quo. The researcher's desire to contribute to social development, can be the driving force to act in the interest of social justice. Despite this, since AR was described by Abraham as being an ethical practice, the dilemma as suggested being experienced by the researcher should not be evident in the research.

The identification of validation, through the learning-action process, was highlighted as a separate characteristic by the other authors presented in Table 4.8. An additional characteristic was identified which spoke to the fact that the results of the research must be shared between clients and researcher, however, this also forms part of the ethics in the research process as presented by Abraham.

The issue of validity in AR has been an ongoing discussion. Heron (1996 cited in Greenwood & Levin 2007) who is particularly attentive to issues of validity makes important contributions to the broader discussions of AR. He makes the connection between inquiry cycles, reflection, action and other elements in the process to an overall view of what constitutes validity in this type of work.

Included in the validity procedures advocated by Heron, are research cycles, balancing divergence and convergence in the process and elements of reflection. The basis for making claims for validity in AR is whether action is warranted or the creation of workable solutions. It was further noted that validity is dealt with differently based on the kind of process and knowledge deployed. Williamson, Bellman and Webster (2012) noted that action researchers must be clear in that they are not simply imposing their majority will on others which could be regarded as oppressive.

In addressing the issue of rigour and validity of AR, authors Sankaran and Dick (2015) reiterated that AR as a form of qualitative research tends to use techniques within qualitative research that would increase validity. It was determined that trustworthiness was proposed as being equivalent to ensuring validity and reliability in research of this nature.

In order to achieve this trustworthiness, there should be the establishment of credibility (internal validity), transferability (external validity), dependability (reliability) and confirmability (objectivity) (Sankaran & Dick 2015, p. 11) Another means by which validity can be achieved in AR as qualitative research is through triangulation by using different methods of data collection (Sankaran & Dick 2015, p. 11).

ACTION RESEARCH ACTION LEARNING (ARAL)

Action Learning (AL) involves the combining of self-development with action for change. Its origin can be traced to Reginald Revans (1907 to 2003) and is probably best understood as a working philosophy instead of a standard practice or a set of techniques (Reason & Bradbury 2013). It was suggested by McNiff (2017, p. 15-16) that AL is actually an off shoot from AR which instead of generating theory actually "emphasises the actions of WBL". It was noted that there is in fact a strong relationship between AR and Work-Based Learning (WBL) (McNiff & Whitehead 2016). Further, it was emphasized that AR is not AL although AL is incorporated in AR and quite frequently the lines between AR and AL are blurred. Moreover, AL is more focussed on improving practice via the collaborative learning process and is not always focused or emphasise research aspects (McNiff & Whitehead 2016, p.17). There was concurrence by Sankaran and Dick (2015) that AR can be combined with AL.

The AL process commences and concludes with purpose initiated by the question "What am I trying to do?" In effect, AL is about helping people "learn how to solve problems". Reason and Bradbury (2013, p. 319) went further to highlight a definition of AL by Pedler (1997) which states:

> *Action learning couples the development of people in work organizations with action on their different problems......*

> *(it) makes the task the vehicle for learning and has 3 main components – people, who accept the responsibility for action on a particular task or issue; problems, or the tasks which are acted on; and the set of six or so colleagues who meet regularly to support and challenge each other to take action and to learn.*

One of the main intents of AL is continuous improvement both at a systems level and self-development which can be achieved through action by both individuals and collectively (Reason & Bradbury 2013). Additionally, it was noted that the purpose and outcome were improvements in person, and collectively learning and action.

A distinctive feature of AL is working practice which is "the set of peers working overtime to provide support and challenge in helping each other achieve their goals" (Reason & Bradbury 2013, p. 322). This set has common practices which include primarily the questions and the provision of feedback. Revans (1998 cited in Reason & Bradbury 2013) described the set as 'the cutting edge' of AL because of the focus on action, pragmatic research, reflection and personal development. He further noted that AL was not a simplistic risk and dilemma free 'learning by doing' as is sometimes depicted, but in fact a moral and practical struggle geared toward progress couched in risk and anxiety.

The emphasis of the concept of a 'set' or group of participants engaged in learning was supported by Sankaran and Dick (2015) where the participants who are volunteers learn with and from each other. It was highlighted that Reginald Revans (1982) used the term 'set' and generated the following equation:

$$L = P + Q$$

where **L** is learning, **P** is programmed instruction and **Q** is questioning insight. Revans suggested that a significant percentage of the learning, even as much as 90% is achieved through insightful questioning of the participants in the set.

AL is faced with quite a few unresolved and developmental issues (Reason & Bradbury 2013). These include the question of definition because according to Weinstein (1995 cited in Reason & Bradbury 2013) AL means different things to different people, what was the best link between individual and organisational learning and the quest for a more critical AL. In order to achieve AL, Greenwood and Levin (2007) suggested that there must be a combination of 3 fundamental elements, action, research and participation.

Some authors addressed the challenge of AL at an organisational level (Revans 1998 cited in Reason & Bradbury 2013). It was theorized that managerial values and the organisational value system are indeed the factors that are most likely responsible for the hindrance of effective action and learning. It was theorized that in order to achieve organisational learning there must be a secured connection between what the AL participants have learnt and other members of the organisation (Donnenberg & De Loo 2004 cited in Reason & Bradbury 2013). The following section will provide an overview of similarities and differences between AR and AL.

AR AND AL SIMILARITIES AND DIFFERENCES

There are obvious similarities and differences between AR and AL. Some of the similarities of AR and AL were highlighted by Reason and Bradbury (2013). One similarity is that both AR and AL share a common origin in that they are both committed to action and pragmatism. Additionally they both react against detached research with the generation of abstract knowledge subsequently being disseminated through teaching from an assumed expertise position.

Other similarities highlighted, include that both AR and AL have genesis in a critique of the application of a positivist, natural sciences approach to social and human settings. Additionally, a common characteristic of both is the cyclical processes that reflect 'the pragmatists' emphasis on the need for experiment, reflection and learning. Finally, they are both concerned with the objective of deriving pragmatic and meaningful solutions to problems of a social nature in organisations, communities and societies (Reason & Bradbury 2013, p. 322).

Some of the differences between AR and AL as indicated by Reason and Bradbury (2013) include the opinion that AR is more developed in both practice and theory than AL and has been developed and perpetuated by a wider community of scholars. Another difference that was noted by Mc Gill and Beaty (2001) cited in Reason and Bradbury (2013) is that the focus of AL is on learning through action as compared to AR which is more research oriented.

The simple distinction between AR and AL may create a false perception of the differences in orientation. This is based on the premise that an argument can be made that the purpose of research in AR is in the main, for the benefit of the group within the area of study (Reason 2006 cited in Reason & Bradbury 2013). However, there seems to be a difference of emphasis in practice on the purpose of research. Additionally, it was noted that AL is associated with people in circumstances of confusion, ambiguity and risk.

REFLECTIVE PRACTICE

Several theorists generally concur that at the centre of professional learning and growth as well as transformation and empowerment is reflection. Quite often the definitions of reflection is strongly related to the cognitive process of the individual, which includes consciousness, analysis, evaluation, questioning and criticizing experiences, assumptions, beliefs and emotions (Hilden & Tikkamaki 2013). The definition of critical reflection as proposed by Grose (2015, p. 315) is:

> *the process by which we self-consciously locate ourselves within the system in which we are operating and in relation to the other players in that system. Through this process, we are able to identify what assumptions are at work and the effect they are having on us, on the other players, and on the system itself*

It has been noted by theorist and authors such as Schon (1983 cited in Tran & Anvair 2014); Blazert, Fettke and Loos (2012 cited in Tran & Anvair 2014) and Embo et al. (2015) that an essential characteristic required for professional competence is reflective capacity. In order to learn from an experience and to gain understanding and awareness from that experience there needs to be the understanding of the difference between just thinking something over and a critical analysis of the experience (Carmel 2006).

There are several definitions of reflection in professional practice presented by a number of authors. For this study, reflection relates to a link between experience and learning (Fletcher & Wilson 2013; Bracci, Bella Owona & Nash 2013) where there is exploration and inquiry based on individual experience and observations, as well as those presented at the research site. The objective of the reflective practice is pertinent in the AR process where there is constant reflection and evaluation in the interest of achieving the desired outcome of the research. The focus is on learning by doing (Edwards 1999).

Schon (1983) introduced the terms 'reflection-in-action' and 'reflection-on-action.' These terms were derived and included by Schon (1983, 1987 cited in Sempowicz & Hudson 2012) by re-phrasing Dewey's model of learning, which involves reflective thinking either while teaching or after teaching. According to Wilkstrom and Jackson (2012), in Schon's (1983) theoretical framework he provided insight into the way professionals think about doing something while they are doing it. This is the concept Schon termed as reflection-in-action and is based on the element of surprise. The surprise element is derived through the fact that more knowledge is obtained out of the situation as compared to what is put in. Reflection-in-action as proposed by Schon is also described as 'thinking on your feet' which involves the thinking and reflecting that occurs in the midst of the current event that is happening (Tran & Anvari 2014).

This concept of 'reflection-in-action' was described by Schon as consisting of: "on-the-spot surfacing, criticizing, restructuring, and testing of intuitive understanding of experienced phenomena" which is in the form of "a reflective conversation with the situation" (Reynolds 2017, p. 2). The element of surprise as described by Schon was supported by Yanow and Tsoukas (2009 cited in Taylor 2010) and further noted that a key element of Schon's reflection-in-action is the ability to be open to being surprised by the world which he referred to as being permeable to surprise.

Schon (1983 cited in Tran and Anvari 2014) describes 'reflection-on-action' as the thinking and reflection that occurs after the event has happened. Additionally, Schon's theory (Wilkstrom & Jackson 2012) gives an insight into how reflection-on-action occurs and is used in the creation of new knowledge. The following section will provide an overview of Work-Applied Learning (WAL).

WORK-APPLIED LEARNING (WAL)

The genesis and development of the WAL for change concept can be attributed in significant part to the work done by Selva Abraham over the last few decades. Fundamental to this concept for change is the ARAL approach. Abraham's work and experience in Work-Based Learning (WBL) gave rise to the extension into WAL which is grounded in a fused ARAL approach. The main features of the WBL platform upon which WBL was developed are presented in Table 4.4 below.

Table 4.4 – Features of WBL

Focuses on tasks
Is a collaborative activity resultant of an experience or problem for which there is a known knowledge base
Is different from what normally happens in business schools
Practical and cognitive process
Is learnt by working, not through reading or observing work
Has a variety of instructional strategies away from the classroom
Is self-directed; creative; expressive; involves feeling; is continual and reflective
Includes action projects, learning teams and other inter-personal experiences, including mentorship
Provides opportunities for professional practice, critical analysis and reflective thinking
Involves knowledge creation and utilisation as collective activates when learning becomes everyone's job

Table 4.4 – (Continued)

Involves thinking and evaluating theory and practice
Links coursework assessment with workplace practices
Can lead to the attainment of qualifications

Source: adapted from McNiff and Whitehead 2016, p.144

However, it was noted by Abraham (2012; 2015, p. 4) that "in addition to creating learning in the workplace by individuals or teams" the WAL model "has also resulted in the collective learning of the teams to create organisational learning and change."

Despite the benefits derived from the incorporation of the features of WBL, it is the addition of the ARAL process in WBL that gives rise to not only learning by individuals such as managers and teams but also "organisational learning and change". This learning is represented in Figure 4.7. This is achieved through the AR cycles of WAL which include plan, act, observe, reflect, evaluate and validate.

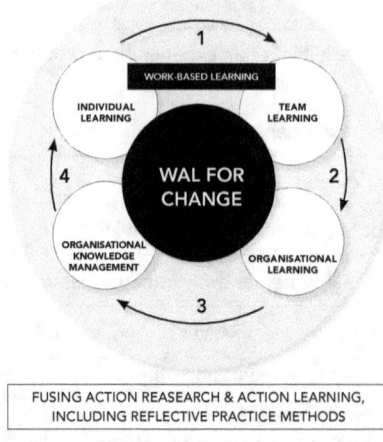

FIGURE 4.7 – Characteristics of action research
Source: Abraham 2012; 2015, p. 5.

Abraham (2012; 2015) noted that there is a distinct difference between AR and AL where AR is a research method and AL is a process. One significant difference as identified by Abraham (2012; 2015) is that the main focus of AL is on questioning as compared to AR which seeks to derive change or noticeable positive difference to "problematic situations" (Abraham 2012; 2015, p. 6).

Based on work conducted by Abraham and other authors in relation to organisational learning and change, a word formula was developed to represent the relationship with AR and AL. These are as follows (Abraham 2012; 2015, p. 9):

$$AL: S + P + A (+F) \longrightarrow AL$$
$$AR: G + P + A + F + C + R \longrightarrow AR$$

It was suggested based on careful analysis that the components of AL that were already considered in or a part of AR as a subset. In this regard, Abraham et al. (1996) suggested that the fusing of AL and AR into an ARAL model can be represented by the following word formula where C represented the cyclical nature of AR and R represented the researcher:

$$ARAL: AL + C + R \longrightarrow AR$$

The fused ARAL approach to WAL has been used extensively to produce organisational learning and change in many industries and organisations. A detailed explanation of the variables of the AR and AL equations is presented in Table 4.5, which is adapted from Abraham (2012; 2015. p 10).

Table 4.5 – Explanation of WAL Symbols

SYMBOLS	DESCRIPTION
S	The AL **set** comprising individuals who come together to investigate solutions to shared problems and to learn from each other.
P	The **problem** to be addressed. Both AL and AR share this problem-focused characteristics.
A	Both AR and AL are **action**-oriented. The group or set takes positive action in response to the ideas and suggestions generated through questioning and addressing.
G	The nature of the AR **group** may be rather different to the set described in AL. The group comprises members of the organisation or community and could also include "Researchers" who may be seen as an integral part of the group since they work in a collaborative manner with the group for change and knowledge development.
F	The term **"Facilitator"** has been placed in brackets in the AL work formula to indicate the disparate view amongst the authors on whether or not a facilitator should be part of the set.
C	The **cyclical** nature of AR. Lewin (1946 and 1947) indicated that the spiral nature of steps was fundamental to AR. His step started with diagnosis, followed by cycles of planning, action and reflection.
R	The **Researcher** in Lewin's original view assisted the group. While some writers question the need for a Researcher, the role of a Researcher as a consultant to the group is widely supported by other authors.

Source: Abraham 2012, p. 10.

Additionally, some of the uses of WAL in industries and organisations were presented by Abraham 2015 and Holyoake 2016 and are reproduced in Table 4.6.

Table 4.6 – Current Applications for the ARAL Approach

APPLICATION	DETAILS
Light Regional Council, Adelaide South Australia	Unique government and community engagement for the Light Regional Council
International Bank	To plan and develop a Customer Relationship Program for bank officers and front line staff across all branches of the bank
Delivery Business unit of Australia Post in South Australia	To develop Delivery Centre Managers and Team Leaders in light of new organisational structure
Global Carriers Group	Applied to manage the impact of the Asian financial crisis on the Global Carriers Group
Internal Revenue Commission (IRC) of Papua New Guinea	Development of a strategic business plan and the implementation of restructuring in the National Revenue Commission (IRC) of Papua New Guinea to bring about change in the delivery of services
Community Development and Employment Program (CDEP) for Aboriginal communities	Evaluate a board management development program which was conducted for the Board members of the Kuju CDEP Inc., an Aboriginal community organisation in Port Lincoln, South Australia
G7 Construction Firm in Malaysia	To develop and implement a WAL facilitative leadership development programme for senior managers in a G7 construction company in Malaysia
Project Management Development Programme for Project Management Practitioners	To develop and implement a work-based project management development programme for project management practitioners in T&T

Source: Abraham 2015 and Holyoake 2016, p. 66.

A word formula was also developed for WAL based on the learning experienced by the learning teams and managers as they go through the cycles and the work-based phases. The word formula is as follows

(Abraham 2012; 2015 p. 16):

$$K + P1 + Q = P2$$

where **K** represents Knowledge, **P1** refers to the Project, **Q** is the questioning nature of the process and **P2** deals with the Performance outcomes.

A description of a typical WAL programme was presented by authors Garnett, Abraham and Abraham (2016, p. 59). It indicated that the WAL programme is made of several AR cycles each of which consists of:

> *AR group meetings (facilitated by a consultant with expertise in WAL and change management), knowledge workshops, work-based application and testing of knowledge, joint observations and reflections and monitoring and evaluation.*

The following sections would discuss the AR method stage.

AR Method Stage
The AR method stage begins with a discussion of the AR site, the AR design, the data collection and data analysis techniques, and finally the techniques that are utilised to evaluate and validate the study.

AR Site
The research site is a Well Workover company in T&T. This site, was selected because of the important service it provides to the larger state owned Petroleum Company in T&T. Currently, the state owned company has approximately 15 Well Workover organisations providing similar services to that of the research site for their land operations.

The prime objective of the research site is to provide the petroleum industry high quality mechanical maintenance, and, well servicing and workover services. Its operations are based in the energy sector, with a staff of approximately 150 employees. The research site provides well services operation primarily to the state owned company in the area of well workover services, but also has other clients in the energy sector.

The research site's operations are based in the southern part of T&T where there is the concentration of both onshore [land-based] and offshore [marine] oil and gas operations (Company Profile 2015). The research site's organisational chart is represented in the Figure 4.8.

The research site currently operates three Well Workover drilling rigs on land: Rig 1, Rig 2 and Rig 4, in the execution of its services. The research site has had in the past and continues to have an accident/incident rate which is seen as unacceptable. This ranges from near misses to actual loss time accidents. There have been many safety initiatives implemented to address these problems, including an OHS management system (OHSMS) aligned to Occupational Health and Safety Assessment Series (OHSAS) 18001 and the Plan-Do-Check-Act model.

However, the research site's OHS performance is one that has continued to cost the organisation significant financial loss both directly from the occurrences of accidents and indirectly from loss of contracts. Additionally, the loss of human resource and its reputation as an organisation that operates in a safe manner in the high risk petroleum industry, has been severely compromised. Despite continued OHS management efforts and initiatives, the accident/incident rate has not shown any reversal in trend which indicates that the desired objective was not being realised. Herein lies the thematic concern, and the problem that has the potential to adversely affect the organisation's sustainability and its ability to provide the necessary Well Workover services that are required in the petroleum industry.

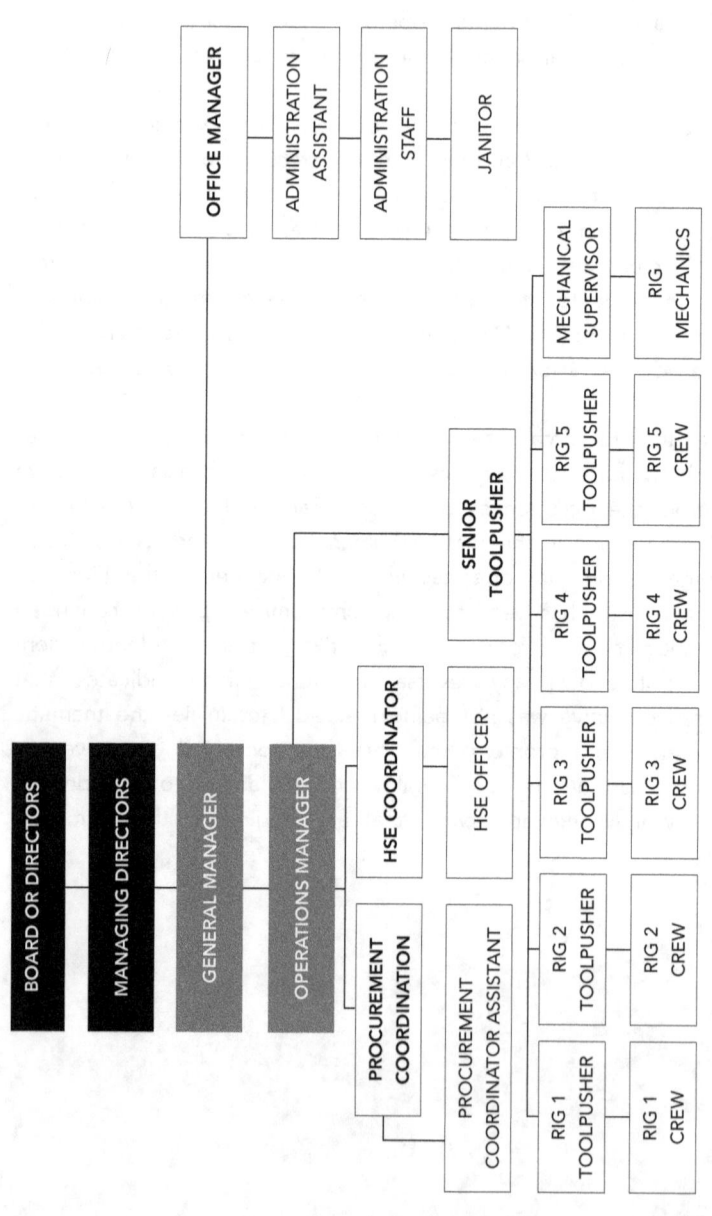

Figure 4.8 – organisational chart
Source: Research site, 2015.

ENTRY TO THE AR SITE

The analysis and justification of the entry and acceptance of the research site is based on research presented by Marshall and Rossman (1989) and adapted in Abraham (1997). This is represented in Table 4.7 below.

Table 4.7 – Justification of Research Site

CRITERIA	JUSTIFICATION
Is entry possible?	Discussions with the MD and other members of Senior Management revealed that entry is not a problem. The agreement between the researcher and the MD who is also the owner of the organisation is twofold. Firstly to produce a reduction in accidents and secondly to provide an enhanced management system for the organisation.
Were processes, people, programmes, interactions and/or structures that were part of the research questions present?	The main research question asks if a WAL approach can be used in the development and implementation of a WAL-OHSMS in a Well Workover company in T&T. The corollary research questions refer to the project, process and learning outcomes as well as the challenges. Since WAL uses a fused ARAL process, AR provides the most appropriate research method. The study relies on interactions with the AR Group, the AL teams, Validation Committee and Senior Management.
Processes?	Major cycles for the processes are planned and evaluated and validation mechanisms established.
People?	The management and staff of the research site.
Interactions?	The interactions between members of the AR Groups, the AL Teams are critical to the study. Additionally, the Validation Committee, which includes Senior Management interact with AR Group members and the researcher during evaluation and validation of the study.

Table 4.7 – (Continued)

CRITERIA	JUSTIFICATION
Structures?	The management structure of the research site include the structure of sub-committees and teams in the organisation, and the structures of the AR Group, teams and Validation Committee.
Was an appropriate role for the researcher possible?	The researcher's role as facilitator, researcher and trainer (in providing Supervisory Training to members of the organisation) enables her to become both a participant observer and direct observer in the ARAL process during the development and implementation of the WAL-OHSMS. Despite the fact that the researcher is an outsider to the research site, an invitation has been extended to her to attend management and operations meetings inclusive of observations and interactions with members of rig crews and middle management during the research process.
Did the choice of site avoid poor sampling decisions?	Sampling is not an issue in the study because only one organisation is used.

Source: adapted from Abraham 1997

When the researcher made contact with the Managing Director (MD) about the possibility of conducting the research, the MD was receptive to the idea and sought further discussion to better appreciate what was involved. This gave rise to a meeting between the researcher, the MD and the Operations Manager (OM).

At this initial meeting the researcher explained the AR method, the AL process, the expected outcome and intent, which is to create organisational change through WAL. The researcher then asked the MD to identify the main OHS challenges being experienced by the organisation. He indicated that there are both major and minor accidents, including vehicular accidents, equipment abuse and employee injuries. He further indicated that the financial loss associated with these accidents and incidents is significant and needs to be addressed. It was recognised that this presented a major concern for management in terms of its impact on the organisation's reputation and the financial impact.

The MD added that they were currently seeking to source and implement a management system as part of a new management structure, because the current structure was poorly implemented and ineffective. Therefore, an agreement was reached between the MD, OM and the researcher that OHSMS project be established with deliverables and outcomes to be twofold:

- *A reduction in accidents and*
- *An enhanced management system for the organisation.*

The researcher confirmed that it would be considered as an OHS consultancy, taking the form of a research project that was of no cost to the organisation. Based on this discussion the possibility of conducting the research was fully accepted.

AR design

The method used for this study is the AR method and consists of two stages, the intervention stage and the planning and implementation stage. The intervention stage consists of the research site intervention, establishment of the AR Group and establishment of the Validation Committee. The planning and implementation stage consists of two Major Cycles and looks at the planning and designing of the WAL-OHSMS (Major Cycle 1) and the implementation of the WAL-OHSMS (Major Cycle 2). The design of the research model takes the following format as seen in Figure 4.9.

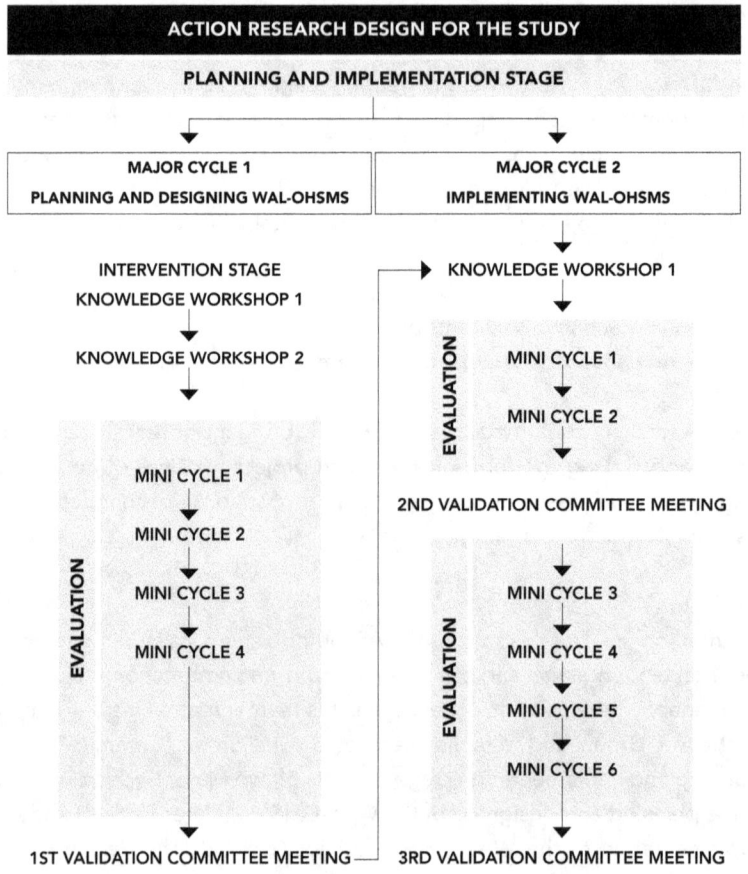

Figure 4.9 – Action research design for the study
Source: adapted from Abraham 2012.

The planning and implementation stage is made up of two Major Cycles with mini cycles within the Major Cycles. Three knowledge workshops are planned, two at the beginning of Major Cycle 1 and one at the beginning of Major Cycle 2. The duration of the first Major Cycle, is three months and focusses on the planning and designing of the WAL-OHSMS. This Major Cycle consists of four mini cycles which take a cyclical format of planning, acting, observing, reflecting, evaluating and re-planning components. At the end of this Major Cycle, the first Validation Committee meeting is held. Continuous evaluation and validation of the data and the research process is conducted within the mini cycles as presented in Figure 4.10.

The second Major Cycle, Major Cycle 2, spans nine months and involves the implementation of the WAL-OHSMS. The Major Cycle 2 consists of six mini cycles. After the plans made at the AR group meetings, the AR group members go back to their respective departments during the Work-Based phase, where they engage the personnel in their different departments (AL Teams) in an attempt to derive the required deliverables to report to the AR group. The number of members in the AL Teams varies from one department to the next, based on the organisational structure and the availability of personnel.

Evaluation will continue throughout the mini cycles. The second Validation Committee process is designed to be conducted at the end of the implementation in this Major Cycle. The third and final Validation Committee meeting was scheduled at the end of Major Cycle 2 which signifies the end of the study. All plans, actions, observations, reflections and re-plans will be documented as the chain of evidence. The structure for this Major Cycle, Major Cycle 2 is presented in Figure 4.11.

162 Chapter 4

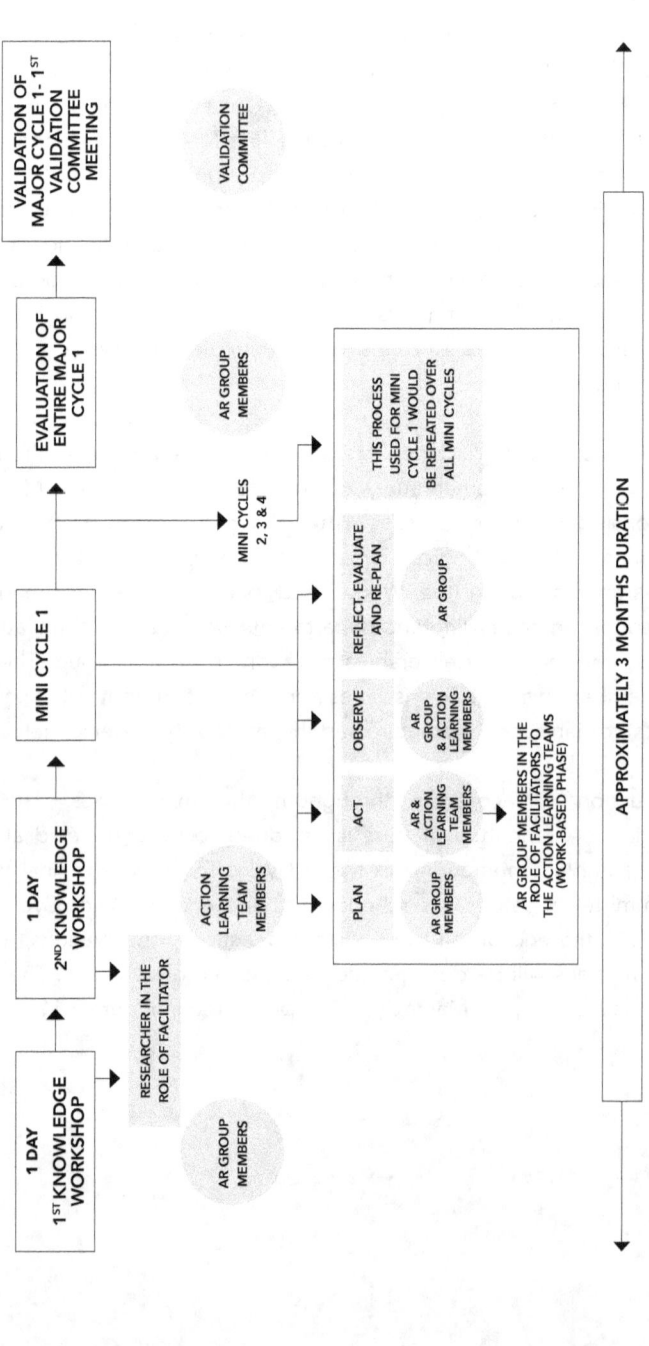

Figure 4.10 – Design of Major Cycle 1

DESIGNING A RESEARCH PLAN FOR AN OHSM SYSTEM 163

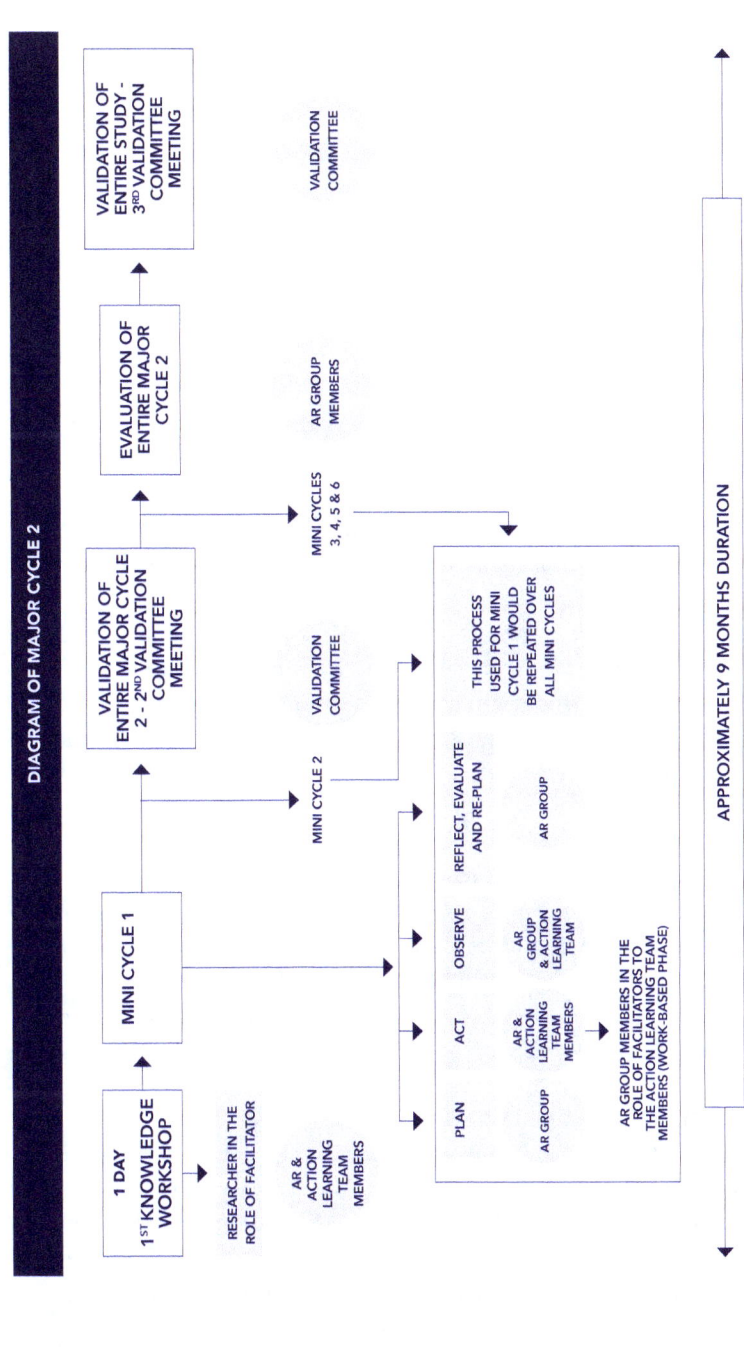

Figure 4.11 – Design of Major Cycle 2

MAJOR CYCLE 1 – PLANNING AND DESIGN OF THE WAL-OHSMS
This cycle commences with a one-day Knowledge Workshop conducted by the researcher in the role of Facilitator and involves all members of the AR Group. Relevant information on specific topics including ARAL, organisational change and reflective practice (Abraham 2012) will be disseminated and discussed. At the end of this session the AR Group members should be able to establish the link between ARAL and change management as well as the process involved.

There will be a second one-day Knowledge Workshop that includes all members of the AR Group and the AL Teams. The main objective of this Knowledge Workshop is to provide guidance on the ARAL process, organisational change and data collection techniques.

The process that involves the actual planning and design of the WAL-OHSMS consists of four mini cycles. There is a Work-Based phase within each mini cycle that involves the AL Teams who work, in collaboration with members of the AR Group to act on the plans made by the AR Group and note relevant observations. On conclusion of the Work-Based phases the researcher will engage the AR Group members in an observation, reflection and evaluation exercise in order to determine if a customisation or re-planning is required before the next mini cycle.

An evaluation exercise is planned for the AR Group, at the end of each mini cycle where data collected is to be discussed, evaluated and triangulated. Additional evaluation also can be conducted through one-on-one discussions with other members of the organisation as well as individual AR Group members. Each mini cycle will end with a re-planning exercise. It must be noted that all the mini cycles adopted the format represented in Figure 4.12 and have specific deliverables.

The intent of deliverable for each mini cycle is specific. The first mini cycle looks at what OHSMS is currently being utilised by the research site and an evaluation of all the accident records within a five-year period. The second mini cycle is used to determine what is required to design the WAL-OHSMS based on the requirements determined through the Work-Based phase and evaluation by the AR Group. The third mini cycle is used to develop a draft of the WAL-OHSMS for analysis and review by both the AL Teams in the Work-Based phase and the AR Group.

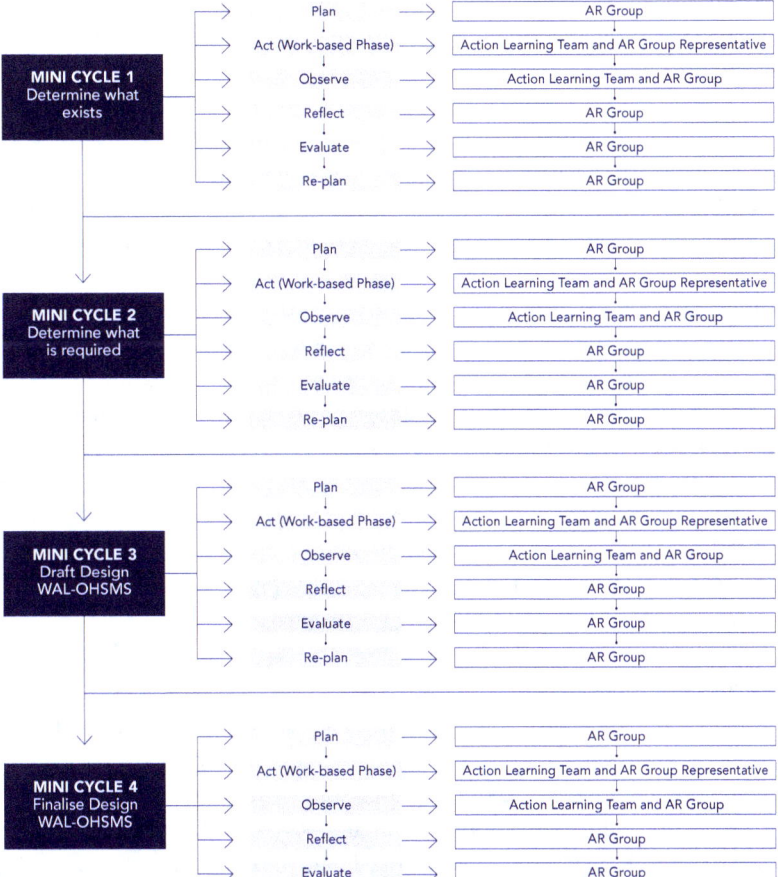

Figure 4.12 – Major Cycle 1 – mini cycle components

Source: Developed for this study

The fourth mini cycle, which is the final mini cycle before the first Validation Committee meeting is used to finalise the WAL-OHSMS before presentation to the Validation Committee members.

At the end of the fourth mini cycle there is an evaluation of the entire Major Cycle 1 and then the first sitting of the Validation Committee. At the Validation Committee meeting, the AR Group is asked to meet with the Validation Committee where the researcher presents a complete documentation of the entire process of Major Cycle 1 for comments and acceptance. Additionally, the challenges faced during the first Major Cycle are identified.

The Validation Committee members are informed as to the findings and outcomes of Major Cycle 1. The Validation Committee validates the process that is used by the AR Group. The result derived at the end of this Major Cycle is the design of a WAL-OHSMS for a Well Workover Company in T&T.

The role of the researcher as a facilitator throughout the entire process involves a close working relationship with the AR Group. Major Cycle 1 spans a period of three months. The design of the entire Major Cycle 1 is represented in Figure 4.10 above. The specific components and deliverables that are required from each mini cycles of Major Cycle 1 is represented in Figure 4.12.

Once the WAL-OHSMS is presented and accepted by the Validation Committee members, the next Major Cycle, Major Cycle 2, the implementation of the WAL-OHSMS, commences.

MAJOR CYCLE 2 – IMPLEMENTATION OF THE WAL-OHSMS
Prior to commencement of this Major Cycle, a meeting will be held with the MD and the OM, and decisions made as to the process of implementation and the proposed time frame. In determining the order in which the different components of the WAL-OHSMS derived during Major Cycle 1 would be implemented, the urgency and the possible impact of each component on the entire management system will be assessed. Components that are deemed critical from an OHS perspective as well as the manner in which the different components may impact the effectiveness of the WAL-OHSMS, need to be considered. An additional consideration is the required resources, both financial and human that would be critical for each component of the implementation.

The result of the first Major Cycle is the design of the WAL-OHSMS for implementation in Major Cycle 2. This was outlined in the previous section and the mini cycles take the format represented in Figure 4.12, the same as described in Major Cycle 1. This second Major Cycle is projected to last a period of approximately nine months. The specific components and deliverables that were required from each mini cycles of Major Cycle 2 is represented in Figure 4.13.

This Major Cycle 2, similar to the previous one, also commences with a one-day Knowledge Workshop. This Workshop involves both members of the AR Group and the AL Teams. At this workshop the participants are exposed to the specific data collection and documentation methods and techniques that are critical for this cycle. Reinforcement of concepts of WAL and the ARAL process are reiterated. Additional discussions need to be conducted specific to OHS, the learning from Major Cycle 1, and the components of the WAL-OHSMS that was designed in Major Cycle 1.

The intent of the deliverables for each mini cycle is specific, as it relates to the implementation and evaluation of the different components. The first mini cycle of the second Major Cycle would be used to determine how the different components of the WAL- OHSMS that was designed in Major Cycle 1, would be implemented. This is based on the discussions held with management prior to the commencement of Major Cycle 2. The order of the components to be implemented and the determined time frame will be used to solicit feedback during this mini cycle in the Work-Based phase to determine how this can be accomplished in an effective manner. Once this is determined, mini cycle two will follow.

Mini cycle two is used to implement the components of the WAL-OHSMS. All the components in the predetermined order are implemented, based on the plan by the AR Group and action taken and executed in the Work-Based phase. The effectiveness of the implementation will be evaluated by the AR Group based on the order of implementation and the agreed time frame. Mini cycle two is followed by the second Validation Committee meeting to validate the WAL-OHSMS components. This is critical to ensure the implementation is conducted in a manner that can be validated, and in accordance with expectation of management.

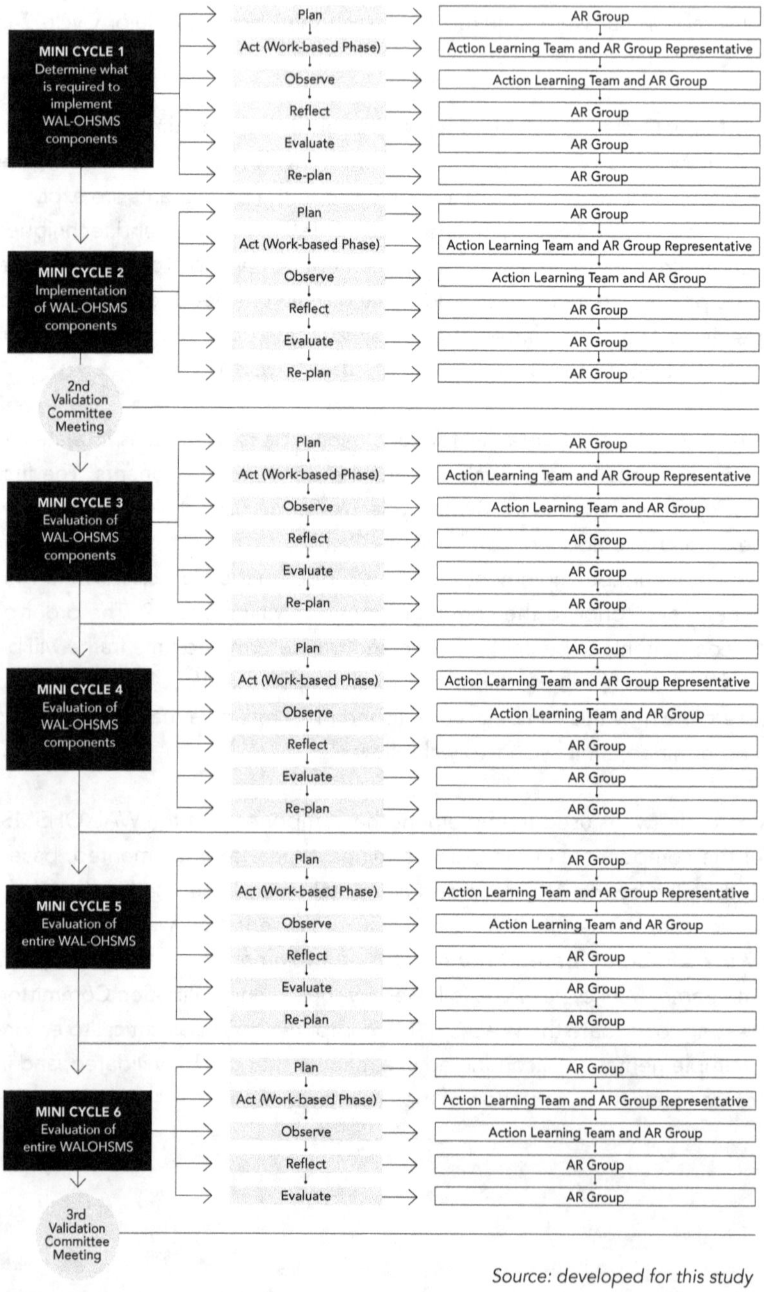

168 Chapter 4

MINI CYCLE 1 Determine what is required to implement WAL-OHSMS components	→ Plan →	AR Group
	→ Act (Work-based Phase) →	Action Learning Team and AR Group Representative
	→ Observe →	Action Learning Team and AR Group
	→ Reflect →	AR Group
	→ Evaluate →	AR Group
	→ Re-plan →	AR Group
MINI CYCLE 2 Implementation of WAL-OHSMS components	→ Plan →	AR Group
	→ Act (Work-based Phase) →	Action Learning Team and AR Group Representative
	→ Observe →	Action Learning Team and AR Group
	→ Reflect →	AR Group
	→ Evaluate →	AR Group
	→ Re-plan →	AR Group
2nd Validation Committee Meeting		
MINI CYCLE 3 Evaluation of WAL-OHSMS components	→ Plan →	AR Group
	→ Act (Work-based Phase) →	Action Learning Team and AR Group Representative
	→ Observe →	Action Learning Team and AR Group
	→ Reflect →	AR Group
	→ Evaluate →	AR Group
	→ Re-plan →	AR Group
MINI CYCLE 4 Evaluation of WAL-OHSMS components	→ Plan →	AR Group
	→ Act (Work-based Phase) →	Action Learning Team and AR Group Representative
	→ Observe →	Action Learning Team and AR Group
	→ Reflect →	AR Group
	→ Evaluate →	AR Group
	→ Re-plan →	AR Group
MINI CYCLE 5 Evaluation of entire WAL-OHSMS	→ Plan →	AR Group
	→ Act (Work-based Phase) →	Action Learning Team and AR Group Representative
	→ Observe →	Action Learning Team and AR Group
	→ Reflect →	AR Group
	→ Evaluate →	AR Group
	→ Re-plan →	AR Group
MINI CYCLE 6 Evaluation of entire WALOHSMS	→ Plan →	AR Group
	→ Act (Work-based Phase) →	Action Learning Team and AR Group Representative
	→ Observe →	Action Learning Team and AR Group
	→ Reflect →	AR Group
	→ Evaluate →	AR Group
3rd Validation Committee Meeting		

Source: developed for this study

Figure 4.13 – Major Cycle 2 – mini cycle components

At the Validation Committee meeting, the AR Group meets with the Validation Committee and the researcher presents a complete documentation of the implementation process of the WAL-OHSMS components.

The Validation Committee members then need to be informed on the findings and outcomes of the implementation process. Each member of the AR Group will be asked to deliver a specific part of the presentation similarly to the format adopted in Major Cycle 1. After this second Validation Committee meeting the study proceeds to mini cycle three.

Both mini cycles three and four will be used to evaluate the effectiveness of the components that were implemented. There will be constant feedback from the Work-Based phase, reflection and evaluation by the AR Group to determine if the individual components are deriving results, either positive or negative. Arising from the reflection and evaluation exercise, decisions can be taken to a re-plan, if required. Once the evaluation of the individual implemented components is completed, the entire WAL-OHSMS will be evaluated during mini cycles five and six.

Mini cycles five and six will see the evaluation of the entire WAL-OHSMS. In addition to the specific mini cycles for evaluation, there will be continued evaluation at the end of each mini cycle by the members of the AR Group, and at times, with individual members of the organisation. This is done to determine if the ARAL process is working and if learning is taking place within the organisation. The evaluation of the implemented components and the entire WAL-OHSMS is conducted over four mini cycles in totality because it allows for ample time to determine the effectiveness of the WAL-OHSMS. This time is important because the impact of an OHSMS on the operations of an organisation cannot be determined immediately after implementation; a period of time would be required. Once mini cycle six is completed the final Validation Committee meeting will be conducted.

The final sitting of the Validation Committee is to be held at the end of this second Major Cycle, Major Cycle 2, after mini cycle six. However, at the final Validation Committee meeting the entire WAL-OHSMS needs to be validated. Once the data on implementation and evaluation of the WAL-OHSMS is presented by the AR Group at the final Validation Committee meeting and accepted by Validation Committee members, this will conclude the study.

The following section looks at the data collection and analysis techniques to be used in this study.

Data collection
The collection and analysis of data is critical to AR. Daton (2007) points out that there are quite a number of researchers who describe a variety of methods for AR (Yin 1994; Taylor, Bogdan & DeVault 2015; Palinkas et al. 2015). Additionally, from a data collection and analysis perspective, data collection and analysis occur simultaneously in the process that takes place as a result of the cyclical nature of AR (Uztosun 2013, p. 81).

The importance of adopting an analytical approach to the data has been well documented. Analysis is described by Merriam (1988) as the movement back and forth between concrete data and abstract concepts. It is a complex process that goes between inductive and deductive reasoning and description and interpretation. The data collection techniques specific to the different components are represented in Figure 4.14. The same techniques will be used during the mini cycle components for both Major Cycle 1 and Major Cycle 2.

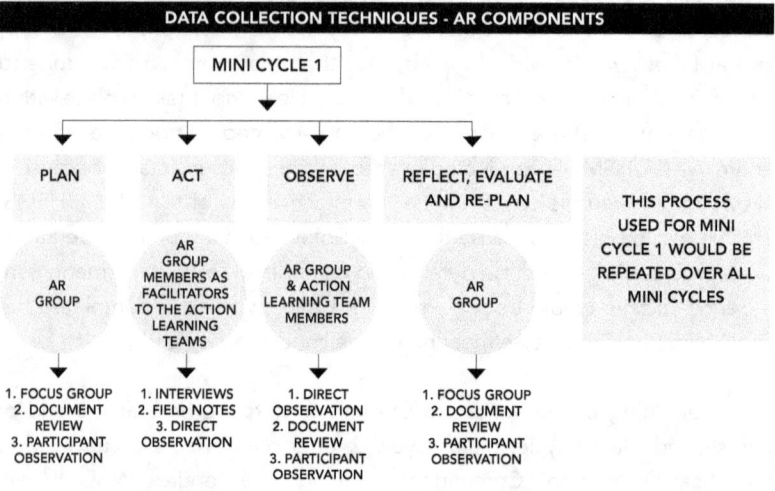

Figure 4.14 – Data Collection Techniques used in this

The data collection techniques to be used during the different components of the mini cycles will vary because of the objective of each component. During the planning component, focus group discussions, document review and participant observations will be used. The action component will use interviews, field notes and direct observation techniques. The observation component will utilise direct observation, document review and participant observation. Finally, the reflection, evaluation and re-planning component will use the focus group, document review and participant observation techniques.

Research needs to be conducted with the use of effective, clear data collection methods. This ensures the accuracy and validity of the information used in the research. Data collection is defined by Nyakundi, Nyamita and Tinega (2014, p. 9) as:

> *The process of gathering and measuring information on variables of interest, in an established systematic fashion that enables one to answer stated research questions, test hypotheses and evaluate outcomes.*

It was further noted that, while there are a variety of methods that are influenced by different disciplines, there is consistence in the emphasis on ensuring accurate and honest collection. In this regard and based on the nature of the study, the data collection methods used in this study are interviews, focus groups, participant observation, direct observation, document review, field notes, and the use of a reflexive Journal.

INTERVIEWS

It has been suggested that the most frequently used data collection method in qualitative research is interviews (Doody & Noonan 2013). Authors Veal (2017) and Norton (2009) compare an interview to a questionnaire in spoken form. The main purpose of conducting an interview in the context of a data collection exercise is to gather more informed responses than can be achieved by a questionnaire, as there is the added advantage of the interview being conducted as individual or as a group (Koshy, Koshy & Waterman 2011), with open-ended questions where the participants are allowed to respond in their own words.

Three types of interviews are highlighted by Norton (2009); Koshy, Koshy and Waterman (2011) and Doody and Noonan (2013). These are structured interviews, semi-structured and open-ended interviews. Structured interviews consist of predetermined questions; semi- structured interviews also have pre-determined questions but are used flexibly, intending to elicit further information if necessary. Open-ended interviews are designed to allow the interviewee to speak more freely.

Semi-structured interviews are frequently used by qualitative researchers, comprising open ended questions in relation to the topics that the researcher is interested in and wants to cover (Hancock, Ockleford & Windridge 2009). An advantage of this method is that it is said to be highly flexible and thus capable of producing data at greater depth. Additionally, the purpose of semi-structured interviews "is to ascertain participants' perspectives on experience pertaining to the research as well as the change outcomes" (McIntosh & Morse 2015, p. 1).

In this study, interviews will be utilised both in a semi-structured and open-ended format. Initially interviews will be used in the intervention stage during the site intervention, establishment of the AR Group, and the establishment of the Validation Committee.

FOCUS GROUP

A focus group discussion is best described as the interaction of people as a single unit, as opposed to individually. With this technique of data collection, the interviewer becomes the facilitator (Veal 2017; Guest, MacQueen & Namey 2012). The group usually consists of four to 10 participants where the research topic is discussed as a group and is sometimes seen as more naturalistic than in-depth interviews. Despite this, the degree of "naturalism" should not be exaggerated because the sole purpose of formulating the group is to explore the research study (Ritchie et al. 2013).

A significant advantage of a focus group as a data collection method is that the analysis of the transcripts can highlight the interaction of the participants and how they influence each other's input and perceptions (Hancock, Windridge & Ockleford 2009; Ritchie et al. 2013).

In this study, focus group discussions will be used as a data collection method at various times. At the evaluation exercise in all the stages of the study, during the mini cycles and at the end of each Major Cycle, focus group discussion will be used to elicit data on the process.

OBSERVATION

Veal (2017) describes observation as a data collection method where the results of observation can be recorded and analysed qualitatively and quantitatively. Lopez and Whitehead (2013) have indicated that observation is more commonly used in qualitative research and can be used to either verify or nullify data that were collected by other methods (Hancock, Ockleford & Windridge 2009). It includes the observational process of watching the behaviours of participants in their natural setting, including social positions, actions and/or interactions (Lopez & Whitehead 2013, p. 132). Two forms of observation for data collection can be participant observation and direct observation (Hancock, Ockleford & Windridge 2009).

Participant observation as a data collection method is seen where, the researcher becomes a participant in the situation being studied (Veal 2017). It additionally involves the observer actually being a part of the group that is being observed or being part of the situation, or living in it (Norton 2009; Koshy, Koshy & Waterman 2011). One of the main advantages noted by Guest, MacQueen and Namey (2012) is that this data collection method can be useful in the generation of topics for subsequent data collection methods and processes. A significant advantage highlighted by Veal (2017) is that the most effective approach to obtaining complex and detailed information in a group or interpersonal context is becoming part of the group.

This data collection method is one of the methods that will feature prominently in this study. In the AR method, the researcher is an active participant in the research process during the different phases. In every

AR Group meeting, including the selection of the Validation Committee members, participant observation is used.

Participant observation will be used as a data collection method in the planning, observation, reflection, evaluation and re-planning phases. The plan is to observe AR Group members and their AL Teams as they interact with the members and crews of the drilling rigs. This interaction is specifically in relation to the conduct of the OHS meetings, as these are intended to address the risk exposure and controls associated with the daily operations.

Observations of the actions of the AL Team members will be documented in order to determine the level of interest, the type of feedback from the participants, the effectiveness of the AL Team members and the quality of the interaction between the AL Team members and the participants.

DOCUMENT REVIEW

Data will be extracted from documentation such as minutes of meetings, policies, records to name a few (Veal 2017; Koshy, Koshy & Waterman 2011). It is a data collection technique which can be used in conjunction with other methods. It is a tool to provide background and context and can critically compare what practically happens and what is happening or likely to happen. It can provide vital information in terms of understanding the philosophy of an organisation (Hancock, Ockleford & Windridge 2009). Consequently, a number of reports and other documents outlining policies, procedure and practices will be identified, collected and analysed.

FIELD NOTES

Field notes involves keeping a record of what happens, why it happened and where. It also includes the evolution of ideas and of the actual research process (Koshy, Koshy & Waterman 2011). There is a link between participant observation and field notes, in that detailed and complete field notes are important to participant observation. This relationship is one where the field notes are the raw data of the participant observation and as such the researcher should as far as possible, make every effort to record complete and comprehensive field notes (Taylor, Bogdan & DeVault 2015, pp. 78-79).

Field notes will be used extensively by the researcher throughout the entire study. Field notes will be kept from the beginning of the process at the intervention phase right through to the last Validation Committee meeting.

During the implementation stage with the agreement of members, all interaction with the AR Group members and the Validation Committee members will be recorded in order to capture all that transpires. This presents insight into how and why certain things happen. All the involvement with the members and crews of the workover rigs will be documented.

REFLEXIVE JOURNALS

Reflexivity was identified as "what has been thought and done in a qualitative research project", inclusive of self-awareness and analysis of the researcher of their role in the research project (Holloway & Galvin 2016, p. 9). As such a reflexive journal would include the feeling and opinions of the researcher and not only a description of the facts. In so doing it creates the avenue for building new experiences and improvement thereof. Further the aim of the reflexive journal "is to improve the learning through the process of thinking and writing about the learning experiences, the good and the bad ones" (Delfino 2015 p. 83).

One concern of reflexive journals as a form of data analysis is that it needs to be considered as the researcher's own social identity and background which may have an impact on the research process. This concern was emphasised by Creswell (2009: 177), Locke et al. (2007 cited in Koshy 2009) and Locke, Spirduso and Silverman (2013), who indicated that:

> *Qualitative research is interpretive research with the enquirer typically involved in a sustained and intensive experience with the participants, which 'introduces a range of strategic, ethical and personal issues into the qualitative research process.'*

This method of analysis involves moving back and forth between experience and awareness in an attempt to study the parts and the whole (Finlay 2005).

Reflexive journals will be used throughout the entire research process where the researcher reflects on the activities and events in the study and recorded perceptions, assumptions, feeling, thoughts and even observations to justify the entries. These entries will be made immediately after the interaction or observation in order to capture data as clearly and concisely as possible.

At the end of every meeting, interaction with management and interaction with AR Group members, crew members and other member of staff, entries will be made to capture the nature, intent and perceptions of the event. The data analysis methods used in this study are discussed in the following section.

Data Analysis
Bryman and Burgess (2002, p.176) have suggested that the relationship between data collection and data analysis needs to be seen in context:

> Material collected through qualitative methods is invariably unstructured and unwieldy. A high portion of it is text based, consisting of verbatim transcriptions of interviews or discussions, field notes or other written documents. Moreover, the internal content of the material is usually in detailed and micro form (e.g. accounts of experiences, descriptions of interchanges, observations of interactions, etc.). The qualitative researcher has to provide some coherence and structure to this cumbersome data set while retaining a hold of the original accounts and observations from which it is derived. Qualitative data analysis is essentially about detection and the tasks of defining, categorizing, theorizing, explaining, exploring and mapping are fundamental to the analyst's role.

Analysis involves a process in which the collected data is inspected, cleaned and transformed in an attempt to assist in the decision-making process about the data and in drawing conclusions (Håkansson 2013, p. 7). Simply put, data analysis is that phase of the research where the main findings are revealed through conducting different data analysis consistent with the research design (Uztosun 2013, p. 81). Some of specific data analysis techniques to be used in this study include chain of evidence, clustering and document analysis.

CHAIN OF EVIDENCE

Yin (1984) points out that a reader of a research document should have a clear understanding of the evidence from the research question to the conclusion. This evidence can be described as the chain of evidence, which contributes to the improvement in the reliability of the data and eventually the outcome of the research. Baskarada (2014) and Moser (2016) simplified the chain of evidence as that which is used to link the questions asked, the data collected, and the conclusions drawn. This contributes to reliability.

All the documentation such as field notes, transcripts from all meeting inclusive of AR Group, Validation Committee and other focus groups, observations that are collected throughout all phases, stages and cycles of the study contributes to the chain of evidence. This chain of evidence is used to assist in the justification and validation of the findings of this study.

CLUSTERING

Clustering is a data analysis technique that seeks to analyse qualitative data at all levels. It involves "clumping" things that go together with each other and can be applied at varying levels of qualitative data (Miles & Huberman 1994). Some of these levels include events or acts, individual participants, process, settings and time periods. The objective of clustering is "to understand a phenomenon better by grouping and then conceptualizing objects that have similar patterns or characteristics" (Miles & Huberman 1994, p. 279). This technique is somewhat similar to content analysis in that there is the grouping of data, just that in this technique the data is analysed qualitatively. Authors Veal (2017) and Guest, MacQueen and Namey (2012) all have endorsed the concept presented by Miles and Huberman (1994).

The analysis of the data collected in this study will be conducted by using this technique with the intent of categorizing data into similar components. It is done in the intervention stage, to establish acceptance and cooperation in the research process, as well as to verify the research problem. Additionally, commonalities in information received from the Validation Committee members, the AR Group members and members of the drilling crews will be categorized from both the development of the WAL-OHSMS in Major Cycle 1 and the implementation/evaluation of the WAL-OHSMS in Major Cycle 2.

DOCUMENT ANALYSIS

Document analysis is described by Yasar (2017) as one of the non-interactive methods used in qualitative research. It includes the analysis of written materials that contain facts and other relevant information about events under investigation (Yildirim & Simsek 2011 cited in Uslu & Cagdas 2017). During the course of the study there will be several sets of data to analyse both prior to and after the implementation of the WAL-OHSMS approach, in an attempt to determine consistence and validity of the reported findings. This data will take various forms, some of which include paper files, transcripts and other company documents.

One of the more important set of documents available for analysis is the accident and near misses reports. These will be reviewed during Major Cycle 1 where the objective is the planning and designing of the WAL-OHSMS. Once the WAL-OHSMS is designed and validated by the Validation Committee, the implementation and evaluation of the WAL-OHSMS will follow. The accident and near misses data will be reviewed at the end of the implementation and evaluation cycle (Major Cycle 2), to help evaluate the effectiveness and success of the WAL-OHSMS. The comparison and analysis of this data will be of significance in determining and analysing the outcomes of this study.

DATA VALIDATION: TRIANGULATION

Given that data is being collected from different sources, triangulation can be used as the data validation technique. Abraham (1997, p. 106) provides a definition:

> *Generally, triangulation refers to the search for consistency of findings from different observers, observing instruments, methods of observation, times, places and research situations.*

Creswell (2009) in defining triangulation described it as a technique where different sources of data after examination are used to build a coherent justification for themes. The author added that once the data is converged from several sources, this process of convergence can be claimed as adding to the validity of the study. This was supported by Guest, MacQueen and Namey (2012) who noted that there is a need to determine the convergence, divergence or contradiction between data sets. Ritchie et al. (2013, p. 276) also notes that data from different sources, such as observation, interviews and document accounts, being compared is a useful form of triangulation. These authors (Ritchie et al. 2013) suggest that the triangulation process be used to check for the integrity of inferences drawn from the data. In summarizing triangulation, Hussein (2015, p. 3) implies that it involves "the combination of two or more methodological approaches, theoretical perspectives, data sources, investigators and analysis methods to study the same phenomenon".

The data collected and analysed in this study comes from different sources through data collection techniques as highlighted in the previous sections. The findings of the analysis, using the different data analysis methods become the sources of input in the validation exercise. Since these findings are derived from more than one source, triangulation of the data can confirm the validity of the research findings.

Data will be sourced and triangulated from the AR group, the Validation Committee and the researcher/observer which is illustrated in Figure 4.15.

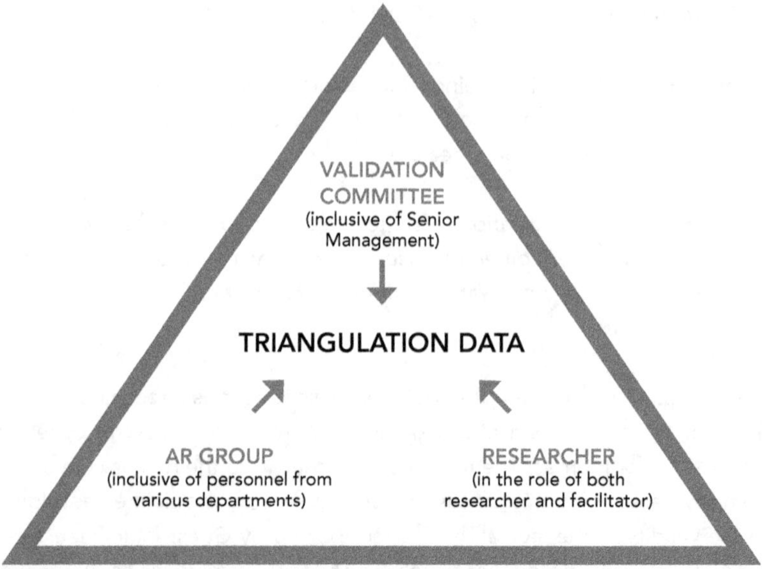

```
                    VALIDATION
                    COMMITTEE
                 (inclusive of Senior
                    Management)
                         ↓

              TRIANGULATION DATA

                 ↗             ↖

       AR GROUP              RESEARCHER
   (inclusive of personnel from   (in the role of both
      various departments)    researcher and facilitator)
```

Figure 4.15 – Sources of Data for Triangulation
Source: Summary of data sources used for triangulation in this study.

The next section looks at the considerations for validity and reliability.

VALIDITY AND RELIABILITY

The importance of validity and reliability in qualitative research has been noted by many authors, for example, Shenton (2004), Zucker (2009), Perry (2013) and Leung (2015).

Shenton (2004) and Zucker (2009) suggest that the concepts of validity, internal and external can be replaced with the concepts of trustworthiness and authenticity. More specifically, internal validity can be contrasted with credibility or authenticity. Moreover, reliability can be contrasted with dependability and auditability.

One idea that has gained some momentum is that validity can be achieved in qualitative research by the creation of an evidence chain, triangulation of data and several layers of analysis (Leung 2015). This validity component is aimed at determining if the study or research makes sense, and if it is credible to the people being studied or others as well as if the conclusions are transferable to other contexts (Zucker 2009).

In this study, there is an establishment of a chain of evidence throughout the entire research process, going through the components of the AR cycles involving planning, acting, observing, reflecting, evaluating and re-planning in both Major Cycles.

Data is collected from a variety of sources for triangulation, inclusive of the researcher in both the roles of researcher/observer and facilitator, the AR group, the AL Teams and the members of the Validation Committee. The data collected and collated is derived from interviews both individually and collectively, focus group meetings, observations, field notes, journals, documents and interaction with members and staff of the research site both administrative and field personnel.

Reliability in qualitative research seeks to determine "if the researcher's processes were consistent and reasonably stable over time and across researchers and methods" (Zucker 2009, p. 11). In order to determine reliability there must be an overlapping of methods such as interviews and focus groups to name two, and reporting on the research in detail (Shenton 2004).

In this study the research methods are multi-layered, refer to Table 4.5 earlier. Additionally, the entire research process will be documented in detail in an attempt to reduce ambiguity.

ETHICAL CONSIDERATION

An important aspect of qualitative research is to ensure credibility in the researcher's role. In this form of research, the researcher can take on a variety of roles while in the research setting (Unluer 2012). The roles as suggested by Adler and Adler (1994) range from being a member of the group being studied (an insider) to complete stranger (an outsider). There is a variety of definitions for insider/outsider researchers, however,

Breen (2007) proposed a generalized definition which suggests that researchers who make a choice to study a group to which they belong are considered insider-researchers as oppose to outsider-researchers who do not belong to the group under study.

Bartunek and Louis (1996) as referenced in O'Leary (2010, p. 1) attempted to define insider and outsider action researchers. This distinction was presented as follows:

> *Insider researchers are practitioners who are invested in the setting and must understand it in order to operate effectively within it. Outsiders, as the term suggests, enter the setting on a temporary basis for the purpose of conducting research, meaning that their more personally consequential settings are elsewhere.*

Based on the role of the researcher as consultant/facilitator in this study, from a research perspective, the researcher can be seen as a friendly outsider as describer earlier since she was not a member of the organisation.

Although the general concept of insider/outsider research still holds today, Milligan (2016) indicated that there is a new thinking in relation to the insider/outsider positions. A key component of this new thinking is that in conducting research, the researcher is neither completely inside nor outside. In this regard, it was theorized that depending on the situations the researcher finds themselves in, the people they interact with and the level of interaction as well as the familiarity of the social norms in the situation, the researcher takes on different positions and roles (Milligan 2016, pp. 239-240) relative to the situation.

Being either an insider or outsider action researcher presents challenges and various ethical issues. Some of the conflicts associated with being an outsider action researcher are highlighted by Coghlan (2012) and include the lack of knowledge of the formal and informal organisation, how it works, who has power and influence, how this power is exercised and who the key players are. Other conflicts include issues of confidentiality, access to data and influence on the group.

In order to address these potential challenges, the researcher's roles and responsibilities need to be clearly defined at the onset of the study, in order to prevent ambiguity. The entire process needs to be conducted in a transparent manner without coercion from any individual or group. Dwyer and Buckle (2009, p. 59) point out that:

> the core ingredient is not insider or outsider status but an ability to be open, authentic, honest, deeply interested in the experience of one's research participants and committed to accurately and adequately representing their experience.

The importance of the role of the participants and the responsibilities the researcher has to them also has been noted by Stevens (2013). Some of the main responsibilities include, voluntary participation, informed decision making, the assurance of confidentiality, and anonymity in relation to data and protection of participants from distress, indignity, discomfort, embarrassment or harm (Stevens 2013, p. 21).

The researcher embraced this sentiment by engaging in this research process in an accurate and responsible manner. All the participants involved in the study were expressly invited to participate, and their decision to participate was of their free will and volition as evident by their signed consent letters. In order to ensure that the participants were willing to participate, the researcher enlisted the assistance of an executive who was not a part of the research, to conduct random interviews with participants to ensure they were satisfied with the process and to determine their willingness to participate. Additionally, any member or members of the Validation Committee were free to attend any AR Group meeting or observe any part of the research process.

Steps are taken to ensure the rights of the research interviewees, AR Group members and AL Team members in conjunction with adherence to all ethical considerations of the AIB. This approach ensures that all participants are assured of their anonymity, privacy and the confidentiality of their involvement. Additionally, the anonymity of individuals is preserved in the data analysis, for example, the identification of employees involved in any specific accidents/incidents is disguised. All data will be stored for five years against loss, unauthorized access, or modification. This will be stored in a locked filing cabinet for that length of time.

JUSTIFICATION OF THE USE OF ACTION RESEARCH

It must be noted that there are many reasons for selecting an AR approach for this study. Abraham (2015 pp. 7 – 9) sets out twelve general characteristics of AR and they are reproduced in Table 4.8.

Table 4.8 – Twelve Characteristics of Action Research

CHARACTERISTICS	SUMMARY DESCRIPTION
Problem Focus	The AR method is problem-focussed in the context of real life situations. The solving of such problems in a research sense would contribute to professional practice and the development of social science knowledge.
Action Orientation	The diagnosis of a problem and the development of a plan to solve the problem can only be considered to be action-oriented if the action becomes part of a process to implement the plan. This brings an action element to the solving of an immediate problem of the organisation which has strategic change implications for the said organisation.
Cyclical Process	The Action Research method involves cycles of planning, action, observation and reflection (evaluation). Thus the cycles of the Action Research method allow the group members to develop a plan, to act, to observe and to reflect on this plan, to implement the plan and then to modify the plan, based on the needs of the group members and the requirements of the organisation and situation. A record of the process of each cycle enables its strengths and weaknesses to be reviewed so that modifications and strategies can be developed for future cycles.
Collaboration	Collaboration is a fundamental ingredient of the Action Research method, because without a team effort to solve problems in an environment of participation, Action Research cannot exist. Collaboration in group problems using Action Research method can be viewed as a continuum from total dependence on the facilitator, who acts as a leader directing the group problem-solving process, through to the total management of the problem by the group members with the facilitator acting as a resource person. The position of the facilitator and the group on this continuum depends on the situation and the needs of the group.

Table 4.8 – (Continued)

CHARACTERISTICS	SUMMARY DESCRIPTION
Ethical Practice	Community interests, improvements in the lives of the group members, justice, rationality, democracy and equality are some of the themes of 'ethical' behaviour. The ethical basis of Action Research is an important characteristic to consider, because the Action Research method involves, to a large extent, groups of people with limited power who are open to exploitation. It requires the researcher to concede their personal needs so that the needs of the group are given the highest priority.
Group Facilitation	The success of the Action Research method will depend on how well the group can operate as an effective team. An understanding of group dynamics therefore seems essential in facilitating this process and dealing with problems that arise during the Action Research cycles.
Creative Thinking	The AR Group members will experience creative thinking as they go through stages of saturation, deliberation, incubation and illumination where the group members look for different options and seek the opinions of different relevant parties to validate those options.
Learning and Re-education	Action Research can be viewed as re-educative, since it contributes to a change in the knowledge base of the organisation, a change in the skills, attitudes and knowledge of the individual group members, and a change in the skills and knowledge of the researcher. It also makes a contribution to several of the social sciences.
Naturalistic	If one accepts that Action Research should be scientific but that there are problems in adopting a positivistic model of science and applying it to social science settings, then it follows that a naturalistic approach is appropriate for the Action Research method. The approach involves qualitative descriptions recorded as case studies rather than laws of cause and effect tested experimentally with statistical analysis of data.

Table 4.8 – (Continued)

CHARACTERISTICS	SUMMARY DESCRIPTION
Emancipatory	The changes experienced by the group members during the Action Research process can contribute to some improvements in their lives and may also have wider social action and reform.
Normative	The normative characteristic of Action Research implies that the social 'norms' of the group are not only considered during the research, but, in order to bring about change in the group, they are modified during the Action Research process.
Scientific	Since the Action Research method can provide an alternative to the positivistic view of science, it is essential that the research be conducted in such a way that is can be defended against criticism of lack of scientific rigour.

Source: Abraham 2015, pp. 7-9.

The approach that will be used in this research include a cyclical collaborative approach that is focussed on a specific workplace problem. It will require the input and expertise from members of the research site that are directly involved in the operations and other departments that can impact the OHS performance. The cyclical approach will be useful in identifying flaws and deficiencies in the process to implement corrective measures in a timely manner.

AR allows for the ultimate transfer of ownership and control of the process to the employees or participants themselves. Israel, Schurman and Hugentobler (1992) describe it as an empowering process where employees gain influence and control through their participation. It was further noted by Cassell and Symon (2006) that AR is primarily used in projects where there is a desire to achieve change through gaining new knowledge and the development of new models of thinking. All of these characteristics are consistent with the intent of this study and the research site.

Since the study is based in a research site where participants from the site are involved in the study, the AR method and AL process, fused into a WAL approach offers an effective way to test a new WAL-OHSMS. This approach allows the researcher to be able to be a participant and be a facilitator in the AR group, despite not being a member of the organisation. This brings a greater understanding of the norms and practices which are key in defining the research problem and the design and implementation of the WAL-OHSMS.

CHAPTER SUMMARY

This chapter has presented a detailed description of the methodology for this study. This was done by outlining the research philosophy behind the study, leading to the adoption of the AR methodology, and presenting the research design. Thereafter, the validity and reliability considerations within the study were outlined and the ethical consideration presented.

The research philosophy was presented and discussions on positivism, interpretivism, quantitative and qualitative research methods were highlighted. The differences between qualitative and quantitative research were noted under the aim, purpose, approach, methods, sampling, data collection, analysis outcomes, results, final report, relationships and rigour of the research. The analysis of these paradigms were used to justify the use of a qualitative research method in this study.

The research design was developed with a recap of the conceptual stage and detailed focus on the AR method stage. The literature in relation to AR, ARAL, reflective practice and WAL was explored in detail to capture theoretical components that formed the basis for the research method for this study.

The research site was presented, highlighting the history and operations of the research site. Additionally, the issues associated with OHS and accident data in relation to the operations of the research site were discussed. Discussion held between management and the researcher produced data that showed the organisation was experiencing financial difficulties as a result of the accidents within its operations. Based on that reality, there was an agreement between the researcher and the MD that the deliverable of the study would be a reduction in accidents and an enhanced management system for the organisation.

The AR design of the study was then presented. The design consisted of a planning and implementation stage that comprised two Major Cycles. The first Major Cycle looked at the planning and design of the WAL-OHSMS and commenced with the intervention stage, followed by two knowledge workshops, four mini cycles and concluded with the first Validation Committee meeting. The second Major Cycle focussed on the implementation of the WAL- OHSMS and commenced with a knowledge workshop, two mini cycles followed by the second Validation Committee meeting. This was followed by four additional mini cycles and concluded with the third Validation Committee meeting. The relationship between the mini cycles and the components as it relates to the involvement of the AR Group and the AL Teams during the Work-Based phases was presented.

The next section was focussed on data collection, analysis and validation in the study. The data collection methods used in this study were interviews, focus group, observation, document review, field notes and reflexive journals. These methods were used at different times throughout the study based on the type of data to be collected and what was required to have the data collected. Data analysis included chain of evidence, clustering and document analysis. Data validation was conducted through triangulation because it allowed for data from different sources to be considered. The data sources included outcomes from the Validation Committee meetings, the AR Group and the researcher in the role of both researcher and facilitator. Ethical consideration in the study was noted as being of significant importance. Insider and outsider researcher perspectives were noted. The credibility and reliability of the data collection and analysis practices in the study were important in ensuring that the study was conducted in an ethical and responsible manner.

The justification for the use of AR in this study was the final section presented. This was mirrored against the 12 characteristics of AR as compiled and presented by Abraham (2015 pp. 7 – 9). The study would be cyclical, collaborative and focussed on a specific work problem. It allowed for the transfer of ownership, knowledge and control of the process to the participants and employees.

CHAPTER 5

PAUL JURMAN

Designing a Research Plan for a Telemonitoring System in a Victorian Health Service Network

INTRODUCTION

This chapter presents the methodology chapter of Paul Jurman's doctoral thesis. It seeks to place this research project in the appropriate research context. It begins with a description of the purpose of the study and the research questions. It will define and justify the action research method within the research paradigm. It will also explain in detail the conceptual and action research stages of the research design. The action research cycles will be further examined and justified in the context of the research techniques utilised to gather and evaluate data as part of the research project. Finally, the chapter will conclude with an examination of the research techniques utilised to ensure the validity, reliability and causality of the effects of the research project.

This chapter will provide an understanding of the research techniques within the AR method. The section on research paradigm, which was included in the original work of the author, has been moved to Appendices 5A and 5B as they will be useful only if you are undertaking doctoral research.

PURPOSE OF THE RESEARCH PROJECT

This research project seeks to:

1) Explore the development and implementation of an action research-oriented Telemonitoring system to enable the home-based monitoring of diabetes patients in a Victorian Health Services Network.

2) Contribute to the literature of health care management globally of an action research-oriented Telemonitoring system for the home-based monitoring of diabetes patients in a Victorian Health Services Network.

3) Contribute to the policy and practice of health care management in Victoria, specifically an action research-oriented Telemonitoring system for the home-based monitoring of diabetes patients.

4) Develop hypotheses and suggestions for further studies relating to the development and implementation of an action research-oriented Telemonitoring system for home-based monitoring of diabetes patients for other Health Services in Australia and globally.

RESEARCH QUESTIONS

The main research question for the research project is:

Can Telemonitoring enable the home-based monitoring of diabetes patients in a Victorian Health Service in Australia (Monash Health) be developed and implemented to improve clinical diabetes management using an action research orientation?

The following corollary research questions have been developed to further guide the collection and analysis of data that will be used in the research project. The corollary research questions have been categorised into four main groups:

Addressing the Development Phase
What was the action research-oriented Telemonitoring system that was developed for use by diabetes patients at Monash Health?

i) What was the action research-oriented Telemonitoring system that was implemented for diabetes patients at Monash Health?

ii) What were the processes that emerged within the action research cycles during the implementation of the Telemonitoring system for diabetes patients at Monash Health?

iii) What were the issues and problems that arose in the implementation of the Telemonitoring system for diabetes patients at Monash Health?

iv) What were the actions taken to overcome these issues and problems during the implementation of the Telemonitoring system for use by diabetes patients at Monash Health?

Addressing the Implementation Phase

i) What was the action research-oriented Telemonitoring system that was implemented for diabetes patients at Monash Health?

ii) What were the processes that emerged within the action research cycles during the implementation of the Telemonitoring system for diabetes patients at Monash Health?

iii) What were the issues and problems that arose in the implementation of the Telemonitoring system for diabetes patients at Monash Health?

iv) What were the actions taken to overcome these issues and problems during the implementation of the Telemonitoring system for use by diabetes patients at Monash Health?

Addressing the Refinement Phase

i) What were the processes that emerged within the action research cycles during the refinement of the Telemonitoring system for diabetes patients at Monash Health?

ii) What were the issues and problems that arose in the refinement of the Telemonitoring system for diabetes patients at Monash Health?

iii) What were the actions taken to overcome these issues and problems during the refinement of the Telemonitoring system for diabetes patients at Monash Health?

Addressing the Outcomes of the Research Project

i) Were improvements observed in participant insulin stabilisation?

ii) Were improvements observed in time spent by clinical staff in obtaining and managing participant insulin data?

RESEARCH DESIGN

The features of the research design for this research project is shown in the Table 5.1.

The research design framework is divided into a Conceptual Stage and an Action Research Method Stage (Abraham 1997; Daton 2007; Hashim 2001; Holyoake 2016) as shown in Table 5.1.

Table 5.1 – Research Design Overview

CONCEPTUAL STAGE	ACTION RESEARCH METHOD STAGE
Researcher's Interest • Experiences and interests of the researcher. • Professional contact with information technology and healthcare professionals. • Attendance at the AIB research seminar. **Literature Review** <u>Healthcare Management</u> <u>Development of Telehealth:</u> • Teleconsulting • Telediagnosis • Telemonitoring • Telehealth and diffusion of innovation <u>Diabetes Management:</u> • Insulin Therapy • Diabetes and Telemonitoring <u>Telehealth for Diabetes Management</u> <u>Action Research in Healthcare and Information Technology</u>	**Action Research Design** • Design of Major Cycles 1, 2 and 3 • Research site of the research project • Unit of Analysis • Ethical Considerations • Validity and Reliability • Control Groups **Data Collection** • Participant Observation • Individual and group discussion • Questionnaires **Data Analysis** • Reflective Practice • Questionnaire data analysis • Content Analysis • Chain of evidence

Table 5.1 – (Continued)

CONCEPTUAL STAGE	ACTION RESEARCH METHOD STAGE
Gap in the literature to be addressed by the research: The design and implementation of a telemonitoring system for Diabetes management using action research.	**Data Evaluation and Validation** • Validation • Triangulation • Control Groups • Independent Review

Source: Adapted from Abraham (1997), Hashim (2001), Daton (2007), Holyoake (2016), Karvinen (2002); Khan (2014); Fng (2014).

The research design framework is divided into a Conceptual Stage and an Action Research Method Stage (Abraham 1997; Daton 2007; Hashim 2001; Holyoake 2016) as shown in Table 5.4.

The following sections address the Conceptual Stage and the Action Research Method Stage.

Conceptual Stage

The Conceptual Stage provides the link between the experience and interests of the researcher that led the researcher to undertake this research project.

This stage consists of literature review (Chapter 2 of this research project) in order to identify gaps in previous research that the current research project would address. The literature review also demonstrates a detailed knowledge of the research area, which provides the basis for the refinement of the research questions. The relevant literature has been reviewed, analysed and critically reflected upon in the context of the research project in the following areas:

- healthcare management and diabetes management
- the Action Research method, including its usage in the creation of new models of care within the healthcare sector
- Action Research usage in the design and implementation of Telemedicine programs

Researcher's Interest

The researcher is a senior information technology (IT) executive working in a major tertiary hospital network in the state of Victoria, Australia. He completed a Bachelor's Degree in Banking and Finance from Victoria University in 2003 and a Master's Degree in Business Administration from Deakin University Australia in 2011. For more than 15 years he worked as an IT professional in public, private, community and acute healthcare settings. In addition, he was also previously the Secretary of the Victorian Healthcare Council of Chief Information Officers.

Through his involvement with IT and clinical service delivery in the healthcare sector, the researcher identified an opportunity for the use of Telemonitoring technology in the management of chronic disease conditions, including diabetes. The researcher identified that the use of such technology had the potential to decrease costs for healthcare providers, as well as provide higher quality care for patients when compared to traditional hospital-centric delivery models. The researcher identified that, despite the potential benefits, there was limited use of Telemonitoring within healthcare organisations (Jennett et al. 2003; Moffatt & Eley 2011; Department of Health 2013). This appears to be as a result of concerns that Telemonitoring is not cost effective (Henderson et al. 2013) and that the potential benefits are overstated (Bergmo 2009; Dávalos et al. 2009; Jennett et al. 2003). Other factors limiting the use of Telemonitoring include technical complexity and legal issues around its use (Kienzle 2001; May et al. 2003; Baker & Bufka 2011; Mars & Jack 2010).

The researcher believed that increased use of Telemonitoring by patients suffering chronic disease conditions within his own organisation would benefit both the organisation and patients. After discussions with experts and having reviewed the current literature in the area of IT and healthcare delivery, the researcher sought to explore the use of an action research-oriented method to develop and implement a Telemonitoring system for diabetes patients. The researcher believed such a research project could contribute not only to the relevant literature, but also to healthcare policy, the practice of healthcare management and the use of technology. This research project could achieve this by identifying an approach that could be utilised by health organisations both locally and nationally within Australia to overcome issues preventing the adoption of Telemonitoring for the management of chronic disease conditions.

The appropriateness of a research project based on the action research method was identified by the researcher as a result of his participation in a research seminar held at the Australian Institute of Business (AIB) in Adelaide, Australia, in August 2013. During the seminar, the researcher had the opportunity to discuss the use of the action research method with Professor Selva Abraham of AIB and compared it to the existing 'gold-standard' of randomised clinical trials for the adoption of new technologies within the healthcare sector.

Based on these discussions, the researcher believed that his objective of increasing the utilisation of Telemonitoring for chronic disease conditions could be achieved by a research project based on the action research method. The project would investigate the development and implementation of an action research-oriented home-based Telemonitoring system for use by diabetes patients in a Victorian Health Services Network.

Literature Review Summary
The second part of the Conceptual Stage was the literature review. The literature review identified gaps in previous research which the current research project would address. In addition, the literature review also demonstrated a detailed knowledge in the areas of:
- Healthcare and diabetes management:
  - Healthcare management
  - Healthcare delivery
  - Diabetes management
  - Use of information technology in healthcare delivery
  - Diffusion of innovation
- Action research:
  - Use of action research in healthcare
  - Use of action research in the creation of new models of care in healthcare
  - Use of action research in the development of Information Technology healthcare delivery models
  - Comparison of action research to traditional healthcare research methods such as randomised clinical trials
- Healthcare management and Telemedicine
- Diabetes and Telemonitoring

The literature review commenced with a keyword database search of electronic databases filtered from peer-reviewed journals. A summary of the databases searched, and the keyword search terms used are presented in Table 5.2.

Table 5.2 — Keyword Database Search

ELECTRONIC DATABASE NAME	Diabetes	Diabetes Management	Insulin Therapy	Healthcare Delivery	Healthcare Management	Telehealth	Telemedicine	Teleconsulting	Telediagnosis	Telemonitoring	Healthcare Management & Telemedicine	Diabetes and Telemonitoring	Action Research & Information Technology & Healthcare Delivery	Diffusion of Innovation
ProQuest Central	x	x	x	x	x	x	x	x	x	x	x	x	x	x
ProQuest Health and Medical Complete	x	x	x	x	x	x	x	x	x	x	x	x	x	x
Scopus (Elsevier)	x	x	x	x	x	x	x	x	x	x	x	x	x	x
MEDLINE/PubMed (NLM)	x	x	x	x	x	x	x	x	x	x	x	x	x	x
OneFile (GALE)	x	x	x	x	x	x	x	x	x	x	x	x	x	x
ProQuest Family Health	x	x	x	x	x	x	x	x	x	x	x	x	x	x
ProQuest Nursing & Allied Health Source	x	x	x	x	x	x	x	x	x	x	x	x	x	x
ProQuest Research Library	x	x	x	x	x	x	x	x	x	x	x	x	x	x
ProQuest Health Management	x	x	x	x	x	x	x	x	x	x	x	x	x	x
SciVerse Science Direct (Elsevier)	x	x	x	x	x	x	x	x	x	x	x	x	x	x
ProQuest Science Journals	x	x	x	x	x	x	x	x	x	x	x	x	x	x
Wiley Online Library	x	x	x	x	x	x	x	x	x	x	x	x	x	x
ProQuest Environmental Science Collection	x	x	x	x	x	x	x	x	x	x	x	x	x	x
ProQuest Psychology Journals	x	x	x	x	x	x	x	x	x	x	x	x	x	x
BMJ Journals (BMJ Publishing Group)	x	x	x	x	x	x	x	x	x	x	x	x	x	x
ProQuest Biology Journals	x	x	x	x	x	x	x	x	x	x	x	x	x	x
ProQuest Career and Technical Education	x	x	x	x	x	x	x	x	x	x	x	x	x	x
Lippincott Williams & Wilkins Journals (Wolters Kluwer Health)	x	x	x	x	x	x	x	x	x	x	x	x	x	x
American Medical Association (CrossRef)	x	x	x	x	x	x	x	x	x	x	x	x	x	x
NEJM (New England Journal of Medicine)	x	x	x	x	x	x	x	x	x	x	x	x	x	x
ABI/INFORM Complete	x	x	x	x	x	x	x	x	x	x	x	x	x	x
ProQuest Environmental Science Collection	x	x	x	x	x	x	x	x	x	x	x	x	x	x
ProQuest Educational Journals	x	x	x	x	x	x	x	x	x	x	x	x	x	x
Taylor & Francis Online - Journals	x	x	x	x	x	x	x	x	x	x	x	x	x	x
ProQuest Social Sciences Journals	x	x	x	x	x	x	x	x	x	x	x	x	x	x
SpringerLink	x	x	x	x	x	x	x	x	x	x	x	x	x	x
Sociological Abstracts	x	x	x	x	x	x	x	x	x	x	x	x	x	x
ERIC (U.S. Dept of Education)	x	x	x	x	x	x	x	x	x	x	x	x	x	x
SAGE Journals	x	x	x	x	x	x	x	x	x	x	x	x	x	x

Source: Table created for this research project (x denotes search conducted).

The literature review then examined the areas of healthcare management, diffusion of innovation, Telehealth, diabetes and action research which can be seen as the parent literature for the research project. It then narrowed its focus to literature central to the research project. For example, the initial literature review of diabetes was narrowed to diabetes management and finally the use of Telehealth to manage diabetes. The results of the parent literature review formed the basis for a review of the immediate literature in the areas of healthcare management and Telemonitoring, diabetes and Telemonitoring, and action research and information technology. The literature review concluded by identifying a specific knowledge gap to be addressed by the research, that being the design and implementation of a Telemonitoring program for diabetes. A diagrammatic summary of the literature review process undertaken appears in Figure 5.1.

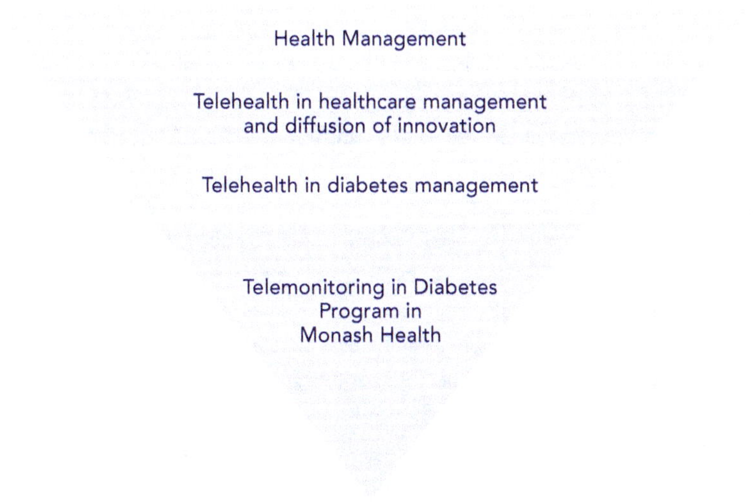

Health Management

Telehealth in healthcare management
and diffusion of innovation

Telehealth in diabetes management

Telemonitoring in Diabetes
Program in
Monash Health

Figure 5.1 – Literature review process

The literature review also examined macro factors impacting healthcare providers. It identified that healthcare policy makers and providers were facing difficulties such as increasing demand for healthcare, higher costs and a diminishing workforce. These difficulties were primarily driven by the decline in mortality rate, which resulted in an aging population as well as an associated increase in age-related chronic diseases such as diabetes.

Through this, it was identified that the management of healthcare organisations and healthcare management theory were subjected to a series of unique constraints not observed elsewhere in the business world Swayne (2008). Walshe and Smith (2006), Swayne (2008), Arndt (2000), Johnson (2009) have identified a number of these constraints which include:

- Healthcare organisations are subject to a high degree of governance and oversight in particular via government health policy.
- Healthcare organisations have unique organisational cultures. On average Healthcare organisations represent eight to fifteen per cent of the Gross Domestic product globally Walshe and Smith (2006, p.2). This makes them significant employers and consequently, the healthcare workforce is a politically powerful group with considerable influence on public opinion.
- Healthcare providers do not have the ability to access strategic alternatives that non-healthcare providers can, for example the ability to refuse to provide treatments that are non-profitable.

In addition, the impact of macro environmental factors (demographic shift, the pace of technological innovation, changing consumer expectations and rising costs) was also examined. This was linked back to the research problem via the concept of diffusion of innovation. The influencers of innovation (Players, Funding, Policy, Technology, Customers, Accountability) Herzlinger (2006) within healthcare were explored and the theory of diffusion of innovation was examined as a solution to the challenges faced by healthcare organisations. In this context, Telemonitoring was identified as one such innovation, both for its innovative use of technology and a new business model for the delivery of clinical services. A more in-depth exploration of the management of healthcare organisations, and innovation is provided in Chapter 2 of this research project.

With this organisational context, the literature search then moved to define and examine the history and development of Telemedicine as a potential solution. It was identified that Telemonitoring is part of a wider field of Telemedicine. This includes sub-specialties such as Teleconsulting, Telediagnosis, and Telepsychiatry. The history, application, efficacy, acceptance and adoption of these specialities were examined. Despite such diversity, Telemedicine and its sub-specialties could be broadly defined as 'different modes of delivering health care services where distance is a critical factor, by all health care professionals using information and communication technologies' World Health Organisation (1998 p.10).

The literature review also revealed that Telemedicine had a long history despite its association with the emerging field of information communication technology. It was identified that the use of Telemonitoring was not without its challenges. These challenges included patients' acceptance and technology issues which were potential barriers to adoption.

Diabetes, the chronic disease condition selected for the research topic, was then examined. The cause, prevalence, cost and clinical outcomes of diabetes were topics that were explored. In examining these factors, the researcher identified that diabetes represented a significant health concern not only locally in the state of Victoria, Australia where the research was to occur but also nationally and globally. The literature review then progressed to examine the treatment of diabetes and the use of insulin therapy. The particulars of insulin therapy were examined from the therapeutic, pharmacological and behavioural perspectives. Treatment protocols for type 2 diabetes were examined, including those of the Australian Diabetes Society which were utilised by patients in this research project.

The literature review concluded by examining the use of action research in the healthcare sector. It was revealed that there was a growing body of literature regarding the use of action research. In particular, the researcher examined the use of action research in the development of new models of care or treatments in the literature. In addition, a comparison of the action research method was made against the traditional medical research approach of randomised clinical trials. It was identified that the action research method had a number of benefits when compared to the traditional approach. The action research method was less expensive, and could be delivered at a faster rate and could be used for immediate operational interventions.

In conclusion, the literature review identified that although there is a body of research on diabetes, there is less research that used the action research method in the development of better clinical outcomes for patients with diabetes. The use of control groups clinically matched to participant groups in the research constitutes a novel approach in the use of the action research method and also appears to address a gap in the literature on action research.

The Action Research Method Stage

Whilst the literature review on action research in the context of healthcare delivery and information technology has been reviewed in Chapter 2 of this research project, the action research method as used in this research project is discussed in this section.

The research method utilised in the research project was action research. The phrase "action research" and the concept of the practical research method of action research have been attributed to Kurt Lewin (Lewin (1946),Lewin (1947), Lewin (1951), Lewin (1952)).

The main tenets of action research have been defined as "problem focussed, context specific, participative, involves a change intervention geared to improvement and a process based on a continuous interaction between research, action, reflection and evaluation" or simply "learning by researching" Hart (1996, p.454). In doing so, action research addresses the gap between the theory and practice of traditional research (O'Brien (1998), Abraham and Daton (2009)).

Despite generally agreed concepts, there exists a lack of consensus concerning a formal definition and an agreed set of characteristics of action research (Cassell and Johnson (2006), Docherty et al. (2006), Reason and Bradbury (2008), Powell (2002)).

For the purpose of this research project, the researcher will be using the definition of action research proposed by Shani and Pasmore (1982 p. 208) as it most closely aligns with the research project and its objective of solving a real organisational problem by bringing about organisational change. Shani and Pasmore defined action research as:

> an emergent inquiry process in which behavioural science knowledge is integrated with existing organizational knowledge and applied to solve real organizational problems. It is simultaneously concerned with bringing about change in organizations, in developing self-help competencies in organizational members and adding to scientific knowledge. Finally, it is an evolving change process which is undertaken in a spirit of collaboration and co-inquiry.

In the research project the organisational problem is the low rate of Telemonitoring adoption, and the change to be introduced is the implementation of a Telemonitoring system for diabetes patients at Monash Health.

The various characteristics of action research described in the literature are summarised in Table 5.3.

Table 5.3 – Summary of Characteristics of Action Research in the Literature

NUMBER OF CHARACTERISTICS	CHARACTERISTICS	REFERENCE
23	Informal, Qualitative, Formative, Subjective, Interpretive, Reflective, Experiential, Involvement/Participative, Framework, Empowerment/Enables, Collaboration, Generates Knowledge/Informs, Democratic, Equity, Liberation, Enhances/Improvement, Action-oriented, Cyclical, Deals with Language, Responsive, Flexible, Developmental, Group Focused.	Powell (2002)
12	Problem focus, Action Orientation, Cyclical process, Collaboration, Ethical Practice, Group facilitation, Creative thinking, Learning and re-education, Naturalistic, Emancipatory, Normative, Scientific.	Abraham (2012)
15	Problem-focused, Action-oriented, Organic process, Collaborative/participatory, Ethically based, Experimental, Scientific, Naturalistic, Normative, Re-educative, Emancipatory, Stresses group dynamic, Concretely critical, Low a priori precision with high accuracy, Unconstrained dialogue.	Peters (1984)

Table 5.3 – (Continued)

NUMBER OF CHARACTERISTICS	CHARACTERISTICS	REFERENCE
4	Addresses a worthwhile practical purpose, encompasses many ways of knowing, is democratic and participative, emergent.	Reason and McKernan (2006)
5	Emergent, engages in unfolding story where it is not possible to control what occurs, focuses on real organizational problems, operates in the people-in-systems domain, applied behavioural science knowledge both engaged and drawn upon.	Coghlan (2011)

Source: Developed for this research project.

The 12 general AR characteristics proposed by Abraham (2016) (Appendix 5B) will be used for the research project as they are most closely aligned to the characteristics of the research project as shown in Table 5.4.

Table 5.4 – Alignment of this research project to Abraham's 12 characteristics of action research

	CHARACTERISTICS	SUMMARY DESCRIPTION	RELEVANCE TO RESEARCH PROJECT
1	Problem Focus	The action research method is problem-focused in the context of real-life situations. The solving of such problems in a research sense would contribute to professional practice and the development of social science knowledge.	The research project will be problem-focused in that it will seek to address a thematic concern of the research organisation, which is the low rate of Telemonitoring adoption. It aims to achieve this via the design and implementation of a Telemonitoring system for use by diabetes patients.
2	Action Orientation	The diagnosis of a problem and the development of a plan to solve the problem can only be considered to be action-oriented if the action becomes part of a process to implement the plan. This brings an action element to the solving of an immediate problem of the organisation, which has strategic change implications for the said organisation.	The research project will be action-oriented in that the action will be part of the process to implement the plan. The research will also be action-oriented in that it will bring an action element to the solving of an immediate problem being the low rate of adoption of Telemonitoring within Monash Health.
3	Cyclical Process	The action research method involves cycles of planning, action, observation, and reflection (evaluation). Thus, the cycles of the action research method allow the action research group members to develop a plan, to act, to observe and to reflect on this plan, to implement and evaluate the plan, then to modify the plan, based on the needs of the action research group members and the requirements of the organisation and situation. A record of the processes of each cycle enables its strengths and weaknesses to be reviewed so that modifications and strategies can be developed for future cycles.	The research project will consist of the design of the Telemonitoring system, its implementation and its subsequent further development. Each of the major cycles will consist of multiple phases. In this way, the research project will demonstrate the action research method of cycles of planning, action, observation, and reflection and evaluation.
4	Collaboration	Collaboration is a fundamental ingredient of the action research method, because without a team effort to solve problems in an environment of participation, action research cannot exist. Collaboration on group problems using the action research method can be viewed as a continuum from total dependence on the facilitator, who acts as a leader directing the group problem-solving process, through to the total management of the problem by the group members with the facilitator acting as a resource person. The position of the facilitator and the group on this continuum depends on the situation and needs of the group.	The research project will require a high degree of collaboration due to the great diversity within the action research group. The action research group will consist of the researcher, the patient advisor, the diabetes unit clinical lead, and a representative from the Telemonitoring system's provider. Collaboration will be required as each of the participants in the research group will be dependent on each other for the overall success of the project.

Table 5.4 – (Continued)

	CHARACTERISTICS	SUMMARY DESCRIPTION	RELEVANCE TO RESEARCH PROJECT
5	Ethical Practice	Community interests, improvements in the lives of the group members, justice, rationality, democracy and equality are some of the themes of 'ethical' behaviour. The ethical basis of action research is an important characteristic to consider, because the action research method involves, to a large extent, groups of people with limited power who are open to exploitation. It requires the researcher to concede their personal needs so that the needs of the group are given the highest priority.	Given the clinical setting, the research project will require a high degree of ethical practice. This will be achieved via formal approvals such as approval by the Human Research Ethics Committee operated by Monash Health and the Ethics Committee of the researcher's academic institution, Australian Institute of Business. In addition, specific representation of groups of people with limited power (in this instance, the patients) will be achieved via the inclusion of a patient advisor role within the action research group.
6	Group Facilitation	The success of the action research method will depend on how well the group can operate as an effective team. An understanding of group dynamics therefore seems essential in facilitating this process and dealing with problems that arise during the action research cycles.	The research project will require the action research group operating as an effective team to ensure success. This will be achieved via the use of multiple group facilitation techniques including setting clear boundaries for interactions, and introducing participants in the action research group to each other in informal settings.
7	Creative Thinking	The action research group members will experience creative thinking as they go through the stages of saturation, deliberation, incubation, and illumination where the group members look for different options and seek the opinions of different relevant parties to validate those options.	The research project will require creative thinking in the solving of issues that will arise during the implementation of the Telemonitoring system.
8	Learning and Re-education	Action research can be viewed as re-educative, since it contributes to a change in the knowledge base of the organisation, a change in the skills, attitudes and knowledge of the individual group members, and a change in the skills and knowledge of the researcher. It also makes a contribution to several of the social sciences.	The research project will be re-educative for the research group and the researcher by exposing them to practice areas outside their traditional areas of expertise or specialisation. In addition, the research project will seek to contribute to the knowledge of the organisation via the implementation of a Telemonitoring system for Diabetes patients.

Table 5.4 – (Continued)

	CHARACTERISTICS	SUMMARY DESCRIPTION	RELEVANCE TO RESEARCH PROJECT
9	Naturalistic	If one accepts that action research should be scientific but that there are problems in adopting a positivistic model of science and applying it to social science settings, then it follows that a naturalistic approach is appropriate for the action research method. The approach involves qualitative descriptions recorded as case studies rather than laws of cause and effect tested experimentally with statistical analysis of data.	The research project will be based on a naturalistic approach inclusive of the collection of qualitative information. Examples of this include the use of participant observation, action research group discussion, and group reflection.
10	Emancipatory	The changes experienced by the action research group members during the action research process can contribute to some improvements in their lives and may also have wider social action and reform.	The research project will be emancipatory in that all of the participants within the action research group will have a personal connection to the treatment of diabetes whether as a clinician, patient or provider. In addition the research project will provide an opportunity for the participants to assist in the development of a Telemonitoring program to manage their own treatment.
11	Normative	The normative characteristic of action research implies that the social 'norms' of the group are not only considered during the research, but, in order to bring about change in the group, they are modified during the action research process.	The research in the design of the Telemonitoring system will incorporate some norms of existing practice. However, the research in particular during the implementation of the Telemonitoring system might challenge other norms by enabling home-based rather than traditional hospital-based care.
12	Scientific	Since the action research method does have a scientific basis and can provide an alternative to the positivistic view of science, it is essential that the research be conducted in such a way that it can be defended against criticisms of lack of scientific rigour.	The research project will ensure scientific rigour via the use of techniques such as content analysis and chain of evidence. Validation techniques such as the use of independent review, triangulation, and a case study protocol will also be utilised. Most notably, the research project will utilise a clinically matched control group that did not undergo Telemonitoring.

Source: Adapted from Abraham (2012 pp. 7-9).

At the core of Lewin's action research method is the action research cycle. In its original Lewinian form, the action research cycle consists of four phases which are summarised in Table 5.5. A key characteristic of Lewin's action research cycle is the continuing 'spiral of steps, each of which is composed of a circle of planning, action and fact-finding about the result of the action' (Lewin 1946, p. 37).

Table 5.5 – The Components of Lewin's Action Research Cycle

PHASE NUMBER	PHASE TYPE	PHASE (PRACTICE)	SUMMARY DESCRIPTION
1	Pre	Objective Setting	Naming the general objective of the research.
2	Core	Planning Action (Action)	Having an overall plan and decision regarding what the first step to take is.
3	Core	Taking Action (Action)	Taking the first step.
4	Core	Fact Finding (Observation/ Reflection on results that follow Action)	Evaluating the first step, seeing what was learned, and creating the basis for correcting the next step.

Source: Adapted from Coghlan (2011 p. 61).

Despite the generally agreed core action research phases of action, observation and reflection, there exists a lack of consensus within the literature concerning the addition of other phases to the action research cycle (Cunningham (1993); Powell (2002); Coghlan (2011); Abraham (1997);Abraham (2012); McGregor & Cartwright (2011), Peters (1984), James(2012)). Holyoake (2016 p. 85) summarised these varied opinions about the composition of the action research cycles as shown in Table 5.6.

Table 5.6 – A Summary of Action Research Cycle Variances

THEORIST	NUMBER OF PHASES IN AR CYCLE	PHASES IN AR CYCLE	REFERENCE
Lewin	4	Objective Setting, Planning Action, Taking Action, Fact Finding.	Coghlan (2011)
Burke	8	Entry, Start-up, Assessment, Action planning, Intervention, Evaluation, Separation, Adoption.	Burke (1994)
Cunningham	6	Initiation, Defining need for change, Focusing and designing a program for change, Planning, Execution, Evaluation or fact-finding.	Cunningham (1993)
Abraham	6	Conceptual Stage, Planning, Action, Observation, Reflection and evaluation, Validation.	Abraham (2012)
McGregor & Cartwright	5	Initial concern or issue, Planning, Action, Monitoring, Reflection.	McGregor and Cartwright (2011)
James, Slater & Bucknam	3	Discovery, Measurable Action, Reflection	James (2012)

Source: Holyoake (2016 p. 85).

The action research cycles in this research project will utilise the model proposed by Abraham (2012) as rationalised in Table 5.7.

Table 5.7 – Alignment of this research project to Abraham's action research cycle phases

PHASE	PHASE	SUMMARY DESCRIPTION	RELEVANCE TO RESEARCH PROJECT
1	Conceptual stage	First phase of the action research cycle: • Researcher conceptualises the introduction of the change to address an issue. Involves the review of current literature, and assessment of the organisational dimensions and the researcher's personal research interest. • Designing of major cycles.	The research project had a clearly defined conceptual phase during which a review of the current literature and the experiences and interests of the researcher was to occur. In addition the following steps were planned to occur during the conceptual phase: • Identify and examine the thematic concern of the research site. In the case of the research project, this was the low rate of Telehealth adoption within Monash Health. • Define the proposed change to address the issue identified. In the case of the research project, which was the design and implementation of a Telemonitoring system for use by Diabetes patients at Monash Health. • Define the main research question. In the case of the research project, this was "Can Australia (Monash Health) be developed and implemented to improve clinical diabetes management using an action research orientation?"
2	Major Cycle 1	Development of an action plan and process for ongoing evaluation.	The research project design consisted of three major AR cycles, the first AR cycle being the design of the Telemonitoring system. Each of the major phases consisted of multiple sub-phases. In this way the research demonstrated the action research method cycles of planning, action, observation, and reflection. (See section entitled Research Design for more detail concerning the AR design for the research project)
3	Major Cycle 2 and 3	Major Cycles 2 and 3 involved the implementation of the AR Cycles.	The second and third AR cycles were about the implementation of the Telemonitoring system. Each of the cycles consisted of multiple mini phases. In this way the research demonstrated the action research method of cycles of planning, action, observation, and reflection. See section on Research Design for more detail concerning the AR design for the research project.

Source: Adopted from Holyoake (2016 p. 85), Abraham (1997 pp. 81-90)

Table 5.7 – (Continued)

PHASE	PHASE	SUMMARY DESCRIPTION	RELEVANCE TO RESEARCH PROJECT
4	Observation	The third phase of the AR cycle: In this phase observations are made of the emerging results of the change implemented. During this phase, observation data is collected.	The research project plan incorporated the following types of data collection and analysis techniques to be utilised: • Reflective practice which was to occur within the AR Group and Validation Committee (VC) meetings and by the researcher during the research project • Triangulation which was to be utilised between AR and VC meetings and their associated questionnaires. • Formal validation which was planned occurred three times during the Action Research Method Stage • Multiple questionnaires which were to be conducted on the AR Group and RC during the research project. • Patient exit questionnaires. • The use of a clinically matched control group of patients that did not undergo Telemonitoring occurred during the Action Research Method Stage to increase reliability and validity.
5	Reflection and evaluation	The fifth phase of the AR cycle: In this phase reflection occurs on the observations made in phase 4. Comparison against the AR plan also occurs to determine the impact of the change (action) and to determine if there is a requirement for further AR cycles.	Reflective practice for this research appears in the research project plan in the form of reflection-in-action and reflection-on-action. The reflective practice of "reflection-in-action" was embedded across all three AR Cycles within the AR group meetings (refer to Table 5.9). Reflection in action practice was selected as the primary reflective practice within the AR group. Reflection-on-action practice was selected as the primary reflective practice within the RC meetings.
6	Validation	The sixth and final phase: Typically occurring at the end of every two AR cycles, the Validation phase concludes Abraham's action research cycle model. This is to ensure that the interpretations reached flow logically from the observation data.	Within the research project plan, validation via peer review was planned to occur three times during the research. The peer review was to take the form of a presentation to the Validation Committee (VC) of Monash Health. During these sessions, the VC consisting of independent stakeholders that were not members of the AR Group would critically assess the program and provided feedback. This assessment was to provide a valuable independent mechanism to validate the data collected by the researcher via observation and group discussions.

Source: *Adopted from Holyoake (2016 p. 85), Abraham (1997 pp. 81-90)*

Action Research Design

The next part of the AR Method Stage was the development of the AR design.

The AR design incorporated the design of three major cycles, the research site of the project, the unit of analysis, ethical consideration, data collection and analysis, and the importance of control groups.

Firstly, Major Cycle 1 showed how the research project came about, the establishment of the Validation Committee and the AR Group and the design and development of the Telemonitoring System. Major Cycle 2 illustrated the implementation of the Telemonitoring System and how the Telemonitoring program was amended based on feedback from the participants. Major Cycle 3 consisted of the second deployment of the Telemonitoring program and the refinement of the research project after an independent review. This approach mirrored the suggestion by Baskerville (1999) to conduct action research in healthcare. Each Major Cycle was made up of a number of phases. Major Cycles 1 and 2 had five phases, while Major Cycle 3 consisted of four phases. Each phase consisted of a number of sub-phases. The design of the research project including Major Cycles, phases, and sub-phases is shown in Figures 5.2 to 5.4.

Figure 5.2 – Action Research Design Major Cycle 1 – Design (4 months)

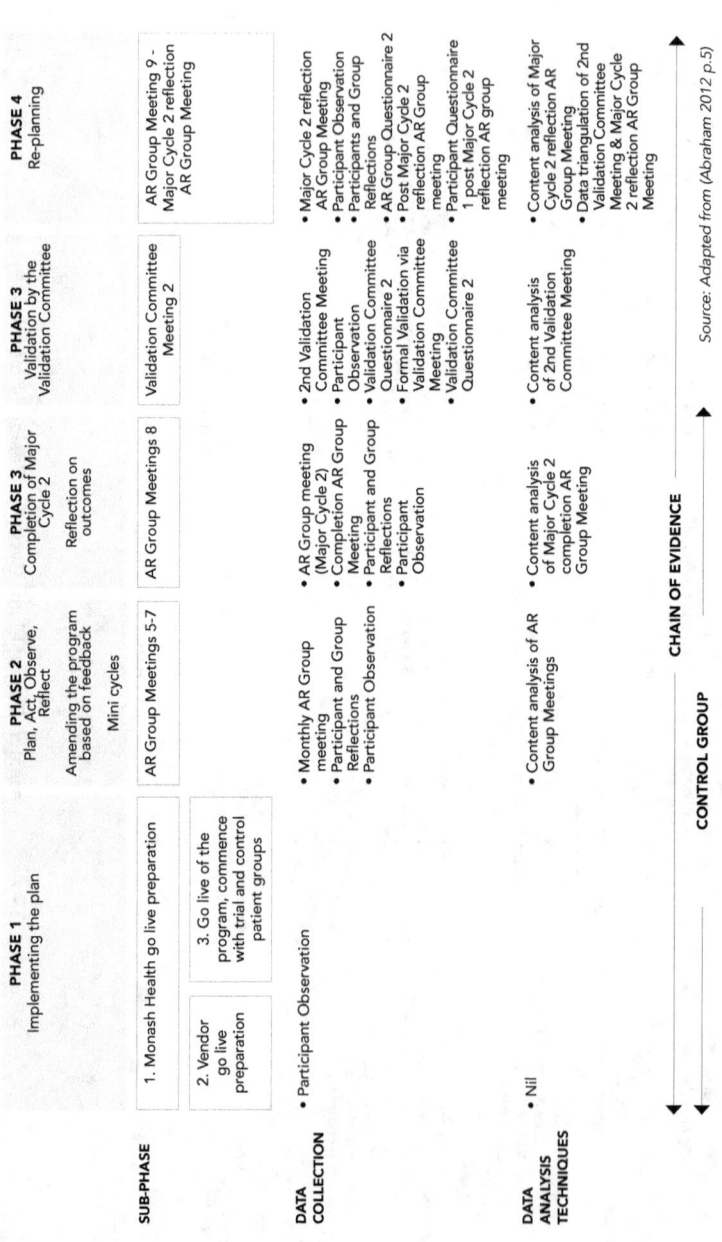

Figure 5.3 – Action Research Design Major Cycle 2 - Implementation (5 Months)

DESIGNING A RESEARCH PLAN FOR A TELEMONITORING SYSTEM 213

Figure 5.4 – Action Research Design Major Cycle 3 - Further Refinement and Implementation (5 Months)

The Telemonitoring program actively monitored participants during Major Cycles 2 and 3 for a total of 10 months. The program was provided for two groups of participants with a maximum of 10 participants per group. The use of a small number of participants in action research is supported by studies undertaken by Mintzberg (1979) and Abraham (1997). The participants were selected from the diabetes outpatient clinics of Monash Health and were patients diagnosed with type 2 diabetes who were commencing insulin stabilisation treatment. The insulin stabilisation treatment would be over a period of 3–5 months, which aligned to the planned major cycle duration of five months.

Participants were either assigned to Telemonitoring insulin stabilisation or to standard insulin stabilisation treatment via e-mail or phone. The group that was provided standard insulin stabilisation treatment was clinically matched to the Telemonitoring participants and acted as a control group to verify results. The use of a control group in an action research project is important as it could provide invaluable insights for future studies. The Telemonitoring system used was My Health Point (http://myhelathpoint.com/en/). The system and equipment was provided by Telstra Corporation Limited.

The following sections will provide more details on the action research design.

Action Research Design Major Cycle 1 – Design
Major Cycle 1 commenced with the support and approval from Monash Health to conduct the research. This was followed by the establishment of the Validation Committee (VC) and the Action Research (AR) Group. The role and composition of the VC and the AR Group including selection rationale is explored in detail in Chapter 4 of this research project. The researcher provided the AR Group with an understanding of the concepts and practice of action research and how it applied to this research project through a series of one-to-one meetings. Next, the researcher selected the Telemonitoring system and recruited the participants for the research project.

The researcher then presented the Telemonitoring system and the research design to the VC. Major Cycle 1 ended with an AR Group reflection based on the feedback by the VC and refinement of the program. Throughout Major Cycle 1, data was collected through a number of ways, such as the researcher's observations and reflections, interviews and group questionnaires. The data collected was analysed using techniques such as content analysis and triangulation. Major Cycle 1 had five phases, with sub-phases over four months as shown in Figure 5.2.

Action Research Major Cycle 2 – Implementation
Major Cycle 2 dealt with the implementation of the Telemonitoring program. Monash Health and the vendor of the Telemonitoring system made preparations to go live in the initial deployment of the Telemonitoring program with the trial and control patient groups. This was followed by the amendment of the program based on feedback by the participants. Next, the outcomes were presented and reflected upon with the VC. The researcher and the AR Group then reflected on the feedback provided by the VC and made further refinement to the program. During Major Cycle 2, data was collected through observations, meetings, reflections and questionnaires. The data collected was then analysed using techniques such as content analysis and triangulation. The five phases and sub-phases for Major Cycle 2 are shown in Figure 5.3.

Action Research Major Cycle 3 – Further Refinement and Implementation
Major Cycle 3 was the further refinement and implementation of the Telemonitoring program. The Telemonitoring program was refined based on the findings from Major Cycles 1 and 2 and re-deployed. New participants and a new control group took part in the second deployment of the Telemonitoring program and the results were collated, reviewed and reflected by the AR Group. In addition, the AR Group also reflected on the overall results from all three major cycles before submitting the results to the VC for an independent review and validation.

Major Cycle 3 ended with an AR Group meeting in which the AR Group reflected on the feedback provided by the VC. During Major Cycle 3, data was collected through meetings, reflections, observations and questionnaires and these were analysed using techniques such as content analysis and triangulation. This cycle had four phases and sub-phases as shown in Figure 5.4.

RESEARCH SITE OF THE RESEARCH PROJECT

A research site may be defined as a small population group with a commonality (such as membership of a social group); the residents of a particular geographic area; an organisation in its entirety or a subset of an organisation (for example a particular workgroup), or unrelated groups of individuals without a commonality that share a common condition such as a chronic illness (Yin 2011). The research site for this research project was Monash Health, and details of the site are provided in Appendix 5C.

In assessing the suitability of a potential research site, Marshall (2016, p. 107) recommends the presence of five characteristics. These characteristics are:
- Entry should be possible.
- High probability that a large mix of people, processes, programs and interactions and structure of interest to the research are present.
- The ability to build trusting relations with the participants in the study.
- The study can be conducted and reported ethically.
- The data quality and credibility of the study are reasonably assured.

The researcher assessed Monash Health against these characteristics to determine its suitability as the research site. The analysis is provided in Table 5.8.

The following sections will elaborate on unit of analysis, ethical consideration, validity and reliability of the research project, data collection, and data analysis techniques.

UNIT OF ANALYSIS

Once the research site was selected, a unit of analysis was determined. A unit of analysis is defined by Collis and Hussey (2013 p. 345) as "the phenomenon under study, about which data are collected and analysed". In essence, the unit of analysis is the "what" that is being analysed (Trochim 2001).

The unit of analysis for the research was the project to design and implement a Telemonitoring system for diabetes patients at Monash Health, not the participants or the research organisation. The use of an IT project as a unit of analysis is established practice (Gillingham 2014; Gillingham 2015; Engwall 1998; Packendorff & Lindgren 2014).

Table 5.8 – Monash Health Research Site Assessment

DESIRABLE RESEARCH SITE CHARACTERISTIC	MONASH HEALTH RESEARCH SITE CHARACTERISTIC EVALUATION
Entry should be possible	At the time of the development of the research proposal, the researcher was the Director of Information Technology at Monash Health. The employment relationship with Monash Health would allow easy entry into the organisation.
	The research proposal received executive support from the Chief Medical Officer and Chief Information Officer of Monash Health. This support was as a result of the low rate of Telehealth adoption being a thematic concern of the organisation (Loh 2014). Such executive support and thematic concern would facilitate easy entry to the required medical programs to conduct the research.
High probability that a large mix of people and processes, programs and interactions and structure of interest to the research are present	Monash Health is a large publicly funded healthcare network based in the state of Victoria, Australia and is a recognised leader in the implementation of new medical technologies and models of health care. Furthermore, Monash Health provides treatment for diabetic patients, the target group of the research. Monash Health provides the full spectrum of clinical services and is a full service "cradle to grave" healthcare provider. Clinical services provided range from research, allied health, all major clinical specialities, mental health, and aged and palliative care in both an inpatient and outpatient context. The organisation's size and clinical variety would provide a large mix of people, process, programs, structures and interactions that would be of interest to the research.

Table 5.8 – (Continued)

DESIRABLE RESEARCH SITE CHARACTERISTIC	MONASH HEALTH RESEARCH SITE CHARACTERISTIC EVALUATION
The ability to build trusting relations with the participants in the research project	The research project will utilise the inherent trust relationship found in the clinician-patient relationship and provider-patient level to establish and maintain trusting relations during the research project. The basis of this clinician-patient relationship is outlined well by Rowe and Calnan (2006) and is caused by information asymmetries, patient dependence on clinical competence, and the inherent vulnerability associated with suffering from an illness.
The research project can be conducted and reported ethically	Ethical practice could be achieved within the research via formal means. The approval of the research by an Australian Government approved Human Research Ethics Committee (HREC) operated by Monash Health and approval from the researcher's academic institution Australian Institute of Business (AIB) were required. In addition specific representation to groups of people with limited power (in this instance the patient group) could be addressed via the inclusion of a patient advisor role within the action research group.
The data quality and credibility of the research project are reasonably assured	In order to ensure data quality and credibility of the research project, the researcher could utilise a number of data analysis techniques including but not limited to content analysis, and chain of evidence. In addition the research project could utilise a clinically matched control group that would not undergo home-based Telemonitoring to verify results.

Source: Adapted from Marshall (2016 p. 107).

ETHICAL CONSIDERATIONS

Having looked at the research design, this chapter now considers the ethical implications of the research project and how they are applied. Ethics have been broadly defined as the norms or standards of behaviour that guide moral choices about our behaviour and our relationships with others (Cooper 2008). Given the nature and context of healthcare, the researcher adopted a more clinically focused definition as proposed by Emanuel et al. (2000). Emanuel et al. suggest that, apart from social norms, clinical research must address seven requirements in order to be considered ethical. These seven requirements and how they were addressed in the research project are shown in Table 5.9.

Table 5.9 – The Seven Factors of Ethical Clinical Research

REQUIREMENT	EXPLANATION	EXPLANATION
Social or scientific value	Evaluation of a treatment, intervention, or theory that will improve health and well-being or increase knowledge.	The research had demonstrable value in the field of diabetes management.
Scientific validity	Use of accepted scientific principles and methods, including statistical techniques, to produce reliable and valid data.	Accepted scientific principles and methods were utilised. This was assured via the formal approval from the Monash Health Human Research Ethics Committee and the Ethics Committee of the researcher's educational institution (The Australian Institute of Business).
Fair subject selection	Selection of subjects so that stigmatised and vulnerable individuals are not targeted for risky research and the rich and socially powerful not favoured for potentially beneficial research.	The research used a case study protocol (research protocol) approved by the Monash Health Human Research Ethics Committee to ensure that vulnerable subjects were not targeted or powerful subjects favoured.
Favourable risk-benefit ratio	Minimisation of risks; enhancement of potential benefits; risk to the subject are proportionate to the benefits to the subject and society.	The research occurred as an adjunct to routine clinical care and was assessed as being of negligible clinical risk by the Monash Health Human Research Ethics Committee. Negligible clinical risk is defined as research where there is no foreseeable risk of harm or discomfort and any foreseeable risk is not more than inconvenience (The National Health and Medical Research Council 2014, pp. 13).

Table 5.9 – (Continued)

REQUIREMENT	EXPLANATION	EXPLANATION
Independent review	Review of the design of the research trial, its proposed subject population, and risk-benefit ratio by individuals unaffiliated with the research.	Formal approval was obtained from the Ethics Committee of the researcher's educational institution, The Australian Institute of Business. In addition, approval was also obtained from the Australian Government in the form of approval by the Monash Health Human Research Ethics Committee (HREC). The Monash Health HREC is certified by the Australian Government National Health and Medical Research Council in accordance with the National Statement on Ethical Conduct in Human Research (The National Health and Medical Research Council et al. 2007, updated March 2014). Ethical conduct of the research was also assured via the periodic review of the research by the Validation Committee. The Validation Committee members were not part of the action research group and acted as a body of review and a form of "cross checking" (Perry 2013, p.143)
Informed consent	Provision of information to subjects about purpose of the research, its procedures, potential risks, benefits, and alternatives, so that the individual understands this information and can make a voluntary decision whether to enrol and continue or participate.	Informed consent was obtained from participants. A participant information sheet was made available to all participants in the research. This sheet contained the details of the proposed research including but not limited to roles and responsibility, data treatment, and purpose. A copy of the participant information sheet appears in Appendix 5D.

Table 5.9 – (Continued)

REQUIREMENT	EXPLANATION	EXPLANATION
Respect for potential and enrolled subjects	Respect for subjects by: 1. Permitting withdrawal from the research; 2. Protecting privacy through confidentiality; 3. Informing subjects of newly discovered risk or benefits; 4. Informing the subjects of results of clinical research; 5. Maintaining welfare of subjects.	1. Withdrawal was permitted and exercised within the research project. 2. All data collected by the research project was made non identifiable prior to being published, shared or re-used. Non-identifiable data is data from which identifiers have been permanently removed, and by means of which no specific individual can be identified (The National Health and Medical Research Council et al., 2007, updated March 2014). Data was made non-identifiable via the methods outlined in Australian Bureau of Statistics National Statistical Service (NSS) Handbook - Techniques to confidentialise data, and The National Health and Medical Research Council et al. (2007, updated March 2014) Section 3.2. 3. Participants were informed of any discovered risk or benefit. 4. Participants were informed of the results of the clinical research. 5. Welfare of participants was maintained at all times with clinical oversight from the clinical lead, and patient advocacy from the patient advisor.

Source: Adapted from Emanuel et al. (2000 p. 2703

ACTION RESEARCH DATA COLLECTION AND ANALYSIS TECHNIQUES

Now that the research design has been examined in greater detail, it is useful to examine what data the research project will collect and how it will be analysed. Within action research, there are a number of methods of data collection available to the researcher. These include participant observation, qualitative interviewing, focus groups and narrative inquiry (Yin 2009; Marshall 1995; Denzin & Lincoln 2008; Bouma 2004; Thomas 2003). Narrative inquiry can be defined as a form of qualitative research that "constructs a narrative rendition of the findings from a real-world setting and participants, to accentuate a sense of 'being there'" (Yin 2011, p. 17). The primary data collection technique employed in this research will be participant observation. This will be supplemented by reflective practice, questionnaires, content analysis and chain of evidence. This will be complemented by quantitative data – specifically, time taken for insulin stabilisation, and number of clinical contacts during insulin stabilisation – recorded for participant and control groups. Quantitative data techniques utilised by this research are explored later in this chapter. The types of data to be collected and analytical techniques to be utilised during the AR method stage will include:

- Reflective practice within the AR Group and VC meetings and by the researcher will occur during the research project
- Multiple questionnaires will be conducted by the AR Group and VC during the research project. Participant exit questionnaires will also be conducted.
- Formal validation will occur three times during the AR method stage.
- Triangulation will be utilised between AR and VC meetings and their associated questionnaires.
- A clinically matched control group of patients will not undergo Telemonitoring to increase reliability and validity.

Participant Observation

Participant observation can be defined as "the systematic description of events, behaviours, and artefacts in the social setting chosen for study" (Marshall, 1989, p. 79). This description has been built on by Schensul (1999, p. 91) in defining the process of participant observation as "the process of learning through exposure to or involvement in the day-to-day or routine activities of participants in the researcher setting".

The researcher will conduct participant observation throughout each of the three major cycles by making detailed field notes. These notes will record the researcher's observations of participants in the research and will cover formal and planned interactions such as AR Group meetings and VC meetings, as well as informal and unplanned interactions such as ad hoc discussions with AR Group members or other individuals involved in the research project.

Participant observation will be utilised by the researcher, who was the Director of Information Technology Services of Monash Health and also assumed the role of internal change agent. As a result, the researcher can be considered an "insider researcher" (Mercer 2007). Given the naturalistic setting of the research, this provides the researcher with the required access to enable the capture of qualitative data required by the action research method.

Reflective Practice

The use of reflective practice is based on the concepts outlined by Schön (1983; 1987; 1994). Reflective practice can be achieved via notes of personal reflections and observations of the researcher during the action research process. Reflective practice for this research project occurred during the participant observation process and took the form of reflection-in-action (reflection while the action is occurring) and reflection-on-action (reflection on actions taken). The reflective practice used by the researcher utilised the techniques of epistemology of practice, artistry of practice, embodied reflection, and frame reflection (Schön 1983; Schön 1987; Kinsella 2010; Kinsella 2007; Schön 1994). Explanations of these techniques are summarised in Table 5.10.

The reflective practice of "reflection-in-action" will be embedded across all three major action research cycles within the AR Group meetings (refer to Table 5.11). Reflection in action has been selected as the primary reflective practice within the AR Group as it best matches the role that researcher is to take in the AR Group (Schön 1983).

Table 5.10 – Reflective Practice Techniques Utilised in the Research Project

CONCEPT	SUMMARY DESCRIPTION
Epistemology of practice	Reflective practice concept which deals with knowledge generated through reflection in and reflection on practice. Epistemology of practice recognizes that through reflection in and on practice, the researcher contributes to their own body of knowledge which in turn influences future practice.
Artistry of practice	Based on John Dewey's work on the relationship between artistry, work, and practice (Dewey 1959). Asserts that professional practice involves not only systematic scientific knowledge but also artistic engagement which enables the researcher to respond in the midst of practice and to improvise particularly in ambiguous, complex, dynamic situations.
Embodied reflection	Based on the ideas of Michel Polanyi, in particular the notion that "we know more than we can tell" (Polanyi 1967, p. 4). A type of reflection that informs intelligent action, but that does not necessarily lend itself to analysis or involve intentional cognitive reflection.
Frame reflection	Based on the work of Nelson Goodman (Goodman 1978), frame reflection recognises that different individuals, disciplines and policy-makers bring different frames to the same event. As a result it is unlikely that disputes can be resolved simply by reference to facts. In this context the researcher's task becomes to set problems with a recognition of the conflicting frames different actors bring.

Source: Adapted from Kinsella (2010, pp. 568–74)

Table 5.11 – Reflective Practice Types selected for use in the Research Project

ACTION RESEARCH MAJOR CYCLE	ACTION RESEARCH MEETING	PRIMARY REFLECTIVE PRACTICE
MAJOR CYCLE 1 - DESIGN	AR Group Meeting 1	Reflection-in-action
	Validation Committee Meeting 1	Reflection-in-action

MAJOR CYCLE 2 - IMPLEMENTATION	AR Group Meetings 2–6	Reflection-in-action
	Validation Committee Meeting 2	Reflection-in-action

MAJOR CYCLE 3 – FURTHER REFINEMENT & IMPLEMENTATION	AR Group Meetings 7–9	Reflection-in-action
	Validation Committee Meeting 3	Reflection-in-action

Source: Table created for this research project

Similarly, the reflective practice of "reflection-on-action" will be embedded across all three major cycles. However, reflection on action in practice has been selected as the primary reflective practice within the VC meetings (see Figure 5.2) at which the researcher will present the outcomes of the cycle and reflect on them with the VC. This has been selected as it best matches the VC's role of an independent reviewer sitting outside the AR Group which "reflect(ed) on action, thinking back on what we have done in order to discover how our knowing-in-action may have contributed to an unexpected outcome" (Schön 1983, p. 26).

Quantitative Data

Two data sets will be collected in order to address the corollary research questions which examined the outcomes of the research project:
i) Were improvements observed in patient insulin stabilisation?
ii) Were improvements observed in time spent by clinical staff in obtaining and managing patient insulin data?

To answer the above questions, two measures are applied as follows.

Measure 1: Time Taken for Insulin Stabilisation
This is a measure (in days) of the time taken for a patient to achieve insulin stabilisation. Decreased time taken to achieve insulin stabilisation is desirable as strict glycaemic control greatly reduces the complications of the disease (UK Prospective Diabetes Study (UKPDS) Group 1998; Diabetes Control and Complications Trial Research Group 1993).

Measure 2: Number of Clinical Contacts During Insulin Stabilisation
This is a measure of the number of times a patient contacts their treating clinician during insulin stabilisation. This is a measure of the efficiency of the delivery of insulin stabilisation via Telemonitoring vs the existing practice. The more time a treating clinician has to spend in direct contact with a patient, the fewer diabetic patients they are able to treat. This results in increased costs to healthcare providers as additional staff are required.

The measures will be used to determine if the introduction of the Telemonitoring system resulted in improvements in patient insulin stabilisation (that is, an improvement in clinical care) and if there was a decrease in time spent by clinical staff in obtaining and managing patient insulin data (that is, an increase in the efficiency in the delivery of insulin stabilisation).

Both the time taken for insulin stabilisation to occur and the number of clinical contacts will be recorded for intervention (Telemonitoring) and control groups. The results will be collated at the end of Major Cycle 2 and again at the end of Major Cycle 3. The mean, median, mode, range and standard deviation will be calculated for both Telemonitoring and control patients for Major Cycles 2 and 3. In addition the mean, median, mode, range and standard deviation for both the time taken for insulin stabilisation to occur and the number of clinical contacts were compared between Major Cycle 2 and Major Cycle 3 to quantify the impact of any changes implemented between Major Cycle 2 and Major Cycle 3. The definitions of these terms and the rationale for their use in the research appears below in Table 5.12.

Table 5.12 – Definitions and Rational of Statistical Calculations Undertaken in the Research

STATISTICAL CALCULATION	DEFINITION	RATIONALE FOR USE
Mean	"The average of a set of measured values. The sum of all the values divided by the number of observations" (Mackridge & Mackridge 2018 p. 202).	Due to the small sample size of 10 or less there is insufficient statistical power to utilise parametric statistics. As a result descriptive statistics such as mean media and mode have been utilised to provide a measure of central tendency (Salkind 2012; Tabachnick 2019).
Median	"The middle ranking observation. Half of the values will be higher and half lower than the median" (Mackridge & Mackridge 2018 p. 202).	See above.
Mode	"The most commonly occurring value in a data set" (Mackridge & Mackridge 2018 p. 202).	See above.
Range	"A measure of dispersion obtained by subtracting the lowest score from the highest score in a distribution" (Zedeck 2013 p. 293).	In order to derive any inference from a data set the measure of central tendency and measure of dispersion is required (Lavrakas 2008; Tabachnick 2019; Salkind 2012). To address the requirement for the measure of central tendency, the mean, median and mode will be calculated. To address the requirement for measure of dispersion both the range and standard deviation will be calculated.

Table 5.12 – (Continued)

STATISTICAL CALCULATION	DEFINITION	RATIONALE FOR USE
Standard Deviation	"A measure of the variability of a set of scores or values, indicating how narrow or broadly they deviate from the mean. A small standard deviation indicates data points that cluster around the mean, whereas a large standard deviation indicates data points that are dispersion across many different values" (Zedeck 2013, p. 349)	See above.

Questionnaires

A total of eight questionnaire cycles will be conducted during the research (refer to Table 5.13). Three main groups will undertake the questionnaire process – the AR Group, the VC and patients participating in the research project.

Table 5.13 – Questionnaires Used in the Research Project

ACTION RESEARCH MAJOR CYCLE	MAJOR CYCLE SUB-PHASE	QUESTIONNAIRE
MAJOR CYCLE 1 - DESIGN	Phase 2: Meeting and Developing AR Group members	AR Group Questionnaire 1
	Phase 2: Meeting and Developing Validation Committee members	VC Questionnaire 1

MAJOR CYCLE 2 - IMPLEMENTATION	Phase 5 – AR Group members' reflection on the Validation Committee review and outcomes.	AR Group Questionnaire 2
	Phase 4 – Presenting and reflecting the outcomes with Validation Committee	VC Questionnaire 2
	Phase 5 – AR Group members' Reflection on the Validation Committee review and outcomes.	Participant Exit Questionnaire 1

MAJOR CYCLE 3 – FURTHER REFINEMENT & IMPLEMENTATION	Phase 4 – AR Group members' reflection on the Validation Committee review and outcomes.	AR Group Questionnaire 3
	Phase 3 – Presenting and reflecting the outcomes of the program with Validation Committee	VC Questionnaire 3
	Phase 4 – AR Group members' reflection on the Validation Committee review and outcomes.	Participant Exit Questionnaire 2

Source: Table created for this research project

AR Group questionnaires and VC questionnaires will be administered at the commencement of the research and the conclusion of Major Cycles 2 and 3 (AR Group Questionnaires 1–3 and VC Questionnaires 1–3). All patient participants who utilise the Telemonitoring system will be provided with exit questionnaires at the conclusion of Major Cycles 2 and 3. The results of these questionnaires appear in Appendices D–F.

The use of questionnaires serves two main purposes. Firstly, they are a secondary data source to enable the researcher to conduct comparative analyses across the AR Group, the Validation Committee, and participants to increase the validity and reliability of the research project. Secondly, they provide a rich source of information for the data analysis technique of content analysis to aid the researcher in answering the corollary research questions.

Content Analysis
The data analysis technique of content analysis will also be utilised. Content analysis can be defined as "a research technique for making replicable and valid inferences from texts (or other meaningful matter) to the contexts of their use" (Krippendorff 2004, p. 19). Put more simply, this technique allows trustworthy inferences to be made from disparate data.

Content analysis will be used on the data gathered from the data collection techniques outlined above in the Action Research Data Collection and Analysis Techniques section of this chapter. The data will be broken down into "meaning units" (Berelson 1952, p. 138) and "context units" (Abraham 1997, p. 118).

The data will be categorised, codified and placed in a matrix to permit additional analysis and synthesis in order to provide meaningful responses to the corollary research questions. This form of content analysis was used in Major Cycles 1–3 as per Table 5.14. See also Figures 5.2-5.4.

Table 5.14 – The Use of Content Analysis in the Research Project

MAJOR CYCLE	USE OF CONTENT ANALYSIS OCCURRED ON THE RESULTS OF
Major Cycle 1	AR Group meeting 1, 1st VC meeting.
Major Cycle 2	AR Group meetings, completion AR Group meeting, 2nd VC meeting, major cycle 2 reflection AR Group meeting.
Major Cycle 3	AR Group meetings, Major Cycle 3 completion AR Group meeting, 3rd VC meeting, final AR Group meeting.

Source: Table created for this research project

Content analysis was selected due to its comparative advantages over other analytical techniques (Berelson 1952; Carney 1972; Krippendorff 1980; O'Brien & Briggs 1987). In particular, it adapts well to unstructured information, is comparatively inexpensive, requires minimal research resources, and is unobtrusive. These were particularly relevant to the proposed research project due to the limited access to resources, the unstructured nature of the delivery of the Telemonitoring system and the requirement for discretion in the delivery of clinical services to patients.

Chain of Evidence
Chain of evidence is a principle of data collection used to address the methodological problem of determining construct validity and reliability of the evidence presented within the research (Yin 2009; Merriam 2009; Stewart 2014). It is based on the principle that "an external observer should be able to follow the derivation of any evidence from initial research questions to ultimate case study conclusions" (Yin 2009, p. 122).

Yin (2009) asserts that in order to maintain a chain of evidence, the evidence presented in the research report should have reliability in that it is the same as the evidence collected during the research and not subject to error or omission. Furthermore, he asserts that the observer should be able to trace the steps either from research questions to conclusions or from conclusions to research questions.

This researcher will adopt the chain of evidence approach as a guiding principle for data collection within the research project. A summary of how the chain of evidence will be used in the research project appears in Figure 5.5 below.

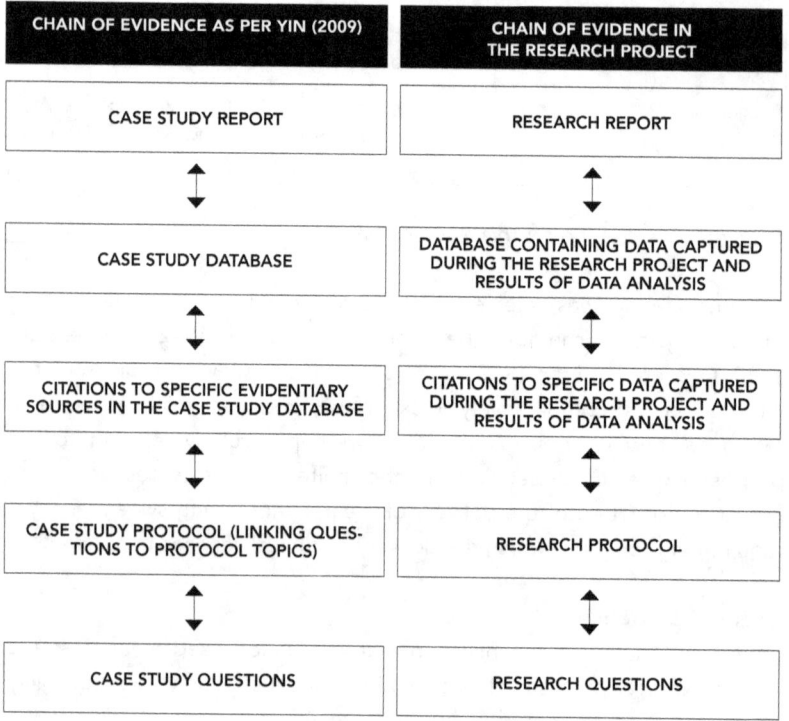

FIGURE 5.5 – Use of chain of evidence within research project
Source: Adapted from Yin (2009 p. 123).

VALIDITY AND RELIABILITY OF THE RESEARCH PROJECT

Validity and reliability are two of the main criteria for judging the quality of a study (Yin 2009, p. 40). Validity can be defined as "the extent to which a test measures what the researcher wants it to measure and the results reflect the phenomena under study" (Collis & Hussey 2013, p. 345). Validity answers the question "Do the interpretations made from the research follow logically from the data?" (Abraham 1997, p. 73).

Reliability can be defined as "the accuracy and precision of the measurement and absence of differences in the results if the research were repeated" (Collis & Hussey 2013, p. 343). Reliability answers the question "Will repeating the research yield similar results?" (Abraham 1997, p. 73). To ensure the validity and reliability of the research project, the research will utilise three main validation techniques:
- Validation via peer review.
- Triangulation.
- Control groups.

The use of multiple validation techniques is particularly important as the researcher is also a participant in the AR Group and therefore there is a risk of researcher bias. Researcher bias is of a particular concern in qualitative research methodologies such as AR. Since "qualitative research is open ended and less structured than quantitative research [it] ... tends to be exploratory" (Johnson 1997, p. 284). In such a setting, researcher bias could result in "selective observation and selective recording of information, and from allowing one's personal views and perspectives to affect how data are interpreted and how the research is conducted" (Johnson 1997 p. 284).

A number of approaches have been developed within qualitative studies to protect against researcher bias and enhance the reliability and validity of such studies. These approaches include statistical sampling methods such as random sampling and systematic non-probabilistic sampling; the use of independent assessment to increase the reliability of analysis; triangulation; grounded theory; direct data collection; peer review; external audit; member checking; and the presentation of qualitative research in a scientific paper format to enabling the reviewer to clearly distinguish between the data, framework and interpretation utilised (Mays & Pope 1995; Cohen & Crabtree 2008; Lincoln 1985; Kirk 1986; Maxwell 1992; LeCompte 1993). The various approaches available are summarised in Table 5.15.

Table 5.15 – Strategies used to promote the validity of Qualitative Research

STRATEGY	DESCRIPTION
Researcher as "Detective"	A metaphor characterising the qualitative researcher as he or she searches for evidence about causes and effects. The researcher develops an understanding of the data through careful consideration of potential causes and effects and by systematically eliminating "rival" explanations or hypotheses until the final "case" is made "beyond reasonable doubt". The "detective" can utilise any of the strategies listed here.
Extended fieldwork	When possible, qualitative researchers should collect data in the field over an extended period of time.
Low inference descriptors	The use of descriptions phrased very close to the participants' accounts and researchers' filed notes. Verbatim (i.e., direct quotations) are a commonly used type of low inference descriptors.
Triangulation	"Cross-checking" information and conclusions through the use of multiple procedures or sources. When the different procedures or sources are in agreement, you have "corroboration".
Data triangulation	The use of multiple data sources to help understand a phenomenon.
Methods triangulation	The use of multiple research methods to research a phenomenon.
Investigator triangulation	The use of multiple investigators (i.e., multiple researchers) in collecting and interpreting the data.
Theory triangulation	The use of multiple theories and perspectives to help interpret and explain the data.
Participant feedback	The feedback and discussion of the researcher's interpretations and conclusions with the actual participants and other members of the participant community for verification and insight.

Table 5.15 – (Continued)

STRATEGY	DESCRIPTION
Peer review	Discussion of the researcher's interpretations and conclusions with other people. This includes discussion with a "disinterested peer" (e.g., with another researcher not directly involved). This peer should be sceptical and play the "devil's advocate", challenging the researcher to provide solid evidence for any interpretations or conclusions. Discussion with peers who are familiar with the research can also help provide useful challenges and insights.
Negative case sampling	Locating and examining cases that disconfirm the researcher's expectations and tentative explanation.
Reflexivity	This involves self-awareness and "critical self-reflection" by the researcher on his or her potential biases and predispositions as these may affect the research process and conclusions.
Pattern Matching	Predicting a series of results that form a "pattern" and then determining the degree to which the actual results fit the predicted pattern.

Source: Johnson (1997, p. 283).

The researcher aims to protect against research bias using a number of techniques. These techniques include peer review via the AR Group and VC meetings as well as reflexivity through personal and group reflective practice in the form of both reflection-in-action (reflection on action while it is occurring) and reflection-on-action (reflection on actions taken) inherent in the action research method.

The following sections elaborate further on the specific techniques used to ensure the validity and reliability of the research project. These techniques were peer review, data triangulation and control groups.

Validation via Peer Review
Validation via peer review will be undertaken three times during the research. The peer review will take the form of a presentation to a

Validation Committee of Monash Health. The Validation Committee performs the role of the "disinterested peer" Johnson (1997, p. 283) as, unlike the researcher, they are not directly involved in the research. The first validation will occur during Major Cycle 1 phase four; the second during Major Cycle 2 phase four; and the third at the conclusion of the trial during Major Cycle 3 phase three.

During these sessions, the VC – consisting of independent stakeholders that are not members of the AR Group – will critically assess the program and provide feedback. These assessments will provide a valuable independent mechanism to validate the data collected by the researcher via observation and group discussions. The use of a Validation Committee as a form of peer review to promote validity in quantitative research follows the model suggested by Johnson (1997 p. 283) and Yin (2011 p. 275).

Data Triangulation
Data triangulation has been defined as "the search for consistency of findings from different observers, observing instruments, methods of observation, times, places and research situations" (Chadwick et al. 1984, p.40). In addition, participant feedback through discussion with the patient representative to ensure participant community insights will also be used. Data triangulation will be undertaken using data from multiple sources including:
- The first, second, and third Validation Committee meetings.
- First AR Group meeting, Major Cycle 2 Close-out AR Group meeting, and Final AR Group meeting.
- The first, second and third Validation Committee questionnaires.
- The first, second and third AR Group questionnaires.

In addition, insights from the patient perspective such as the personal experience of diabetes and factors which impact on insulin stabilisation will be obtained through discussion with the Patient Advisor and used in the data triangulation.

This triangulation will enable the groups participating in the research (such as the AR Group and Validation Committee) to identify systemic issues or themes for further investigation.

Control Group as Applied in this Research Project

Although there is a body of research on diabetes, there is less research that uses the AR method in conjunction with the use of participant and control groups (Baillargeon et al. 2007; De Las Nueces et al. 2012; Ramli et al. 2016).

Control groups are a critical component in both the randomised control trial and randomised clinical trial experimental methods. They consist of a group of research participants who are not subject to the research intervention (i.e., factor or phenomena being studied) but are subject to the same procedures as the intervention group (Elliot et al. 2016). In the case of this research project, a clinically identical control group of patients that will not use the Telemonitoring system (the intervention) will be established. The control group will increase the internal validity of the Telemonitoring intervention and increase the likelihood that observed differences can be attributed to the Telemonitoring system.

There will be two groups of participants – one group for Major Cycle 2 and one for Major Cycle 3 – with a maximum of 20 participants per cycle. Each cycle will last five months. There are no participants in Major Cycle 1, as this cycle is responsible for the implementation of the Telemonitoring. As a result, during this cycle there is no system available for participant use.

The participants in Major Cycle 2 and 3 will be selected from the diabetes outpatient clinics of Monash Health and will be patients diagnosed with type 2 diabetes newly commencing on insulin who require insulin stabilisation. Within each group of 20 participants, 10 will be assigned to Telemonitoring insulin stabilisation and 10 will assigned to standard insulin stabilisation treatment. The group provided standard insulin stabilisation treatment will be clinically matched to the Telemonitoring participants and act as a control group. A summary of the duration, number and breakdown of participants per major AR cycle appears below in Table 5.16.

Table 5.16 – Research participant numbers per Major AR Cycle

Action Research Cycle	Duration of Cycle	No. of participants to undergo Telemonitoring insulin stabilisation (Telemonitoring group)	Number of participants to undergo standard insulin stabilisation (Control group)	Total Number of participants per AR cycle.
Major Cycle 1 – Design	4 months	0	0	0
Major Cycle 2 – Implementation	5 months	10	10	20
Cycle 3 – Further Refinement	5 months	10	10	20

Source: Developed for this research

Within the literature, there are a number of views concerning the potential use of control groups within action research (see e.g. Cook 1979; Festinger & Katz 1966; Campbell 1966; Beer & Walton 1987). Beer and Walton (1987) argue that one of the major discrepancies between action research and the scientific method is the inherent incompatibility between the AR method and the use of control groups. A notable example is the findings of Blumberg and Pringle from their Rushton Coal Mine action research experiment that "the use of formal control groups in field research may actually impede progress" and "can lead to incomplete and erroneous data and can even force termination of the experiment" (Blumberg & Pringle 1983, p. 409). In their action research experiment, control group hostility led to the eventual termination of the research. The hostility resulted from the loss of a perceived benefit as the control group did not receive the same treatment as their colleagues undergoing the program. This perceived loss of benefit or so called "resentful demoralisation" (Cook 1979, p. 79) is hypothesised to have occurred as a consequence of the control group becoming aware of the treatment group due to the setting of the research (Aguinis 1993). This suggestion is supported by Harrison (1971), who notes that it is often not possible to isolate the control group from influence by the experimental group. Examples such as these highlight the underlying reason for the incompatibility of control group use with AR – namely, that AR interventions occur in field settings and, as a consequence, they exist in an open, dynamic, naturalistic, organisational context subject to environmental variables. It then follows that such a setting is incompatible with control groups, which traditionally are utilised in controlled laboratory or clinical settings (Grant & Wall 2009; Aguinis 1993).

In a healthcare setting, as in the research project, the scientific mode of inquiry is most analogous to that of the testing of an entirely new drug or clinical therapy utilising a randomised controlled trial. Randomised controlled trials are considered the "ultimate highest quality proof" (Takala 2009, p. 80) within health research.

In contrast, a number of medical specialties – such as behavioural, psychosocial and critical care (Schwartz et al. 1997; Parshuram & Kavanagh 2004; Takala 2009) – are grappling with the effective use of control groups within research. Many of these specialties are facing the same challenges as identified by Aguinis (1993) and Blumberg and Pringle (1983) in conducting research in a field setting. Some have gone so far as to suggest that in certain circumstances, randomised controlled trials no longer represent "the gold standard for research design" (Grant & Wall 2009, p. 672) and that in such circumstances the use of experimental designs such as control groups is potentially "illusory" in attempting to establish causation (Kember 2003, p. 99).

Particularly within the field of healthcare delivery, there exist significant ethical considerations in that any participant should be assured of receiving the best available standard therapy in any therapeutic study – or, more simply, any research must minimise the potential risk of patient harm (Freedman 1987). This often precludes the use of no-treatment control conditions or placebo control conditions (Schwartz et al. 1997; Berkman & Syme 1979). This requirement has seen the emergence of therapeutic studies in which a new treatment is compared with an existing therapy or treatment. The adoption of such "comparison" control groups is supported by some (Campbell 1966; Cook 1979; Festinger & Katz 1966) as a viable alternative to no-treatment or placebo controls. Such proponents argue that the physical setting of the experiment is not as important as other factors, and a no-treatment condition is not a critical component of control group design. Instead, there should be at least two groups that can be compared to each other (Aguinis 1993). Kember (2003) additionally asserts that this, combined with alternative strategies such as triangulation from multiple sources and methods including meta-analysis, may provide more reliable outcomes.

Within the context of this research project, the researcher will attempt to mitigate against each of these factors via the control group design, as summarised below in Table 5.17.

Table 5.17 – Mitigating controls utilised within the Action Research Project

RISK OF CONTROL GROUP USE IN ACTION RESEARCH	CONSEQUENCE	MITIGATING CONTROL WITHIN PROJECT
Unable to isolate control group from influence by participant group.	Communication between control and participant groups results in perception that an unequal distribution of valuable resource has occurred resulting in "resentful demoralisation" Cook 1979, p. 79), erroneous data and possible termination of research project.	Medical treatment and discussion concerning the project with participants occurred in an individual not a group setting isolating participant and control groups. Confidentiality of the medical treatment process was utilised to ensure that control and participant groups were isolated from each other.
Study control group design inadequate.	Weak claim of causality for the intervention.	Established two groups within the research project to enable comparison. Established a control group that did not undertake Telemonitoring-based treatment.

Table 5.17 – (Continued)

RISK OF CONTROL GROUP USE IN ACTION RESEARCH	CONSEQUENCE	MITIGATING CONTROL WITHIN PROJECT
Study control group design not compatible with medical ethical requirements to protect the patient from harm.	Potential exists to cause patient harm and ethical breaches if selection for control group precludes the administration of existing treatment.	Ensured the proposed research project was approved by an Australian government approved Human Research Ethics Committee. Research project was conducted so that the control group would undergo existing standard treatment and participant group would undergo existing treatment supplemented with Telemonitoring.
Comparison between the participant and control group can only be reliably achieved via a no-treatment or placebo control condition.	Weak claim of causality for the intervention.	Established a control group that did not undertake Telemonitoring-based treatment

Source: Adapted from Bärnighausen et al. (2017, pp. 23–27).

Research Protocol

To further strengthen the reliability of the research, a case study protocol (also known as a research protocol) was developed. The case study protocol for this research project will be a modification of the format proposed by Yin (2009) and will describe how the trial is to be conducted, including the design, methodology, data collection and manipulation methods. The research protocol also has an important secondary function in that it ensures the safety of participants and the integrity of the data collected. The overall objective of the research protocol is to improve the quality of the research, with particular reference to its reliability.

The research protocol for this research will be designed in accordance with the requirements of the National Statement on Ethical Conduct in Human

Research (National Health and Medical Research Council et al. 2007, updated March 2014) and the Australian Code for Responsible Conduct of Research (National Health and Medical Research Council 2018).

SUMMARY

This chapter commenced with an examination of the purpose of the research project and the main research question:

> *Can a home-based Telemonitoring system for use by diabetes patients in a Victorian Health Service in Australia be developed and implemented, using action research, to improve the efficiency and effectiveness of clinical diabetes management?*

The corollary research questions to be addressed in the development and implementation phases, and that identify the characteristics of the research project, were explored. The researcher then examined the six principal research paradigms and the four research approaches. In doing so the researcher justified the use of an interpretivist approach and, more specifically, of the action research (AR) method as appropriate for the research project. This was followed by an exploration of the AR method as it applied to the research project. Next, the researcher examined in detail the features of the research design, including the literature review approach taken within the conceptual stage. This was followed by a detailed examination of the AR method stage and the application of AR into the research project including; the AR design for the research project, the techniques utilised for data collection, data analysis, and data evaluation and validation. The research site, unit of analysis, ethical considerations and use of control groups were also examined.

The following chapter of this research project will address the findings and analysis of the research project in the context of the development and implementation of the Telemonitoring system. The planning of the research project is reflected upon and recorded as Cycle 1, and the implementation is reflected upon and recorded as Cycles 2 and 3.

CHAPTER 6

ALAN BARNES

Future Directions
The Ongoing Evolution of Work-Applied Learning

Two major dimensions emerge from the considerations of work applied learning in these pages. The first is the effectiveness of work applied learning across the many contexts of its implementation. The second is the development of the theory and understanding of work applied learning. Why should work applied learning be effective in organisational change? After all it is just one of many different approaches to and theories about organisational change. What are the theoretical aspects of work applied learning that underpin such success and how has that theory been evolving? Perhaps most importantly how should work applied learning respond to the many profound challenges of our age, including generative artificial intelligence? The answers to such questions lie partly in the chapters in the book and partly in the praxis of those who engage in work applied learning in their current and future workplaces.

THE DEVELOPMENT OF WORK-APPLIED LEARNING

Chapter 1. A Conceptual Framework for Work-Applied learning for Developing Managers as Practitioner Researchers

This introductory chapter, by Ortrun Zuber-Skerritt and Selva Abraham, carefully builds the conceptual basis of Work Applied Learning from the early and varied notions of "action" to a sound conceptual model of Work-Applied Learning and its relationship to theories of knowing and learning. It demonstrates how Work-Applied Learning integrates the concepts of Work-Based Learning and Action Research and Action Learning as well as lifelong learning, reflective practice and action leadership. It points to the collaborative, equitable, and emancipatory aspects of Work-Applied

Learning. Importantly it argues the need for such an innovative conceptual approach in current and future times, outside of the standard academic approaches, and reflecting a more relevant view of knowledge creation through work-based praxis.

Chapter 2. Work-Applied Learning Model

Written by its author, Selva Abraham, the chapter develops the Work-Applied Learning model by detailing the concept and the process of Work-Applied Learning. It begins with the extension of Work-Based Learning through fusing action research, action learning and reflective practice into a coherent Work-Applied Learning model. It shows how this leads from individual and team learning of Work-Based Learning to organisational and community change and learning that is characteristic of Work-Applied Learning. It outlines the twelve general characteristics of Action Research and emphasises the cyclical creative thinking and learning processes as the integrated action research and action learning method is applied interactively through the change process. Importantly the chapter uses diagrams and symbolic formulae to graphically describe the processes in play when the Work-Applied Learning approach is used, demonstrating clearly the dynamic nature of those processes. Detailed explanations provide guidance to those new to these approaches, and the practice of Work-Applied Learning is described at length. The role of the action learning group in the process is described and the function of evaluation and validation is discussed. The chapter concludes with a flowchart of a typical Work-Applied Learning change programme.

Chapter 3 Designing Work-Applied Learning Research Plans

This chapter continues the development of Work-Applied Learning through the designing of action research and action learning research plans. This is essential reading for managers considering how to deal with a persistent organisational thematic concern. The chapter outlines a structured model research plan in diagrammatic form and then describes in detail the design phases involved in stage 1, the conceptual stage and in stage 2, the Action Research stage. It illustrates each of these planning phases with relevant examples from three research projects: Kuju CDEP in South

Australia, Well Worker Company in Trinidad and Tobago and Monash Health in Victoria, Australia. This grounding of research design within extant real world research problems should help readers to appreciate the many subtleties in the contextually dependent Action Research Action Learning research design. The chapter broadens the consideration of real-world approaches to Action Research Action Learning research design by considering some thirty-six projects which provide a bird's eye view of a variety of methodological approaches including data collection, data analysis and validation techniques. It also brings into focus emancipatory and participatory aspects of the Action Research Action Learning research process.

Chapter 4. Implementing Work-Applied Learning in Trinidad and Tobago

This chapter presents the methodology section of Lisa Mohammed's doctoral thesis. It provides a straightforward model and sequence of topics that will need to be addressed by the methodological section of any research project. It is particularly relevant to those in industries where work-based praxis must address issues of human safety.

The chapter begins with a purpose for the study that lies in improving the Occupational Health and Safety Management System of a company servicing the petroleum industry in Trinidad and Tobago. It then outlines the associated research questions which are framed within the Work-Applied Learning paradigm. Key concepts and terms needed later in the research are explained. Major and minor cycles of the Action Research Action Learning process are detailed. These discussions see an increasing contextualisation of the research to aspects of the company's workplace. The various types of data collection are discussed and as are data analysis techniques including chain of evidence, clustering and document analysis. Data validation through triangulation is discussed as is validity and reliability. An ethics section considers the role of participants and the responsibilities of the researcher, especially in relation to the Action Research and Action Learning approach. There are final considerations of the justification of the use of action research and the chapter ends with an extensive list of references, many of which will find relevance in similar future studies.

Chapter 5. Design and Research Plan for a Telemonitoring System in a Victorian Health Network.

This chapter presents the methodology section of Paul Jurman's doctoral thesis. The purpose of the study is the implementation of an action research oriented telemonitoring system for home-based diabetes patients in Monash Health within the Victorian Health Services network in Victoria, Australia and in doing so to contribute to policy development in health care management. It is particularly relevant to those considering the types of work-based praxis needed for change in the health industry. The major research question is: can such a system be developed and implemented to improve outcomes. The research design section outlines a conceptual stage and an action research stage. It critically considers the alignment of the proposed research to Abraham's twelve characteristics of action research providing the readers with a useful template for their own research design. The action research design is considered in detail and demonstrates the contextualisation of the study to the Monash Health workplace. Ethical practices are considered as are data collection and analysis techniques. These include reflective practices, questionnaires, triangulation and a matched control group. Detailed consideration is given to validating the study including chain of evidence, reliability, validity, peer review and data triangulation.

DEMONSTRATED EFFECTIVENESS OF WORK-APPLIED LEARNING ACROSS DIVERSE SETTINGS

It is clear from chapters three, four and five that Work-Applied Learning can be effective in very different contexts. This gives hope to managers globally that there is an effective change process that might suit their unique circumstances. This is no more evident than in the Kuju CDEP Work-Applied Learning Research Project and it is illustrative to reconsider it here.

Tackling an issue as complex as Aboriginal employment in Australia is a daunting task, even more so in 1992. The many realities of lack of education, language barriers, historical prejudice and neglect, encouragement of a welfare ideology, intercultural misunderstanding and distrust and so on, make for a challenging environment for organisational change that might improve indigenous employment. Uniquely across many different approaches to organisational change, Work-Applied Learning embeds people in all its processes. It was essential that community leaders were not only included and consulted but co-designed the project processes and participated in the recursive change model. Indeed, indigenous perceptions of their locus of control and their understanding was a vital research question of such a project. In contemporary language, Work-Applied Learning is effective at giving rise to real change at the intersection of post-colonial power and indigenous culture. This project marks a watershed in theoretical developments, it deliberately asked: Can an Action Research method work to implement a management training and development programme congruent with the needs of indigenous community leaders? The project clearly demonstrated the efficacy of Action Research in this context. Reflections on this project lead directly to the fusion of action learning and action research within the research process outlined in chapter three.

WORK-APPLIED LEARNING: AN ADAPTIVE ROBUST CHANGE PROCESS

The diversity of workplaces across the thirty-six theses referred to in chapter three demonstrate the robust relevance of the Work-Applied Learning approach to diverse organisations. These include corporations, community organisations, oil companies, health organisations, large housing construction companies, sporting clubs, government, and quasi government organisations. The projects are equally diverse including Occupational Health and Safety Management System, project management, worker retention, total quality management, conflict management, employment development, and organisational survival. Importantly many of these work contexts are non-western in their cultural, linguistic and social values.

The efficacy of the Work-Applied Learning approach across so many different organisational types and research foci is testament to an approach that while well-structured is very adaptive to its context. The theoretical concepts outlined in chapter two seem to apply across these organisational types, research foci and cultural differences. Importantly the cycles of action research, action learning and reflective practice produce relevant and valued outcomes for these organisations. As an adaptive robust change process developed over the last few decades, the question now becomes just how Work-Applied Learning will stack up against the massive structural, technological, intellectual, geopolitical and environmental changes that are a feature of today's world.

FUTURE PROOFING WITH WORK-APPLIED LEARNING

The global Covid pandemic seems to be the watershed for many changes and trends to become more firmly established around the world. It is as though the global disruption of the pandemic has catalysed all sorts of nascent influences into becoming major trends shaping organisational behaviour into the future. These include sustainability, remote and distributed work, diversity and inclusivity, skills shortage, geopolitical ructions and so on. As well as these trends, there are recent technological developments that will have long-term impacts, with artificial intelligence the foremost amongst them.

Overwhelmingly, generative artificial intelligence is seen as the mega trend impacting organisations in the future (McKinsey Group, 2024). It will permeate all organisational types, education, business, government, religious and non-government organisations (the third sector) and the wider community including disadvantaged communities. Artificial intelligence will impact organisational types differentially, in terms of depth, breadth, productivity, creativity, and eventually, role. In its adoption, there will be opportunities to build a more humane future. It is already clear that artificial intelligence will be a great leveller in the workplace (Kanbach et al, 2023), that technologies can have a democratising effect, and that artificial intelligence can raise workplace productivity. No organisation will be untouched by artificial intelligence and organisations failing to strategically plan for artificial intelligence now are at risk of failure (Boston Consulting Group 2024). A recent book called Work + Learning (Fergusson, Baker, van de Lann, 2024) argues, and demonstrates through its examples, the usefulness of Work Based Learning in dealing with these trends. However, there are reasons to think that Work-Applied Learning itself is uniquely positioned to help organisations evolve to adapt to these global trends, especially to generative artificial intelligence.

WORK-APPLIED LEARNING AND THE EMANCIPATORY AND PARTICIPATORY PARADIGM

The Work-Applied Learning approach sees human action as pivotal to organisational change. Even more so, it adopts an emancipatory view of the participants in the change process. The participants, as Taddeo (2023, p 39) puts it, are "immersed in the work setting and culture of (research) interest, with an aim to achieve collective ownership both of the problem identified and of the approaches/solutions considered and implemented to address the identified challenge". Such participants may be aware of the "importance of addressing power imbalances, positions of privilege and social structures, throughout the research process, along with associated implications for those involved with, and potentially impacted by, the research". It is a feature of this participatory and emancipatory approach that ethical issues are dealt with dynamically through the change process. This will be critical in an age where artificial intelligence is part and parcel of many change processes, and the ethical impact of decisions made with artificial intelligence's help needs to be carefully evaluated.

The type of knowledge generated by emancipatory research is contextual, not likely to be generalisable (Marsh, 2014) and not reducible to neural network parameters critical to artificial intelligence's functionality. Such "know how" or "praxis" will emerge as a prominent way of knowing in an artificial intelligence age. But just as an emancipatory paradigm resists reducibility of knowledge to artificial intelligence, it allows for the extensive use of artificial intelligence in the human interest. This is the inner power of the Work-Applied Learning approach: Work-Applied Learning can embrace the advantages that artificial intelligence can offer while engendering a humane change process.

FUTURE DIRECTIONS FOR WORK-APPLIED LEARNING

Work-Applied Learning offers a paradigm and a method of change that is emancipatory, ethically sound, involves human knowledge production and is profoundly in consonance with a humane future in an age of artificial intelligence. The congruence of Work-Applied Learning and the democratising influence of various trends and technologies opens up vast opportunities for humane change across contemporary organisations. For Work-Applied Learning to become a major management practice broadly across contemporary organisations, it will need to evolve new learnings and new practices. Specifically, Work-Applied Learning needs to embrace and evolve learnings from the adoption of artificial intelligence in a way that leads to it as the preferred approach to organisational change.

Strategically, Work-Applied Learning needs to look at various organisational types and examine the sorts of "know how" that can produce humane outcomes when artificial intelligence is introduced and adopted. An excellent sector to examine would be the "not for profit" sector. The acute financial, human and resource needs of this sector can be partially alleviated through the application of artificial intelligence to decrease costs, to accelerate human potential and performance, and to lessen resources needed. The advantages for effective artificial intelligence use in this sector are considerable. Of course, issues necessarily arise, for example, the resistance of this sector to technological change, the role of volunteers and volunteering within the sector and a public perception that there must be a human face behind every service. But once understood, such difficulties can be addressed by the Work-Applied Learning approach while still gaining the advantages of changes in a humane fashion.

Work-Applied Learning itself needs to develop a robust literature of case studies demonstrating the Work-Applied Learning approach and the positive adoption of artificial intelligence. The case study model itself needs to adapt to artificial intelligence as a knowledge generator and the participatory paradigm needs to consider artificial intelligence as an actor. Sector case studies would be an excellent place to start. Moreover, Work-Applied Learning needs to argue for its epistemological superiority to other methods by identifying and lauding the development of its "know how".

Work-Applied Learning is a relevant management approach in a world of profound and rapid change and hopefully readers of this book will be empowered and motivated in adopting and adapting Work-Applied Learning for a more humane future.

REFERENCES

CHAPTER 1

Abraham, S. (Ed.) (2015), *Work-Applied Learning for Change*, WAL Publications Pty Ltd., Adelaide.

Adorno, T. (2008), *Lectures on Negative Dialectics*, Polity, Cambridge.

Aspin, D., Chapman, J., Hatton, M. and Sawano, Y. (Eds) (2001), *International Handbook of Lifelong Learning*, Vols 1/2, Kluwer Academic Publishers, Dordrecht.

Bawden, R. and Williams, M. (2017), "The learning conference and worldview transformations", in Zuber-Skerritt, O. (Ed.), *Conferences as Sites of Learning and Development: Using Participatory Action Learning and Action Research Approaches*, Routledge, London, pp. 74-85.

Bhaskar, R. (2008), *A Realist Theory of Science*, Verso, London (first published in 1975).

Biggs, J. (2005), *Teaching for Quality Learning at University*, 2nd ed., SRHE and Open University Press, Maidenhead.

Billet, S. (2010), "The perils of confusing lifelong learning with lifelong education", *International Journal of Lifelong Learning*, Vol. 29 No. 4, pp. 401-418.

Boud, D. and Solomon, N. (Eds) (2001), *Work-Based Learning: A New Higher Education?*, Open University Press, Buckingham.

Boud, D., Keogh, R. and Walker, D. (1985), *Reflection: Turning Experience into Learning*, Routledge, London.

Bradbury, H. (Ed.) (2015), *The Sage Handbook of Action Research*, 3rd ed., Sage, London.

Bryant, A. and Charmaz, K. (Eds) (2007), *The Sage Handbook of Grounded Theory*, Sage, Thousand Oaks, CA.

Burns, D. (2007), *Systemic Action Research: A Strategy for Whole System*

Change, Policy Press, Bristol.

Cantwell, J. (2015), *Leadership in Action*, Melbourne University Publishers, Melbourne.

Carr, W. and Kemmis, S. (1986), *Becoming Critical: Education, Knowledge and Action Research*, Falmer Press, London.

Charmaz, K. (2006), *Constructing Grounded Theory: A Practical Guide through Qualitative Analysis,* Sage, London.

Coghlan, D. and Brydon-Miller, M. (Eds) (2014), *The Sage Encyclopedia of Action Research*, Sage, London.

Corbin, J. and Strauss, A. (2013), *Basics of Qualitative Research: Techniques and Procedures for Developing Grounded Theory,* 4th ed., Sage, Thousand Oaks, CA.

Dahlberg, L. and McCraig, C. (Eds) (2010), *Practical Research and Evaluation: A Start-to-Finish Guide for Practitioners*, Sage, London.

Dick, B. (2012), "Action research and action learning for an uncertain and turbulent world", in Zuber-Skerritt, O. (Ed.), *Action Research for Sustainable Development in a Turbulent World,* Emerald Group Publishing Limited, Bingley, pp. 29-44.

Drake, P. and Heath, L. (2011), *Practitioner Research at Doctoral Level: Developing Coherent Research Methodologies*, Routledge, Abington.

Fox, M., Martin, P. and Green, G. (2007), *Doing Practitioner Research*, Sage, London.

Garnett, J. (2012), "Authentic work-integrated learning", in Hunt, L. and Chalmers, D. (Eds), *University Teaching in Focus: A Learning-centred Approach*, ACER Press, Melbourne, pp. 164-179.

Gibbs, G. and Garnett, J. (2007), "Work-based learning as a field of study", *Research in Post-compulsory Education*, Vol. 12 No. 3, pp. 409-421.

Gibson, B. and Hartman, J. (2013), *Rediscovering Grounded Theory*, Left Coast Press, Walnut Creek, CA. Glaser, B. and Strauss, A. (1967), The Discovery of Grounded Theory: Strategies for Qualitative Research, Aldine, New York, NY.

Godin, S. (2008), *Tribes: We Need You to Lead*, Penguin, London.

Greenwood, D. (2012), "Reflective practice: a critique of the work of Argyris and Schön", *Journal of Advanced Nursing*, Vol. 18 No. 8, pp. 1183-1187.

Habermas, J. (1974), *Theory and Practice*, Heinemann, London.

Habermas, J. (1978), *Knowledge and Human Interest*, 2nd ed., Heinemann, London.

Harvey, M. (2014), "Strengths-based approach", in Coghlan, D. and Brydon-Miller, M. (Eds), *The Sage Encyclopedia of Action Research*, Vol. 2, Sage, London, pp. 732-735.

Jackson, S. (Ed.) (2011), *Lifelong Learning and Social Justice: Communities, Work and Identities in a Globalised World*, NIACE, Leicester.

Jarvis, P. (Ed.) (2001), *The Routledge International Handbook of Lifelong Learning*, Routledge, London.

Kemmis, S., McTaggart, R. and Nixon, R. (2014), The Action Research Planner: Doing Critical Participatory Action Research, Springer, Singapore.

Knott, C. and Scragg, T. (2011), *Reflective Practice in Social Work*, 2nd ed., Learning Matters, Exeter.

Kolb, D. (1984), Experiential Learning: Experience as the Source of Learning and Development, Prentice Hall, Upper Saddle River, NJ.

Kuhn, T.S. (1970), *The Structure of Scientific Revolutions*, 2nd ed., The University of Chicago Press, Chicago, IL.

Lewin, K. (1926), *Vorsatz, Wille und Bedürfnis (Intention, Will and Need)*, Springer, Berlin.

Lewin, K. (1948), *Resolving Social Conflict: Selected Papers on Group Dynamics*, Harper and Brothers, New York, NY.

Lewin, K. (1951), *Field Theory in Social Science: Selected Theoretical Papers*, Harper and Row, New York, NY.

McCashen, W. (2005), *The Strength Approach: A Strength-based Resource for Sharing Power and Creating Change*, St Luke's Innovative Resources, Bendigo.

Maxwell, J.C. (1995), *Developing the Leaders Around You: How to Help Others Reach their Full Potential*, Thomas Nelson Publishers, Nashville, TN.

Moon, J. (2006), *Learning Journals: A Handbook for Reflective Practice and Professional Development*, 2nd ed., Routledge, London.

Reason, P. and Bradbury, H. (2001), "Introduction: inquiry and participation in search of a world view worthy of human aspiration", in Reason, P. and Bradbury, H. (Eds), *Handbook of Action Research: Participatory Inquiry and Practice*, Sage, London, pp. 1-14.

Reason, P. and Bradbury, H. (Eds) (2006), *Handbook of Action Research: Concise Paperback Edition*, Sage, London.

Reason, P. and Bradbury, H. (Eds) (2008), *The Sage Handbook of Action Research: Participative Inquiry and Practice*, 2nd ed., Sage, London.

Reason, P. and Bradbury, H. (Eds) (2013), *The Sage Handbook of Action Research: Participatory Inquiry and Practice*, 3rd ed., Sage, London.

Revans, R. (1971), *Developing Effective Managers: A New Approach to Business Education*, Longmans, London.

Revans, R. (1982), *The Origins and Growth of Action Learning*, Chartwell-Bratt, Bromley.

Revans, R. (1991), "The concept, origin and growth of action learning", in Zuber-Skerritt, O. (Ed.), *Action Learning for Improved Performance*, AEBIS Publishing, Brisbane, pp. 14-25.

Revans, R. (1998), *ABC of Action Learning: Empowering Managers to Act to Learn from Action*, 3rd ed., Lemos and Crane, London.

Revans, R. (2006), *Action Learning: Reg Revans in Australia*, DVD, based on the video program produced by Ortrun Zuber-Skerritt in 1991, Video Vision, ITS, University of Queensland, Brisbane. Available through open access: https://www.youtube.com/watch?v=4_1klQcSmnE

Saleebey, D. (2005), *The Strength Perspective in Social Work Practice*, 4th ed., Allyn and Bacon, Boston, MA.

Schön, D.A. (1983), *The Reflective Practitioner: How Professionals Think in Action*, Temple Smith, London.

Schön, D.A. (1987), *Educating the Reflective Practitioner*, Jossey-Bass, San Francisco, CA.

Senge, P. (1990), *The Fifth Discipline: The Art and Practice of the Learning Organisation*, Doubleday, New York, NY.

Sheehan, P. (2001), "Foreword", in Aspin, D., Chapman, J., Hatton, M. and Sawano, Y. (Eds), *International Handbook of Lifelong Learning*, Vol. 1, Kluwer Academic Publishers, Dordrecht, pp. xi-xii.

Smith, D.W. (2013), "Phenomenology", in Zalta, E.N. (Ed.), *The Stanford Encyclopedia of Philosophy*, The Metaphysics Research Lab, Center for the Study of Language and Information, Stanford University, Stanford, CA, available at: http://plato.stanford.edu/archives/win2013/entries/phenomenology/ (accessed 12 January 2017).

Taylor, B. (2000), *Reflective Practice*, Open University Press, Buckingham.

Trilling, B. and Fadel, C. (2009), *21st Century Skills: Learning for Life in Our Times*, Jossey-Bass, San Francisco, CA.

Van Manen, M. (2014), *Phenomenology of Practice: Meaning-giving Methods in Phenomenological Research and Writing*, Left Coast Press, Walnut Creek, CA.

Wood, L. & Zuber-Skerritt, O. (Eds). (2024). *Shaping the future of higher* education: Positive and sustainable frameworks for navigating constant change. Helsinki, Finland: Helsinki University Press. Available through open access: http://doi.org/10.33134/HUP-25

Yin, R.K. (2013), *Case Study Research: Design and Methods*, 5th ed., Sage, London.

Zohavi, D. (2003), *Husserl's Phenomenology*, Stanford University Press, Stanford, CA.

Zuber-Skerritt, O. (2002a), "The concept of action learning", *The Learning Organisation*, Vol. 9 No. 3, pp. 114-124.

Zuber-Skerritt, O. (2002b), "The concept of action research", *The Learning Organisation*, Vol. 9 No. 3, pp. 125-131.

Zuber-Skerritt, O. (2009), *Action Learning and Action Research: Songlines through Interviews*, Sense Publishers, Rotterdam.

Zuber-Skerritt, O. (2011), *Action Leadership: Towards a Participatory Paradigm*, Springer, Dordrecht.

Zuber-Skerritt, O. and Teare, R. (2013), *Lifelong Action Learning for Community Development: Learning and Development for a Better World*, Sense Publishers, Rotterdam.

Zuber-Skerritt, O., Wood, L. and Louw, I. (2015), *A Participatory Paradigm for an Engaged Scholarship in Higher Education: Action Leadership from a South African Perspective*, Sense, Rotterdam.

Corresponding author

Ortrun Zuber-Skerritt can be contacted at: ortrun@mac.com

For instructions on how to order reprints of this article, please visit our website: *www.emeraldgrouppublishing.com/licensing/reprints.htm* Or contact us for further details: *permissions@emeraldinsight.com*

CHAPTER 2

Abraham, S 1993, *A Management Training and Development Programme for Indigenous Community Leaders. A Case Study*, PhD thesis, The Flinders University of South Australia.

Abraham, S 1994, *Board Management Training for Indigenous Community Leaders Using Action Research, The Kuju CDEP Learning Experience*, Port Lincoln Kuju CDEP Inc., South Australia.

Abraham, S 2012, *Work-Applied Learning for Change*, AIB Publications Pty Ltd, Adelaide, Australia.

Abraham, S, Arnold, G & Oxenberry, R 1996, 'The Self-Discovering Organisation: Fusing Action Research to the Learning Organisation', presented at the conference on *Developing a Learning Organisation through Action Learning and Action Research*, organised by Action Learning, Action Research & Process Management Association Inc., Singapore Institute of Management, Singapore, 25-26 October 1996.

Boud, D & Solomon, N (eds) 2001, *Work-Based Learning: A New Higher Education*, Buckingham: SRHE and OU Press.

Costley, C 2015, 'Educational Knowledge in Professional Practice: A Transdisciplinary Approach', in Gibbs P (ed) 2015, *Transdisciplinary Learning and Professional Practice*, London, Springer.

Fergusson, L, van der Laan, L & Baker, S 2024, *Work + Learning A Knowledge Base of Theory and Practice in Australia*, Peridis Publishing, Queensland Australia.

Garnett, J 2012, 'Authentic work integrated learning', in Hunt, L. & Chalmers, D (eds), *University teaching in focus: A learning centred approach*, Melbourne: ACER Press.

Helyer, R, Wall, T, Minton, A & Lund, A 2021, *The Work-based Student Learning Handbook*, 3rd edn, Palgrave Macmillan, London.

Lewin, K 1946, 'Action research and Minority Problems', Journal of Social

Issues, vol. 2, pp. 34-46, in Kemmis, S & McTaggart, R (eds) 1988, *The Action Research Reader*, 3rd edn, Deakin University Press, Melbourne.

Lewin, K 1947, 'Frontiers in Group Dynamics II. Channels of Group Life, Social Planning and Action Research', *Human Relations*, vol. 1, pp. 143-153.

Lewin, K 1951, *Field Theory in Social Sciences: Selected Theoretical Papers*, Cartwright, D. (ed), Harper, New York.

Lewin, K 1952, 'Group Decisions and Social Change', in Swanson, G, Newcombe, T & Hartley E (eds), *Readings in Social Psychology*, Henry Holt, New York; and in Kemmis, S & McTaggart, R 1988, *The Action Research Reader*, 3rd edn, Deakin University Press, Melbourne, pp. 47-56.

Peters, M & Robinson, V 1984, 'The Origins and Status of Action Research', *Journal of Applied Behavioural Science*, Vol. 20, Issue 2, pp.113-124.

Quick, JT 1963, 'Creativity, a Pursuit of Excellence', *Military Review*, Vol.43, no.10, pp. 28-33.

Raelin, JA 2000, Work-based Learning: *The New Frontier of Management Development*, Prentice Hall, Upper Saddle River, New Jersey.

Raelin, J 2008, *Work-Based Learning: Bridging Knowledge and Action in the Workplace*, Jossey-Bass, San Francisco.

Revans, R 1982, 'What is Action Learning?', *Journal of Management Development*, vol. 1, no. 3, pp. 64-75.

Revans, R 1983, 'Action Learning: Its origins and nature', in Pedler, M (ed) *Action Learning in Practice*, Gower, Aldershot, Hants.

Roodhouse, S & Mumford, J 2010, *Understanding work-based learning*, Gower, Surrey.

Schön, D 1983, *The Reflective Practitioner*, Basic Books, New York.

Tripathi, P & Reddy, P 2007, *Principles of Management*, 3rd edn, Tata

McGraw-Hill Publishing, New Delhi, India.

Wallace, G 1926, *The Art of Thought*, J Cape, London.

Wenger, E 1999, *Communities of Practice: Learning, Meaning and Identity*, Cambridge University Press, Cambridge.

Wimmer, R 2011, *The Five Stages of Communication/Persuasion*, http://www.rogerwimmer.com/mmr10e/fivestagesofcommunication.pdf

CHAPTER 3

Australian Government Department of Human Services 2014, *Medicare telehealth*, viewed 9 March 2014, http://www.medicareaustralia.gov.au/provider/incentives/telehealth/index.jsp.

Baker, DC & Bufka, LF 2011, 'Preparing for the telehealth world: Navigating legal, regulatory, reimbursement, and ethical issues in an electronic age', *Professional Psychology: Research and Practice*, vol. 42, pp. 405-411.

Bergmo, T 2009, 'Can economic evaluation in telemedicine be trusted? A systematic review of the literature', *Cost Effectiveness and Resource Allocation*, vol. 7, p. 18.

Bonner, A & Tolhurst, G 2002, 'Insider-outsider perspectives of participant observation', *Nurse Researcher*, vol. 9, no. 4, pp 7-19 DOI:10.7748/nr2002.07.9.4.7.c6194.

Bowen, G 2009, 'Document Analysis as a Qualitative Research Method', *Qualitative Research Journal*, vol 9, pp 27-40. 10.3316/QRJ0902027.

Bowes, A & McColgan, G 2006, *Smart technology and community care for older people: Innovation in West Lothian Scotland*, Age Concern Scotland, Edinburgh.

Commonwealth of Australia 1987, *Aboriginal Employment Development Policy Papers*, papers 1-5.

Crowe, S, Cresswell, K, Robertson, A, Huby, G, Avery, A & Sheikh, A 2011, 'The case study approach', *BMC Medical Research Methodology*, Jun 27;11:100. doi: 10.1186/1471-2288-11-100.

Cryer, L, Shannon, SB, Van Amsterdam, M & Leff, B 2012, 'Costs for 'hospital at home' patients were 19 percent lower, with equal or better outcomes compared to similar inpatients', *Health Affairs*, vol. 31, pp. 1237-1243.

Dávalos, ME, French, MT, Burdick, AE & Simmons, SC 2009, 'Economic evaluation of telemedicine: Review of the literature and research guidelines for benefit-cost analysis', *Telemedicine & e-Health*, vol. 15, pp. 933-948.

Department of Health 2013, *Supporting the implementation of telehealth in Victoria: The Victorian government's response to the recommendations of the Health Innovation and Reform Council*, Government of Victoria, Melbourne.

Diabetes Australia 2014a, *Living with diabetes: Type 2 diabetes*, viewed 22 November 2015, http://www.diabetesaustralia.com.au/Living-with-Diabetes/Type-2-Diabetes/.

Diabetes Australia 2014b, *National diabetes data snapshot*, Diabetes Australia, Canberra.

Dinneen, SF 2010, 'What is diabetes?' *Medicine*, vol. 38, no. 11, p. 589-591, doi: 10.1016/j.mpmed.2010.08.004.

Gläser-Zikuda, M 2012, 'Self-Reflecting Methods of Learning Research' in NM Seel (ed), Encyclopedia of the Sciences of Learning, Springer, Boston, MA, available at https://doi.org/10.1007/978-1-4419-1428-6_821.

Gogus, A 2012, 'Brainstorming and Learning' in NM Seel (ed), *Encyclopedia of the Sciences of Learning*, Springer, Boston, MA, available at https://doi.org/10.1007/978-1-4419-1428-6_491.

Graham, I, Filippatos, G, Atar, D, Vardas, PE, Pinto, FJ & Fitzsimons, D 2017, 'Patient engagement', *European Heart Journal*, vol. 38, pp. 3114-3115.

Grundy, S 1982, 'Three modes of action research', *Curriculum Perspectives*, vol. 2, no. 3, pp. 23–34.

Henderson, C, Knapp, M, Fernández, J-L, Beecham, J, Hirani, SP, Cartwright, M, Rixon, L, Beynon, M, Rogers, A, Bower, P, Doll, H, Fitzpatrick, R, Steventon, A, Bardsley, M, Hendy, J & Newman, SP 2013, 'Cost effectiveness of telehealth for patients with long term conditions (Whole Systems Demonstrator telehealth questionnaire study): Nested economic evaluation in a pragmatic, cluster randomised controlled trial', *BMJ Clinical Research*, vol. 346, p. f1035.

House of Representatives Standing Committee on Aboriginal Affairs 1989, *A Chance for the Future: Training in Skills for Aboriginal and Torres Strait Island Community Management and Development.*

Htong Kham, S 2024, Outsider From Within, Insider From Without: Negotiating Researcher Positionality in Comparative Social Research', *International Journal of Qualitative Methods*, vol. 23, pp.1-10. https://doi.org/10.1177/16094069241254004

Husserl, E 1965 'Phenomenology and the crisis of philosophy: Philosophy as a rigorous science, and Philosophy and the crisis of European man' available at https://philpapers.org/rec/HUSPAT.

Industrial Court of Trinidad and Tobago 2016, *Special Sitting of the Industrial Court of Trinidad and Tobago for the opening of the 2016-2017 Law Term*, address by Her Honour Debra Thomas-Felix, President, Industrial Court of Trinidad and Tobago.

Institute Of Medicine (U.S.) Committee on Evaluating Clinical Applications of Telemedicine 1996, *Telemedicine: A guide to assessing telecommunications in health care*, N. A. Press, Washington, DC.

Jennett, PA, Hall, LA, Hailey, D, Ohinmaa, A, Anderson, C, Thomas, R, Young, B, Lorenzetti, D & Scott, RE 2003, 'The socio-economic impact of telehealth: a systematic review,' *Journal of Telemedicine & Telecare*, vol. 9, pp. 311-320.

Jennett, PA, Scott, RE, Hall, LA, Hailey, D, Ohinmaa, A, Anderson, C, Thomas, R, Young, B & Lorenzetti, D 2004, 'Policy implications associated with the socioeconomic and health system impact of telehealth: A case study from

Canada', *Telemedicine & e-Health*, vol. 10, pp. 77-83.

Johnson, A 2003, 'Measuring DM's net effect is harder than you might think', *Managed Care*, vol. 12, pp. 28-32.

Jupp, V (ed) 2006, *The SAGE dictionary of social research methods*, vols. 1-0, SAGE Publications Ltd, available at https://doi.org/10.4135/9780857020116.

Kienzle, M 2001, 'Coming up short: Telemedicine's promise in perspective', *Journal of Rural Health*, vol. 17, pp. 14-15.

Macia, L 2015, 'Using Clustering as a Tool: Mixed Methods in Qualitative Data Analysis', *The Qualitative Report*, vol. 20, no 7, pp 1083-1094, available at https://doi.org/10.46743/2160-3715/2015.2201.

Mars, M & Jack, C 2010, 'Why is telemedicine a challenge to the regulators?' *South African Journal of Bioethics and Law*, vol. 3, p. 55.

Marshall, C & Rossman, GB 1989, *Designing Qualitative Research*, 1st edn, Sage Publications, California.

Marshall, C, Rossman, GB & Blanco, GL 2022, *Designing Qualitative Research*, 7th edn, Sage Publications, California.

May, C, Harrison, R, Macfarlane, A, Williams, T, Mair, F & Wallace, P 2003, 'Why do telemedicine systems fail to normalise as stable models of service delivery?' *Journal of Telemedicine and Telecare*, vol. 9, pp. 25-26.

Milligan, L 2016, 'Insider-outsider-inbetweener? Researcher positioning, participative methods and cross-cultural educational research', *Compare: A Journal of Comparative and International Education*, vol. 46, no. 2, pp. 235-250.

Meystre, S 2005, 'The current state of telemonitoring: A comment on the literature', *Telemedicine & e-Health*, vol. 11, pp. 63-69.

Ministry of Labour and Small and Micro Enterprise Development Republic of Trinidad and Tobago, 2011, *Feature address by The Honourable Errol McLeod, Minister of Labour and Small and Micro Enterprise Development*, at the Observance of World Day for Safety and Health at Work 2011.

Ministry of Labour and Small and Micro Enterprise Development Republic of Trinidad and Tobago, 2014, *Remarks by the Honourable Errol McLeod, Minister of Labour and Small and Micro Enterprise Development*, at the Launch of National Occupational Safety and Health Week 2014.

Moffatt, JJ & Eley, DS 2011, 'Barriers to the uptake of telemedicine in Australia: A view from providers', *Rural and Remote Health*, vol. 11, pp. 1581.

Motta, R, Barbosa, CE, Lyra, A, Oliveira, J, Zimbrão, G, & Souza, J 2022, 'Extracting Knowledge from and for Meetings.' https://doi.org/10.1109/ICSTE57415.2022.00019.

Moss, S 2020, 'Introduction to case studies, the Yin Approach' https://www.cdu.edu.au/files/2020-07/Introduction%20to%20case%20studies%20-%20the%20Yin%20approach.docx

Mühleisen, S 2001, 'Is 'Bad English' dying out? A diachronic comparative study of attitudes towards Creole versus Standard English in Trinidad', *PhiN*, vol. 15, pp. 43-78.

Nehez, J 2022, 'To be, or not to be, that is not the question: External researchers in emancipatory action research', *Educational Action Research*, https://doi.org/10.1080/09650792.2022.2084132.

Orlikowski, WJ & Baroudi, JJ 1991, 'Studying Information Technology in Organizations: Research Approaches and Assumptions' https://doi.org/10.1287/isre.2.1.1.

Pare, G, Jaana, M & Sicotte, C 2007, 'Systematic review of home telemonitoring for chronic diseases: the evidence base', *Journal of the American Medical Informatics Association*, vol. 14, no. 3, p. 269.

Patton, MQ 1990, *Qualitative Evaluation and Research Methods*, 2nd edn, Sage Publications, California.

Rabinowitz, P n.d., 'Section 4. Techniques for Leading Group Discussions', *Centre for Community Health and Development*.

https://ctb.ku.edu/en/table-of-contents/leadership/group-facilitation/group-discussions/main

Report of The Committee of Review of Aboriginal Employment and Training Programmes, (The Miller Report), 1985, Commonwealth Government of Australia.

Rowe, R & Calnan, M 2006, 'Trust relations in health care: The new agenda', *European Journal of Public Health*, vol. 16, pp. 4-6.

Schofield, RS, Kline, SE, Schmalfuss, CM, Carver, HM, Aranda, JM, Pauly, DF, Hill, JA, Neugaard, BI & Chumbler, NR 2005, 'Early outcomes of a care coordination-enhanced telehome care program for elderly veterans with chronic heart failure', *Telemedicine & e-Health*, vol. 11, pp. 20-27.

Sheikhattari, P, Wright, MT, Silver, GB, van der Donk, C & van Lanen, B 2022, 'Practitioner research for social work, nursing and the health professions', *Journal of Social Work*, 23(2), pp. 404-407. https://doi.org/10.1177/14680173221109408.

Simmons, N 2017, 'Axial coding' The Sage Encyclopedia of Communication Research Methods (Vol. 4, pp. 80-82). SAGE Publications, Inc, https://doi.org/10.4135/9781483381411

Spalding, NJ 2009, 'Improving practice through involvement in action research', *International Journal of Therapy and Rehabilitation*, vol. 16, pp. 130-138.

Stanberry, B 2001, 'Telemedicine: Barriers and opportunities in the 21st century', *Journal of Internal Medicine*, vol. 249, pp. 109-120.

Taddeo, CM 2023, 'Practitioner Researcher: Insights into methodologies employed in action research and work applied learning contexts: A report prepared by CMT Accessible Research for the Global Centre for Work Applied Learning' (unpublished).

Taddeo, CM 2024, 'A revised final commentary prepared by CMT Accessible Research for the Global Centre for Work Applied Learning' as further amended in February 2025 and (unpublished).

Vitale, G 2023, 'Research Methodology' in *Understanding Supply Chain Digitalization Through Actor-Network Theory*, SIDREA Series in Accounting and Business Administration. Springer, Cham. https://doi.org/10.1007/978-3-031-30988-5_3.

World Health Organisation 1998, *A health telematics policy in support of WHO's Health-for-All Strategy for global health development: Report of the WHO Group Consultation on Health Telematics*, 11–16 December, Geneva, 1997, WHO, Geneva.

Williams, M & Moser, T 2019, 'The art of coding and thematic exploration in qualitative research'. International Management Review, vol.15, no. 1, pp.45-55.

Williamson, GR 2012, *Action research in nursing and healthcare*, SAGE, London.

World Health Organisation 2005, *Preventing chronic diseases: a vital investment: WHO global report*, WHO, Geneva.

World Health Organisation 2006, *Facts related to chronic diseases*, WHO, Geneva.

Yin, RK 1981, 'The case study crisis: Some answers', *Administrative Science Quarterly*, vol. 26, no. 1, pp. 58-65.

Yin, RK 1989, *Case study research: Design and methods*, Sage Publications, London.

Zedeck, S (ed) 2014, *APA Dictionary of Statistics and Research Methods*, 1st edn, American Psychological Association, Washington DC, US.

Zuber-Skerritt, O (ed) 2003, *New Directions in Action Research*, Routledge, London.

Zuber-Skerritt, O & Abraham, S 2017, 'A conceptual framework for work-applied learning for developing managers as practitioner researchers,' *Higher Education, Skills and Work-Based Learning*, vol. 7, no.1, pp. 35-50. https://doi.org/10.1108/HESWBL-05-2016-0037.

CHAPTER 4

Abraham, S 1997, *Exploratory Action Research for Manager Development, Action Learning*, Action Research and Process Management Association (ALARPM) Inc. and Gibaran Action Research Management Institute Pty Ltd, Toowang, Queensland, Australia.

Abraham, S 2012, *Work-Applied Learning for Change*, AIB Publications Pty Ltd, Adelaide, Australia.

Abraham, S 2015, *Work-Applied Learning for Change, Work-Applied Learning Series*, AIB Publications Pty Ltd, Adelaide, Australia.

Abraham, S 2016, *Action Research Characteristics: In a Work - Applied Learning for Change Context*, Adelaide: WAL Publications.

Abraham, S, Arnold, G & Oxenberry, R 1996, T*he Self-Discovery Organisation: Fusing Action Research to the Learning Organisation*, presented at a conference on Developing a Learning Organization through Action Learning and Action Research, 25 & 26 October, organised by Action Learning, Action Research & Process Management Assoc. Inc. & Singapore Institute of Management, in Singapore.

Abraham, S & Daton, A 2009, 'Using action research in the restructure of a public service department in Papua New Guinea', *Gibaran Journal of Applied Management*, vol. 2, pp. 1-19.

Adler, PA & Adler, P 1994, 'Observational techniques', in NK Denzin & YS Lincoln (eds), *Handbook of qualitative research*, pp. 377–392, Thousand Oaks, CA: Sage.

Altrichter, H, Feldman, A, Posch, P & Somekh, B 2013, *Teachers investigate their work: An introduction to action research across the professions*, Routledge.

Amaratunga, D, Baldry, D, Sarshar, M & Newton, R 2002, 'Quantitative and qualitative research in the built environment: application of "mixed" research approach', *Work study*, vol. 51, no. 1, pp. 17-31.

Antonellis Jr, PJ & Berry, G 2017, 'Practical Steps for the Utilization of Action Research in Your Organization: A Qualitative Approach for Non-Academic Research', *International Journal of Human Resource Studies*, vol. 7 (2), 41.

Antwi, SK & Hamza, K 2015, 'Qualitative and quantitative research paradigms in business research: A philosophical reflection', *European Journal of Business and Management*, vol. 7, no. 3, pp. 217-225.

Avison, D, Lau, F, Myers, M & Nielsen, P 1999, 'Action Research', *Communications of the ACM*, vol. 42, no. 1.

Bainbridge, R, Tsey, K, McCalman, J, Kinchin, I, Saunders, V, Lui, FW & Lawson, K 2015, 'No one's discussing the elephant in the room: contemplating questions of research impact and benefit in Aboriginal and Torres Strait Islander Australian health research', *BMC Public Health*, vol. 15, no. 1, p. 696.

Baškarada, S 2014, 'Qualitative case study guidelines', *The Qualitative Report*, vol. 19, no. 40, pp. 1-18. http://nsuworks.nova.edu/tqr/vol19/iss40/3

Basri, H 2014, 'Using qualitative research in accounting and management studies: Not a new agenda', *Journal of US-China Public Administration*, vol. 11, no. 10, pp. 831-838.

Bracci, L, Bella Owona, JM & Nash, E J 2013, 'Community engagement through international service-learning: How a foreign student can become a social actor in the host society', *Intercultural Communication Studies*, vol. 22, no. 1, pp. 195-215.

Breen, LJ 2007, 'The researcher 'in the middle': Negotiating the insider/outsider dichotomy', *The Australian Community Psychologist*, vol. 19, no. 1, pp. 163-174.

Bryman, A & Bell, E 2007, *Business Research Methods*, 2nd edn, Oxford University Press, USA.

Bryman, A & Burgess, RG 2002, *Analyzing qualitative data*. Routledge London.

Burns, RB 1997, *Introduction to research methods*, 3rd edn, Australia: Longman.

Carmel, A 2006, 'Models for reflective practice', *Practice Nurse*, vol. 32, no. 10, pp. 28-32.

Cassell, C & Symon, G 2006, *Essential guide to qualitative methods in organizational research,* Sage, London.

Chandler, D & Torbert, B 2003, *Transforming Inquiry and Action*, SAGE Publications London, Thousand Oaks CA, New Delhi.

Cleaver, E, Lintern, M & McLinden, M 2014, *Teaching and Learning in Higher Education: Disciplinary Approaches to Educational Enquiry*, London: Sage.

Coghlan, D 2012, *The dynamics of insider action research, doing action research in your own organisation*, 31 October 2012, http://hls.uwe.ac.uk/research/Default.aspx?pageid=222

Creswell J 2009, *Research Design: Qualitative, Quantitative and Mixed Methods Approaches*, 3rd edn, Sage, Los Angeles.

Danuwar, RK 2014, *A study on socio-economic status of Doney (Raidanuwar) tribe*, Doctoral dissertation, Central Department of Economics Faculty of Humanities and Social Sciences Tribhuvan University, Kirtipur, Kathmandu.

Daton, A 2007, *Restructuring a Government Department in Papua New Guinea Public Services using the Action Research Approach*, DBA thesis, Gibaran Business School, Australia.

Delfino, MCN 2015, 'Designing English teaching activities based on popular music lyrics from a corpus perspective', *Domínios de Lingu@ gem*, vol. 9, no. 2, pp. 76-95.

Donnellan, D, Murray, CD & Holland, J 2014, 'Couples' experiences of their relationship surrounding trauma', *Traumatology*, vol. 20, no. 4, p. 262.

Doody, O & Noonan, M 2013, 'Preparing and conducting interviews to collect data', *Nurse researcher,* vol. 20, no. 5, pp. 28-32.

Dwyer, S & Buckle, J 2009, 'The space between: On being an insider – outsider in qualitative research', *International Journal of Qualitative Methods,* vol. 8, no. 1, pp. 54-63.

Edwards, A, 1999, 'Reflective Practice in Sport Management', *Sport Management Review,* vol. 2, pp. 67-81.

Embo, M, Driessen, E, Valcke, M & van der Vleuten, CPM 2015, 'Relationship between reflection ability and clinical performance: A cross-sectional and retrospective-longitudinal correlational cohort study in midwifery', *Midwifery,* vol. 31, no. 1, pp. 90-94.

Farren, M 2005, *A brief history of action research,* viewed on 21 November 2012, <http://www.innovateonline.info/extra/exhibit2422.htm >.

Finlay, L 2005, 'Reflexive embodied empathy: a phenomenology of participant-researcher intersubjectivity', *Methods Issue: The Humanistic Psychologist,* vol. 33, no. 4, pp. 271-292.

Fletcher, T & Wilson, A 2013, 'The transformative potential of reflective diaries for elite English cricketers', *Leisure/Loisir,* vol. 37, no. 3, pp. 267-286.

Garnett, J, Abraham, S & Abraham, P 2016, 'Using work-based and work-applied learning to enhance the intellectual capital of organisations', *Journal of Work-Applied Management,* vol. 8. no. 1, pp. 56-64.

Greenwood, DJ & Levin, M 2007, *Introduction to action research,* Thousand Oaks, CA: SAGE Publications, Inc. doi: 10.4135/9781412984614.

Grose, C 2015, 'Uncovering and Deconstructing the Binary: Teaching (and Learning) Critical Reflection in Clinic and Beyond', *Clinical L. Rev.,* vol. 22, no. 301.

Guba, EG & Lincoln, YS 1994, 'Competing paradigms in qualitative research', *Handbook of qualitative research,* vol. 2, pp. 163-194, 105.

Guest, G, MacQueen KM & Namey EE 2012, *Applied Thematic Analysis,* Sage Publications, Los Angeles.

Hakansson, A 2013, 'Portal of research methods and methodologies for research projects and degree programs', in *Proceedings of the international conference on frontiers in education: Computer science and computer engineering (FECS)* (p. 1). The Steering Committee of the World Congress in Computer Science, Computer Engineering and Applied Computing (WorldComp).

Hancock, B, Windridge, K & Ockleford, E 2009, *'An Introduction to Qualitative Research'*, The NIHR RDS EM / YH.

Hashim, M 2001, *Introducing change in a Bumiputra shipping organisation in Malaysia*, an Action Research case study, DBA thesis, Southern Cross University, Australia.

Hepworth, M 2016, *Research 1 Course (R1): Pre-online Handout: Glossary of key concepts in research*, The Institute of Development Studies, http://creativecommons.org/licenses/by-sa/3.0/

Hilden, S & Tikkamaki, K 2013, 'Reflective practice as a fuel for organizational learning', *Administrative sciences*, vol. 3, no. 3, pp. 76-95.

Hofstee, E 2006, *Constructing a good dissertation: A practical guide to finishing a Masters, MBA or PhD on schedule*, Sandton: EPE.

Holden, MT & Lynch, P 2004, 'Choosing the appropriate methodology: Understanding research philosophy', *The marketing review*, vol. 4, no. 4, pp. 397-409.

Holloway, I & Galvin, K 2016, *Qualitative research in nursing and healthcare*, John Wiley & Sons.

Holyoake, N unpub., 14 August 2016, *To investigate a continuous improvement approach using a work-applied action research and and action learning (ARAL) design in the defence industry of Australia*, Doctor of Business Administration Thesis, Australian Institute of Business

Hussein, A 2015, 'The use of triangulation in social sciences research: Can qualitative and quantitative methods be combined?' *Journal of Comparative Social Work*, vol. 4, no. 1.

Inbaraj, J 2018, Action Research - *Key to Teaching & Learning*, Lulu Publication, USA.

Iofrida, N, De Luca, AI, Strano, A & Gulisano, G 2014, 'Social life cycle assessment in a constructivist realism perspective: a methodological proposal', in *Social LCA in progress, Pre-Proceedings of the 4th International Seminar in Social LCA. Montpellier, France*, pp. 44-50.

Israel, B, Schurman, S & Hugentobler, M 1992, 'Conducting action research: Relationships between organization members and researchers', *Journal of Applied Behavioral Science*, pp. 74-101.

Kemmis, S., & McTaggart, R 1982, *The Action Research Planner*, Deakin University.

Kemparaj, U & Chavan, S 2013, 'Qualitative research: A brief description', *Indian Journal of Medical Sciences*, vol. 67, no. 3/4, p. 89.

Khan, JI, unpub., 2015, *To investigate the development and implementation of Work-Based Project Management Development Programme for project management practitioners in Trinidad and Tobago*, DBA Thesis, Australian Institute of Business, Adelaide, Australia.

Koshy, V 2009, *Action Research for improving educational practice, A step by step guide*, 2nd edn, Sage Publication.

Koshy, E, Koshy, V & Waterman, H 2011, 'What is action research?' *Action research in healthcare*, pp. 1-24, London: SAGE Publications Ltd doi: 10.4135/9781446288696.n1.

Lester, PE, Inman, D & Bishop, LK 2014, *Handbook of tests and measurement in education and the social sciences*, Rowman & Littlefield.

Leung, L 2015, 'Validity, reliability, and generalizability in qualitative research', *Journal of Family Medicine and Primary Care*, vol. 4, no. 3, pp. 324-327.

Lewin, K 1946, Action research and minority problems. *Journal of Social Issues*, 2, 34-46. in S. Kemmis & W. McTaggart (eds), *The action research reader* (3rd edn), Deakin University Press.

Lewin, K 1947, *Frontiers in group dynamics II. Channels of group life, social planning and action research*, Human Relations, 1, 143-153.

Locke, LF, Spirduso, WW & Silverman, SJ 2013, *Proposals that work: A guide for planning dissertations and grant proposals*, 6th edn, Thousand Oaks, CA: Sage.

Lopez, V & Whitehead, D 2013, 'Sampling data and data collection in qualitative research', *Nursing and Midwifery Research: Methods and Critical Appraisal for Evidence-based Practice*, pp. 124-140, Elsevier Health Sciences, London.

Mackenzie, N & Knipe, S 2006, 'Research dilemmas: Paradigms, methods and methodology', *Issues in Educational Research*, vol. 16, no. 2, pp. 193-205, 20 April 2015, http://www.iier.org.au/iier16/mackenzie.html

Marshall, C & Rossman, G 1989, *Designing qualitative research*. Sage Publications Inc.

McGrath, JE & Johnson, BA 2003, *Methodology makes meaning: How both qualitative and quantitative paradigms shape evidence and its interpretation*.

McIntosh, MJ & Morse, JM 2015, 'Situating and constructing diversity in semi-structured interviews', *Global qualitative nursing research*, vol. 2, p. 2333393615597674.

McNiff, J 2017, *Action Research: All you need to know*, SAGE.

McNiff, J & Whitehead, J 2016, *You and your action research project*, Routledge, New York, NY.

Merriam, SB 1988, *Qualitative research and case study applications in education*, San Francisco: Jossey-Bass.

Mertens, DM 2005, *Research methods in education and psychology: Integrating diversity with quantitative and qualitative approaches*, 2nd edn, Thousand Oaks: Sage.

Miles, MB & Huberman, AM 1994, *Qualitative data analysis: An expanded sourcebook*. Sage.

Miller, M, Greenwood, D & Maguire, P 2003, *Why Action Research*, SAGE Publications London, Thousand Oaks, CA, New Delhi.

Milligan, L 2016, 'Insider-outsider-inbetweener? Researcher positioning, participative methods and cross-cultural educational research', *Compare: A Journal of Comparative and International Education*, vol. 46, no. 2, pp. 235-250.

Molineux, J 2018, 'Using action research for change in organizations: processes, reflections and outcomes', *Journal of Work-Applied Management*, 10(1). https://doi.org/10.1108/JWAM-03-2017-0007

Moser, R 2016, *Quantitative and qualitative research in management (and Computer Science)*, Conference or Workshop Item, Research Workshop – Canossa Sisters, St. Gallen, https://www.alexandria.unisg.ch/publications/249515

Myers, MD 1997, 'Qualitative research in information systems', *Management Information Systems Quarterly*, vol. 21, no. 2, pp. 241-242.

Norton, LS 2009, *Action research in teaching and learning: A practical guide to conducting pedagogical research in Universities*, Routledge, London and New York.

Nyakundi, DO, Nyamita, MO & Tinega TM 2014, 'Effect of internal control systems on financial performance of small and medium scale business enterprises in Kisumu, City, Kenya', *International Journal of Social Sciences and Entrepreneurship*, vol. 1, no. 11.

O'Brien, R 1998, *An Overview of the Methodological Approach of Action Research*, Faculty of Information Studies, University of Toronto.

O'Leary, D 2010, 'Outsider positioning in action research: Struggling with being on the outside looking in', *Undoing privilege: Unearned advantage in a divided world*, pp. 39-52.

Orlikowski, W & Baroudi, J 1991, 'Studying information technology in organizations: research approaches and assumptions', *The Institute of Management Sciences*, Information Systems Research, vol. 2, no. 1.

Palinkas, LA, Horwitz, SM, Green, CA, Wisdom, JP, Duan, N & Hoagwood, K 2015, 'Purposeful sampling for qualitative data collection and analysis in mixed method implementation research', *Administration and Policy in Mental Health and Mental Health Services Research*, vol. 42, no. 5, pp. 533-544.

Pedler, M 1997, *Action learning in practice*. Gower Publishing, Ltd.

Perry, C 2013, *Efficient and Effective Research: Work-Applied Learning Series*, AIB Publications Pty Ltd, Adelaide, South Australia.

Pietkiewicz, I & Smith, JA 2014, 'A practical guide to using interpretative phenomenological analysis in qualitative research psychology', *Psychological Journal*, vol. 20, no. 1, pp. 7-14.

Ponterotto, J 2005, 'Qualitative research in counseling psychology: A primer on research paradigms and philosophy of science', *Journal of Counseling Psychology*, vol. 52, no. 2, pp. 126-136.

Ramos, J 2002, 'Action Research as Foresight Methodology', *Journal of Future Studies*, vol. 7.

Reason, P & Bradbury, H 2001, Introduction: Inquiry and participation in search of a world view worthy of human aspiration in P. Reason & H. Bradbury (eds) 2001, *Handbook of action research: Participatory inquiry and practice* (pp. 1-14). Sage.

Reason, P & Bradbury, H. (eds) 2006, *Handbook of action research: Concise paperback edition*. Sage.

Reason, P & Bradbury, H 2013, *Handbook of Action Research: Participative inquiry and practice*, Sage Publications.

Revans, R 1982, *The origins and growth of action learning*. Chartwell-Bratt, Bromley.

Reynolds, M 2017, *Organizing reflection*, Routledge.

Ritchie, J, Lewis, J, Nicholls, CM & Ormston, R 2013, *Qualitative research practice: A guide for social science students and researchers*, Sage.

Rubin, A & Babbie, ER 2016, *Empowerment series: Research methods for social work*, Cengage Learning.

Russell, N 2014, *Approaching educational enquiry*. Higher Education Academy. https://www.sheffield.ac.uk/polopoly_fs/1.592717!/file/ApproachingEducationalEnquiry.pdf

Sankaran, S & Dick, B 2015, 'Linking theory and practice in using action-oriented methods', *Designs, methods and practices for research of project management*, pp. 211-224.

Seale, C 1999, 'Quality in qualitative research', *Qualitative Inquiry*, vol. 5, no. 4, pp. 465-478.

Sempowicz, T & Hudson, P 2012, 'Mentoring Pre-Service Teachers' Reflective Practices towards producing teaching outcomes', *International Journal of Evidence Based Coaching and Mentoring*, vol. 10, no. 2, p. 52.

Seng, FA, unpub. 2014, *To investigate the development and implementation of a WAL facilitative leadership development programme (FLDP) for senior managers in a G7 construction firm in Malaysia*, Australian Institute of Business, South Australia.

Shahzad, WM 2016, *Comparative analysis of the productivity levels achieved through the use of panelised prefabrication technology with those of traditional building system: a thesis submitted in fulfilment of the requirements for the degree of Doctor of Philosophy (PhD) in Construction*, School of Engineering & Advanced Technology, Massey University, Albany, New Zealand, Doctoral dissertation, Massey University.

Shenton, AK 2004, 'Strategies for ensuring trustworthiness In qualitative research projects', *Education in information*, vol. 22, no. 2, pp. 63-75.

Solomonidou, G 2015, *A mixed methods investigation into the perceptions of lower secondary school students and teachers in Cyprus on the purposes and approaches of assessment*, Doctoral dissertation, School of Education.

Stevens, M 2013, *Ethical issues in qualitative research*, King's College London.

Susman, G & Evered, R 1978, 'An Assessment of the Scientific Merits of Action Research', *Administrative Science Quarterly*, pp. 582-603.

Taylor S 2010, 'Negative Judgements: Reflections on Teaching Reflective Practice', *Organisation Management Journal*, vol.7, pp. 5-12.

Taylor, SJ, Bogdan, R & DeVault, M 2015, *Introduction to qualitative research methods: A guidebook and resource*, John Wiley & Sons.

Thompson, F 2003, *An action research analysis of factors involved in Australian small to medium-sized enterprises planning and tendering for overseas development aid projects*, PhD thesis, South Cross University, Lismore.

Tran, HMT & Anvari, F 2014, *Reflective frameworks for change management*, Proc. 8th European Conference on IS Management and Evaluation: ECIME, Ghent, Belgium, pp. 253-261.

Tromp, C, Beukema, L & Almekinders, C 2009, 'Research in action, Theories and practice for innovation and social change', pp. 221-241.

Unluer, S 2012, 'Being an insider researcher while conducting case study research', *The Qualitative Report*, vol. 17, no. 29, p. 1.

Uslu, B & Cagdas, A 2017, 'Content analysis of the Turkish course books for pre-school children (50-74 months old)' *Research Highlights in Education and Science*, pp. 33.

Uztosun, MS 2013, *The role of student negotiation in improving the speaking ability of Turkish university EFL students: An action research study*.

Veal, AJ 2017, *Research methods for leisure and tourism*, Pearson U. K.

Wilkstrom, A & Jackson M 2012, 'Visualization in Reflective Practice – Support for Management', *The Design Management institute*, pp. 62-73.

Williamson, GR, Bellman, L & Webster, J 2012, *Action research in nursing and healthcare* London: SAGE Publications Ltd doi: 10.4135/9781446289112.

Winkler, DM 2016, *A new approach to parental involvement: The role of virtual parent-teacher conferences*, Doctor of Education in Educational Leadership for Learning Dissertations. 3, https://digitalcommons.kennesaw.edu/educleaddoc_etd/3

Yasar, MD 2017, 'Brain Based Learning in Science Education in Turkey: Descriptive Content and Meta Analysis of Dissertations', *Journal of Education and Practice*, vol. 8 (9), pp.161-168.

Yin, RK 1984, *Case study research, design and methods*, Sage Publications, Beverly Hills, California, 1984.

Yin, R 1994, *Case study research, Design and Methods*, 2nd edn, Thousand Oaks: Sage.

Yin, R 2018, *Case study research designs and applications.* 6edn, SAGE Publications, Los Angeles, United States of America.

Zucker, D 2009, *How to do a case study*, University of Massachusetts Amherst, Scholar Works @ UMass Amherst, College of Nursing Faculty Publication Series, College of Nursing.

CHAPTER 5

Abraham, S 1997, *Exploratory action research for manager development*, Action Learning, Brisbane.

Abraham, S 2012, *Work-applied learning for change*, AIB, Adelaide.

Abraham, S 2016, *Action research characteristics : in a work-applied learning for change context / Selva Abraham.* Adelaide, SA, WAL

Publications Pty Ltd.

Abraham, S & Daton, A 2009, 'Using action research in the restructure of a public service department in Papua New Guinea', *Gibaran Journal of Applied Management*, vol. 2, 1-19.

Aguinis, H 1993, 'Action research and scientific method: Presumed discrepancies and actual similarities', *Journal of Applied Behavioral Science*, vol. 29, pp. 416-431.

Arndt, M 2000, 'The transfer of business practices into hospitals: History and implications, Advances in Health Care Management', vol. 1, 339-368, http://dx.doi.org/10.1016/S1474-8231(00)01013-2

Australian Government National Statistical Service 2014, *National Statistical Service handbook Australia*, viewed 15/10/2016, http://www.nss.gov.au/nss/home.NSF/pages/NSS+Handbook

Babbie, ER 2004, *The practice of social research*, Thomson/Wadsworth, Belmont, CA.

Baillargeon, J-P, Carpentier, A, Donovan, D, Fortin, M, Grant, A, Simoneau-Roy, J, St-Cyr-Tribble, D, Xhignesse, M & Langlois, M-F 2007, 'Integrated obesity care management system -implementation and research protocol', *BMC Health Services Research*, vol. 7, p. 163.

Baker, DC & Bufka, LF 2011, 'Preparing for the telehealth world: Navigating legal, regulatory, reimbursement, and ethical issues in an electronic age', Professional Psychology: Research and Practice, *vol. 42, pp. 405-411*.

Bärnighausen, T, Tugwell, P, Shemilt, I, Rockers, P, Geldsetzer, P, Lavis, J , Grimshaw, J, Daniels, K, Brown, A, Bor, J, Tanner, J, Rashidian, A, Barreto, M, Vollmer, S & Atun, R 2017, 'Quasi-experimental study designs series-paper 4: Uses and value', *Journal of Clinical Epidemiology*, vol. 89, pp. 21-29.

Baskerville, R 1999, 'Investigating information systems with action research', *Communications of the Association of Information Systems*, vol. 2, pp. 1-31.

Beer, M & Walton, A 1987, 'Organization change and development', *Annual Review of Psychology*, vol. 38, pp. 339-367.

Berelson, B 1952, *Content analysis in communication research*, Hafner Publishing Company, New York.

Bergmo, T 2009, 'Can economic evaluation in telemedicine be trusted? A systematic review of the literature', *Cost Effectiveness and Resource Allocation*, vol. 7, p. 18.

Berkman, LF & Syme, SL 1979, 'Social networks, host resistance, and mortality: A nine-year follow-up study of Alameda County residents', *American Journal of Epidemiology*, vol. 109, p. 186.

Blumberg, M & Pringle, C 1983, 'How control groups can cause loss of control in action research: The case of Rushton Coal Mine', *Journal of Applied Behavioral Science*, vol. 19, pp. 409-425.

Boland, R 1985, 'Phenomenology: A preferred approach to research in information systems', in E Mumford, RA Hirschheim, G Fitzgerald & T Wood-Harper (eds), *Research methods in information systems*, NorthHolland, Amsterdam.

Bouma, GD 2004, *The research process*, Oxford University Press, South Melbourne.

Bryman, A & Bell, E 2015, *Business research methods*, Oxford University Press, Oxford.

Burke, WW 1994, *Organization development: A process of learning and changing*, Addison-Wesley, Reading, MA.

Burns, D, Hyde, P, Killett, A, Poland, F & Gray, R 2014, 'Participatory organizational research: Examining voice in the co-production of knowledge', *British Journal of Management*, vol. 25, pp. 133-144.

Campbell, D. T 1966, *Experimental and quasi-experimental designs for research.*, R. McNally, Chicago, IL.

Carney, TF 1972, *Content analysis: A technique for systematic inference from communications*, University of Manitoba Press, Winnipeg.

Cassell, C & Johnson, O 2006, Action research: Explaining the diversity, *Human Relations*, vol. 59, pp. 783-814.

Chadwick, BA, Bahr, HM & Albrecht, SL 1984, *Social science research methods*, Prentice-Hall, Englewood Cliffs, NJ.

Coghlan, D 2011, *Action research: Exploring perspectives on a philosophy of practical knowing*, Sage, Thousand Oaks, CA.

Cohen, D & Crabtree, B 2008, 'Evaluative criteria for qualitative research in health care: Controversies and recommendations', *Annals of Family Medicine*, vol. 6, pp. 331-339, doi: 10.1370/afm.818. vol. pp.

Collis, J & Hussey, R 2013, *Business research: A practical guide for undergraduate and postgraduate students*, Palgrave Macmillan, Basingstoke.

Cook, TD 1979, *Quasi-experimentation: Design & analysis issues for field settings*, Rand McNally, Chicago, IL.

Cooper, DR 2008, *Business research methods*, McGraw-Hill, New York, NY.

Creswell, JW 2007, *Qualitative inquiry & research design*, Sage Publications, Thousand Oaks, CA.

Creswell, JW 2009, *Research design: Qualitative, quantitative, and mixed methods approaches*, Sage Publications, Thousand Oaks, CA.

Cunningham, JB 1993, *Action research and organizational development*, Praeger, Westport, CT.

Daton, A 2007, *Restructuring a government department in the Papua New Guinea public service using the action research approach*. Doctorate of Business Administration, Australian Institute of Business.

Dávalos, ME, French, MT, Burdick, AE & Simmons, SC 2009, 'Economic evaluation of telemedicine: Review of the literature and research guidelines for benefit-cost analysis', *Telemedicine & e-Health*, vol. 15, pp. 933-948.

De Las Nueces, D, Hacker, K, Digirolamo, A & Hicks, LS 2012, 'A systematic review of community-based participatory research to enhance clinical trials in racial and ethnic minority groups', *Health Services Research*, vol. 47, p. 1363.

Denzin, NK & Lincoln, YS 2008, *Collecting and interpreting qualitative materials*, Sage Publications, Thousand Oaks, CA.

Department Of Health 2013, *Supporting the implementation of telehealth in Victoria: The Victorian government's response to the recommendations of the Health Innovation and Reform Council*, Government of Victoria, Melbourne.

Dewey, J 1959, *Art as experience*, Capricorn Books, New York, NY.

Diabetes Control And Complications Trial Research Group 1993, 'The effect of intensive treatment of diabetes on the development and progression of long-term complications in insulin-dependent diabetes mellitus', *New England Journal of Medicine*, vol. 329, pp. 977-986.

Docherty, P, Ljung, A & Stjemberg, Y 2006, 'The changing practice of action research', in J Lowstedt & T Stjernberg (eds), *Producing management knowledge*, Routledge, Abingdon.

Easterby-Smith, M 2012, *Management research: An introduction*, SAGE, London.

Elliot, ME, Fairweather, IE, Olsen, WKE & Pampaka, ME 2016, *A dictionary of social research methods*, Oxford University Press, Oxford.

Emanuel, E, Wendler, D & Grady, C 2000, 'What makes clinical research ethical?', *JAMA*. vol. 283, pp. 2701-2711

Engwall, M 1998, 'The project concept(s): On the unit of analysis in the study of project management', in RA Lundin & C Midler (eds), *Projects as arenas for renewal and learning processes*, Springer, Boston, MA.

Festinger, L & Katz, D 1966, *Research methods in the behavioral sciences*, Holt, Rinehart and Winston, New York, NY.

Fng Ah, S 2014, *To investigate the development and implementation of a WAL Facilitative Leadership Development Programme (FLDP) for senior managers in a G7 construction firm in Malaysia*, Doctor of Business Administration, Australian Institute of Business.

Freedman, B 1987, 'Equipoise and the ethics of clinical research', *The New England Journal of Medicine*, vol. 317, pp. 141-5.

Gable, GG 1994, 'Integrating case study and survey research methods: An example in information systems', *European Journal of Information Systems*, vol. 3, pp. 112.

Gillingham, P 2014, 'Repositioning electronic information systems in human service organizations', *Human Services Organizations: Management, Leadership & Governance*, vol. 38, p. 125.

Gillingham, P 2015, 'Electronic information systems in human service organisations: The what, who, why and how of information', *British Journal of Social Work*, vol. 45, pp. 1598.

Goodman, N 1978, *Ways of worldmaking*, Hackett, Indianapolis, IN.

Grant, AM & Wall, TD 2009, 'The neglected science and art of quasi-experimentation', *Organizational Research Methods*, vol. 12, pp. 653-686.

Gummesson, E 2000, *Qualitative methods in management research*, Sage Publications Thousand Oaks, CA

Harrison, R 1971, 'Research on human relations training: Design and interpretation', *Journal of Applied Behavioral Science*, vol. 7, no. 1, pp. 71-85.

Hart, E 1996, 'Action research as a professionalizing strategy: Issues and dilemmas', *Journal of Advanced Nursing*, vol. 23, pp. 454-461.

Hashim, M 2001, *Introducing change in a bumiputera shipping organisation in Malaysia: An action research case study*, Doctorate of Business Administration, Australian Institute of Business.

Henderson, C, Knapp, M, Fernández, J-L, Beecham, J, Hirani, SP, Cartwright, M, Rixon, L, Beynon, M, Rogers, A, Bower, P, Doll, H, Fitzpatrick, R, Steventon, A, Bardsley, M, Hendy, J & Newman, SP 2013, 'Cost effectiveness of telehealth for patients with long term conditions (Whole Systems Demonstrator telehealth questionnaire study): Nested economic evaluation in a pragmatic, cluster randomised controlled trial', *BMJ Clinical Research*, vol. 346, p. f1035.

Henderson, KA 2011, 'Post-positivism and the pragmatics of leisure research', *Leisure Sciences*, vol. 33, pp. 341-346.

Herzlinger, RE 2006, 'Why innovation in health care is so hard', *Harvard Business Review*, vol. 84, pp. 58.

Holyoake, N 2016, *To investigate a continuous improvement approach using a work-applied action research and action learning (ARAL) design in the defence industry of Australia*, Doctor of Business Administration, Australian Institute of Business.

Hughes, JA 1997, *The philosophy of social research*, Longman, London.

James, EA 2012, *Action research for business, nonprofit, & public administration: a tool for complex times*, SAGE Publications, Thousand Oaks, CA.

Jennett, PA, Hall, LA, Hailey, D, Ohinmaa, A, Anderson, C, Thomas, R, Young, B, Lorenzetti, D & Scott, RE 2003, 'The socio-economic impact of telehealth: a systematic review', *Journal of Telemedicine & Telecare*, vol. 9, pp. 311-320.

Johnson, JA 2009, *Health organizations: Theory, behavior, and development*, Jones and Bartlett, Sudbury, MA.

Johnson, RB 1997, 'Examining the validity structure of qualitative research', *Education*, vol. 118, no. 2, pp. 282.

Kaplan, B & Duchon, D 1988, 'Combining qualitative and quantitative methods in information systems research: A case study', *MIS Quarterly*, vol. 12, pp. 571-586.

Karvinen, K 2002, *Developing and implementing a process of integration: Internal and external customers and technology in the building components industry*, Doctor of Business Administration, Australian Institute of Business.

Kember, D 2003, 'To control or not to control: The question of whether experimental designs are appropriate for evaluating teaching innovations in higher education', *Assessment & Evaluation in Higher Education*, vol. 28, pp. 89-101.

Khan, JI 2014, *To investigate the development and implementation of a work-based project management development programme for project management practitioners in Trinidad and Tobago*, Doctor of Business Administration, Australian Institute of Business.

Kienzle, M 2001, 'Coming up short: Telemedicine's promise in perspective', *Journal of Rural Health*, vol. 17, pp. 14-15.

Kinsella, EA 2007, 'Technical rationality in Schön's reflective practice: Dichotomous or non-dualistic epistemological position', *Nursing Philosophy*, vol. 8, pp. 102–113.

Kinsella, EA 2010, 'The art of reflective practice in health and social care: Reflections on the legacy of Donald Schön', *Reflective Practice*, vol. 11, pp. 565-575.

Kirk, J 1986, *Reliability and validity in qualitative research*, Sage Publications, Beverly Hills, CA.

Kleinberg-Levin, DM 1988, *The opening of vision: Nihilism and the postmodern situation*, Routledge, New York, NY.

Krippendorff, K 1980, *Content analysis: An introduction to its methodology*, Sage Publications, Thousand Oaks, CA.

Krippendorff, K 2004, *Content analysis: An introduction to its methodology*, 2nd edn, Sage, Thousand Oaks, CA.

Kuhn, TS 1962, *The structure of scientific revolutions*. Chicago, London, Chicago, London : University of Chicago Press.

Lavrakas, PJ 2008, *Encyclopedia of survey research methods*, SAGE Publications, Thousand Oaks, CA.

Lecompte, MD 1993, *Ethnography and qualitative design in educational research*, Academic Press. San Diego, CA.

Lee, AS 1991, 'Integrating positivist and interpretive approaches to organizational research', *Organization Science*, vol. 2, pp. 342-365.

Lewin, K 1946, 'Action research and minority problems', *Journal of Social Issues*, vol. 2, pp. 34-36.

Lewin, K 1947, 'Frontiers in group dynamics II. Channels of group life social planning and action research', *Human Relations*, vol. 1, pp. 143-153.

Lewin, K 1951, *Field theory in social sciences: Selected theoretical papers*, Harper, New York, NY.

Lewin, K 1952, 'Group decisions and social change', in G Swanson, T Newcombe & E Hartley (eds), *Readings in social psychology*, Henry Holt, New York, NY.

Lincoln, YS 1985, *Naturalistic inquiry*, Sage Publications, Beverly Hills, CA.

Loh, E 2014, personal communication, 1 September.

LOH, E. September 2014. RE: Telehealth at Monash Health. Type to JURMAN, P.

Long, T & Johnson, M 2000, 'Rigour, reliability and validity in qualitative research', *Clinical Effectiveness in Nursing*, vol. 4, pp. 30-37.

Mackridge, A & Mackridge, A 2018, *A practical approach to using statistics* in health research: From planning to reporting*, John Wiley & Sons Newark, NJ.

Mars, M & Jack, C 2010, 'Why is telemedicine a challenge to the regulators?', *South African Journal of Bioethics and Law*, vol. 3, p. 55.

Marsden, D & Littler, D 1996, 'Evaluating alternative research paradigms: A market-oriented framework', *Journal of Marketing Management*, vol. 12, pp. 645-655.

Marshall, C 1989, *Designing qualitative research*, Sage Publications, Newbury Park, CA.

Marshall, C 1995, *Designing qualitative research*, 2nd edn, Sage Publications, Thousand Oaks, CA.

Marshall, C 2016, *Designing qualitative research*, 3rd edn, SAGE, Thousand Oaks, CA.

Maxwell, J 1992, 'Understanding and validity in qualitative research', *Harvard Educational Review*, vol. 62, pp. 279-300.

Maxwell, JA 2012, *A realist approach for qualitative research*, SAGE Publications, Thousand Oaks, CA.

May, C, Harrison, R, Macfarlane, A, Williams, T, Mair, F & Wallace, P 2003, 'Why do telemedicine systems fail to normalise as stable models of service delivery?', *Journal of Telemedicine and Telecare*, vol. 9, pp. 25-26.

Mays, N & Pope, C 1995, 'Rigour and qualitative research', *BMJ*, vol. 311, pp. 109-112.

Mcgregor, D & Cartwright, L 2011, *Developing reflective practice: A guide for beginning teachers*, Open University Press, Maidenhead.

Mercer, J 2007, 'The challenges of insider research in educational institutions: Wielding a double-edged sword and resolving delicate dilemmas', *Oxford Review of Education*, vol. 33, pp. 1-17.

Merriam, SB 2009, *Qualitative research: A guide to design and implementation*, Jossey-Bass, San Francisco, CA.

Mingers, J 2001, 'Combining IS research methods: Towards a pluralist methodology', *Information Systems Research*, vol. 12, pp. 240-259.

Mintzberg, H 1979, 'An emerging strategy of "direct" research', *Administrative Science Quarterly*, vol. 24, pp. 582-589.

Moffatt, JJ & Eley, DS 2011, 'Barriers to the up-take of telemedicine in Australia: A view from providers', *Rural and Remote Health*, vol. 11, pp. 1581.

Morgan, G & Smircich, L 1980, 'The case for qualitative research', *The Academy of Management Review*, vol. 5, pp. 491-500.

Myers, MD & Avison, DE 2002, *Qualitative research in information systems: A reader*, SAGE, London.

Myers, MD 1997, 'Qualitative research in information systems', *MIS Quarterly*, vol. 21, pp. 241-242.

National Health And Medical Research Council 2014, *National statement on ethical conduct in human research*, Commonwealth of Australia, Canberra.

National Health And Medical Research Council 2018, *Australian code for responsible conduct of research*, Commonwealth of Australia, Canberra.

National Health And Medical Research Council, The Australian Research Council & The Australian Vice-Chancellors Committee 2007 (Updated March 2014), *National statement on ethical human research*, Commonwealth of Australia, Canberra

Normann, R 1970, *A personal quest for methodology*, Scandinavian Institute for Administrative Research, Stockholm.

O'Brien, R 1998, *An overview of the methodological approach of action research*, viewed 02/04/2016, http://www.web.ca/~robrien/papers/arfinal.html [Accessed].

O'Brien, PW & Briggs, DK 1987, 'Content analysis of motivational appeals for sociocultural forecasting', in RJS Macpherson (ed), *Ways and meanings of research in educational administration*, University of New England, Armidale.

Ozanne, Julie L & Saatcioglu, B 2008, 'Participatory action research', *Journal of Consumer Research*, vol. 35, no. 3, pp. 423-439

Packendorff, J & Lindgren, M 2014, 'Projectification and its consequences: Narrow and broad conceptualisations', *South African Journal of Economic and Management Sciences*, vol. 17, pp. 7-21.

Parshuram, CS & Kavanagh, BP 2004, 'Positive clinical trials: Understand the control group before implementing the result', *American Journal of Respiratory and Critical Care Medicine*, vol. 170, pp. 223.

Perry, C 2013, *Efficient and effective research: A toolkit for research students and developing researchers*, AIB Publications, Adelaide.

Peters, M 1984, 'The origins and status of action research', *Journal of Applied Behavioral Science*, vol. 20, pp. 113-124.

Polanyi, M 1967, *The tacit dimension*, Routledge & K. Paul, London.

Powell, W 2002, 'Organizational change models', *Futurics*, vol. 26, pp. 20-45.

Ragin, CC 1987, *The comparative method: Moving beyond qualitative and quantitative strategies*, University of California Press, Berkeley, CA.

Ramli, A, Selvarajah, S, Haniff, J, Abdul-Razak, S, Rahman, T, Tong, S, Lee, V, Ng, K & Ariffin, F 2016, 'Effectiveness of the EMPOWER-PAR intervention in improving clinical outcomes of type 2 diabetes mellitus in primary care: A pragmatic cluster randomised controlled trial', *BMC Family Practice*, vol. 17, p. 157.

Reason, P & Bradbury, H 2008, *The SAGE handbook of action research: Participative inquiry and practice*, SAGE, London.

Reason, P & Mckernan, J 2006, 'Choice and quality in action research practice: A response to Peter Reason/A response to J.A. McKernan', *Journal of Management Inquiry*, vol. 15, pp. 187-208.

Robson, C 2011, *Real world research: A resource for users of social research methods in applied settings*, Wiley Chichester.

Rowe, R & Calnan, M 2006, 'Trust relations in health care: The new agenda', *European Journal of Public Health*, vol. 16, pp. 4-6.

Salkind, NJ 2012, *Exploring research*, Prentice Hall, Boston, MA.

Schensul, SL 1999, *Essential ethnographic methods: Observations, interviews, and questionnaires*, AltaMira Press, Walnut Creek, CA.

Schön, DA 1983, *The reflective practitioner: How professionals think in action*, Basic Books, New York, NY.

Schön, DA 1987, *Educating the reflective practitioner*, Jossey-Bass, San Francisco, CA.

Schön, DA, & Rein, M 1994, *Frame reflection: Toward the resolution of intractable policy controversies*, Basic Books, New York.

Schwartz, C, Chesney, M, Irvine, M & Keefe, F 1997, 'The control group dilemma in clinical research: Applications for psychosocial and behavioral medicine trials', *Psychosomatic Medicine*, vol. 59, pp. 362-371.

Shani, AB & Pasmore, WA 1982, 'Towards a new model of the action research process', *Academy of Management Proceedings*, 1982, pp. 208-212.

Smith, JK 1983, 'Quantitative versus qualitative research: An attempt to clarify the issue', *Educational Researcher*, vol. 12, pp. 6-13.

Sobh, R & Perry, C 2006, 'Research design and data analysis in realism research', *European Journal of Marketing*, vol. 40, pp. 1194-1209.

Stewart, A 2014, 'Case study', in JB Mills (ed), *Qualitative methodology: A practical guide*, SAGE, Thousand Oaks, CA.

Swayne, LE 2008, *Strategic management of health care organizations*, Wiley, Hoboken, NJ.

Tabachnick, BG 2019, *Using multivariate statistics*, Pearson, New York, NY.

Takala, J 2009, 'Better conduct of clinical trials: The control group in critical care trials', *Critical Care Medicine*, vol. 37, pp. S80.

Taneja, S, Taneja, P & Gupta, R 2011, *Researches in corporate social responsibility: A review of shifting focus, paradigms, and methodologies*, Springer, Dordrecht.

Thomas, RM 2003, *Blending qualitative & quantitative research methods in theses and dissertations*, Corwin, Thousand Oaks, CA.

Travers, M 2001, *Qualitative research through case studies*, SAGE, Thousand Oaks, CA.

Trochim, WMK 2001, *Research methods knowledge base*, Atomic Dog Publishing, Cincinnati, OH.

UK Prospective Diabetes Study (UKPDS) Group 1998, 'Intensive blood-glucose control with sulphonylureas or insulin compared with conventional treatment and risk of complications in patients with type 2 diabetes (UKPDS 33)', *The Lancet*, vol. 352, pp. 837-853.

Van Maanen, J 1983, *Qualitative Methodology*. London, SAGE.

Wahyuni, D 2012, 'The research design maze: Understanding paradigms, cases, methods and methodologies', *Journal of Applied Management Accounting Research*, vol. 10, pp. 69-80.

Walshe, K & Smith, J 2006, *Healthcare management*, Open University Press, Maidenhead.

Weber, R 2004, 'The rhetoric of positivism versus interpretivism', *MIS Quarterly*, vol. 28, p. iii-xii.

Williams, M 2000, 'Interpretivism and generalisation', *Sociology*, vol. 34, pp. 209-224.

World Health Organisation 1998, *A health telematics policy in support of WHO's Health-for-All Strategy for global health development: Report of the WHO Group Consultation on Health Telematics, 11–16 December, Geneva, 1997*, WHO, Geneva.

World Health Organisation 2006, *Facts related to chronic diseases*, WHO, Geneva.

Yin, RK 2009, *Case study research: design and methods*, Sage Publications, Thousand Oaks, CA.

Yin, RK 2011, *Qualitative research from start to finish*, Guilford Press, New York, NY.

Zedeck, S 2013, *APA dictionary of statistics and research methods*, American Psychological Association, Washington, DC.

CHAPTER 6

Boston Consulting Group 2024, *Generative AI*. https://www.bcg.com/capabilities/artificial-intelligence/generative-ai

Fergusson, L, Baker, S & van der Lean, C 2024, *Work + Learning: A Knowledge Base of Theory and Practice in Australia*. Periods Publishing.

Forbes 2024, 'The 10 biggest business trends for 2024 everyone must be ready for now by Bernard Marr', *Forbes*. https://www.forbes.com/sites/bernardmarr/2023/09/25/the-10-biggest-business-trends-for-2024-everyone-must-be-ready-for-now/

Karpathy, A 2023, 'Intro to Large Language Models' http://www.youtube.com/watch?v=zjkBMFhNj_g&t=1s

Kanbach, DK, Heiduk, L, Blueher, G, Schreiter, M & Lahmann, A 2024, 'The

GenAI is out of the bottle: generative artificial intelligence from a business model innovation perspective', *Review of Managerial Science*, 18, pp. 1189–1220. https://doi.org/10.1007/s11846-023-00696-z

Mash, B 2014, 'African primary care research: participatory action research', *African Journal of Primary Health Care and Family Medicine*, 6(1), pp. 1–5.

McHugh, ML 2012, 'Interrater reliability: the kappa statistic', *Biochemia Medica*, 22(3), pp. 276–282.

McKinsey Group 2024, *McKinsey Technology Trends Outlook 2024*. https://www.mckinsey.com/capabilities/mckinsey-digital/our-insights/the-top-trends-in-tech#/

APPENDICES

APPENDIX 3A: DOCTORAL RESEARCH PROJECTS

METHOD	Candidate 27	Candidate 28	Candidate 29	Candidate 30	Candidate 31	Candidate 32	Candidate 33	Candidate 34	Candidate 35	Candidate 36
Interviews	2	1	2	2	1	1	2	2	2	2
Questionnaires	1	1	1	1	2	2	1	1	1	1
Surveys	1	1	1	1	1	2	1	1	1	1
Participant Observation	2	1	1	1	2	2	2	2	2	2
Researcher's Observation	2	2	2	2	2	2	2	2	2	2
Document Collection	2	2	1	2	1	2	1	2	2	1
Document Analysis	2	2	2	2	1	2	1	2	2	2
Triangulation	2	2	1	2	2	2	2	2	2	2
Content Analysis	2	2	1	1	2	2	1	1	2	1
Researcher's Reflection	1	1	2	2	2	1	1	2	2	1
Participants' Reflection	1	1	2	2	1	1	1	2	2	1
Statistics	1	1	1	1	1	1	1	1	1	1
Evaluation	1	1	1	1	1	1	1	1	2	1
Validation	1	1	1	1	1	1	1	1	2	1
Discussion	1	2	1	1	1	1	1	1	2	1
Tape/Video Recordings	1	1	1	1	2	1	1	1	1	1
Brainstorming	1	1	1	1	1	1	1	1	2	1
Meetings	1	1	1	1	1	1	1	2	2	2
Focus Group	2	1	2	2	1	1	1	2	1	1
Emancipatory Method	1	1	1	1	1	1	2	2	1	2
Chain of Evidence	2	2	2	2	2	2	2	2	2	2
Clustering	1	2	2	2	1	1	2	2	2	2
Researcher's Personal Diary	1	1	2	2	1	1	2	2	2	1
Participant's Personal Diary	1	1	1	1	1	1	1	1	1	1
Participant's Written Description	1	1	1	1	1	1	1	1	2	1

1 – No (Not included as a method); 2 – Yes (included as a method)

APPENDIX 3A: DOCTORAL RESEARCH PROJECTS

METHOD	Candidate 27	Candidate 28	Candidate 29	Candidate 30	Candidate 31	Candidate 32	Candidate 33	Candidate 34	Candidate 35	Candidate 36
Researcher's Visit To Relevant Sites	2	1	1	1	1	1	2	2	1	1
Participant's Visit To Relevant Sites	1	1	1	1	1	1	1	1	1	1
Reflexivity	2	2	2	2	2	2	1	2	1	2
Recording Non-Verbal Communication	2	2	2	1	1	1	1	1	2	1
Anal_OpnAxialSel	1	1	1	1	1	1	1	1	2	1
Assessment	1	1	1	1	2	1	1	1	2	1
Participant CndtIntrvws	1	1	1	1	1	1	1	1	2	1
Mind Mapp & FloCht	1	1	1	1	1	1	1	1	2	1
Root-Cause Analysis	1	1	1	1	1	1	1	1	2	1

1 – No (Not included as a method); 2 – Yes (included as a method)

APPENDIX 3B: MASTERS RESEARCH PROJECTS

METHOD	C1	C2	C3	C4	C5	C6	C7	C8	C9	C10	C11	C12	C13
Interviews	2	2	2	1	1	2	1	1	1	2	2	2	2
Questionnaires	2	1	2	1	1	2	1	1	2	2	1	2	2
Surveys	1	1	2	1	2	1	1	1	1	1	1	1	1
Participant Observation	1	1	1	1	2	1	1	1	2	2	2	1	2
Researcher's Observation	2	2	2	2	2	2	1	2	2	2	2	2	2
Document Collection	2	2	1	1	1	1	1	1	1	1	2	2	1
Document Analysis	2	1	1	1	2	2	1	1	1	1	2	2	1
Triangulation	2	2	2	2	2	1	1	2	2	2	1	1	2
Content Analysis	2	2	1	1	1	1	1	1	2	1	1	1	2
Researcher's Reflection	2	1	2	1	1	2	1	1	1	2	1	2	2
Participants' Reflection	2	1	2	1	1	2	1	1	1	2	1	2	2
Statistics	2	1	2	1	1	1	1	1	1	1	1	1	1
Evaluation	1	2	1	1	1	1	1	1	1	2	1	2	2
Validation	1	2	1	1	1	1	1	1	1	1	1	1	1
Discussion	1	2	2	1	1	1	1	1	2	1	1	1	2
Tape/Video Recordings	2	2	1	1	1	2	1	1	1	1	2	1	2
Brainstorming	1	2	1	1	1	2	1	1	2	1	1	1	2
Meetings	2	1	1	1	1	2	1	1	2	1	2	1	2
Focus Group	1	1	2	1	1	1	1	1	1	2	1	1	1
Emancipatory Method	1	2	2	2	2	2	2	2	2	2	2	1	2
Chain of Evidence	1	1	1	1	1	1	1	1	1	1	1	1	1
Clustering	1	1	1	1	1	1	1	1	1	1	1	1	1
Researcher's Personal Diary	2	2	1	1	2	2	1	1	1	1	1	1	2
Participant's Personal Diary	2	1	1	1	1	2	1	2	2	2	1	1	2
Participant's Written Description	2	1	2	1	1	1	1	1	2	1	1	1	2

1 – No (Not included as a method); 2 – Yes (included as a method)

C = CANDIDATE

APPENDIX 3B: MASTERS RESEARCH PROJECTS

METHOD	C1	C2	C3	C4	C5	C6	C7	C8	C9	C10	C11	C12	C13
Researcher's Visit To Relevant Sites	1	1	1	1	1	1	1	1	1	1	1	1	2
Participant's Visit To Relevant Sites	2	1	1	1	1	1	1	1	1	1	1	1	1
Reflexivity	1	1	1	1	2	1	1	1	1	1	1	1	2
Recording Non-Verbal Communication	1	1	1	1	1	2	1	1	1	1	1	1	2
Anal_OpnAxialSel	1	1	1	1	1	1	1	1	1	1	1	1	1
Assessment	1	1	1	1	1	1	1	1	1	1	1	1	1
Participant Cndtintrvws	1	1	1	1	1	1	1	1	1	1	1	1	2
Mind Mapp & FloCht	1	1	1	1	1	1	1	1	1	1	1	1	1
Root-Cause Analysis	1	1	1	1	1	1	1	1	1	1	1	1	1

1 – No (Not included as a method); 2 – Yes (included as a method)

C = CANDIDATE

APPENDIX 3B: MASTERS RESEARCH PROJECTS

METHOD	C14	C15	C16	C17	C18	C19	C20	C21	C22	C23	C24	C25	C26
Interviews	2	2	2	2	1	1	1	1	1	1	1	1	1
Questionnaires	1	2	1	1	1	1	1	1	2	1	1	1	1
Surveys	1	1	1	1	1	2	2	1	1	2	2	1	1
Participant Observation	2	2	1	1	1	1	2	2	1	2	2	1	2
Researcher's Observation	2	2	2	2	1	2	2	2	2	2	2	2	2
Document Collection	2	1	1	1	1	2	2	2	1	1	1	1	1
Document Analysis	1	1	1	1	2	2	1	2	1	1	2	1	2
Triangulation	2	2	2	1	1	2	1	2	2	2	2	2	2
Content Analysis	2	1	1	2	1	1	1	1	1	1	1	1	1
Researcher's Reflection	1	1	1	1	2	2	2	2	2	2	2	2	2
Participants' Reflection	1	1	1	1	2	2	2	1	1	2	2	2	2
Statistics	1	1	1	1	1	1	1	1	1	1	1	1	1
Evaluation	1	2	1	1	1	1	2	2	2	1	2	2	2
Validation	1	2	1	1	1	1	1	2	2	1	2	2	2
Discussion	2	1	1	1	1	1	1	2	1	1	1	1	1
Tape/Video Recordings	2	1	1	1	1	1	1	1	2	1	1	1	1
Brainstorming	1	1	1	1	1	1	1	1	1	1	1	1	1
Meetings	1	1	2	1	1	1	1	2	1	1	1	1	1
Focus Group	1	1	1	1	1	2	1	2	1	2	2	2	2
Emancipatory Method	2	1	2	2	1	1	2	2	2	1	2	1	2
Chain of Evidence	1	1	1	1	1	2	1	2	2	2	2	2	2
Clustering	2	1	1	1	1	1	1	1	2	2	2	2	2
Researcher's Personal Diary	2	2	1	1	1	1	2	2	2	1	2	1	2
Participant's Personal Diary	2	2	1	1	1	1	1	1	1	1	2	1	1
Participant's Written Description	1	1	1	1	1	1	1	2	1	1	1	1	1

*1 – No (Not included as a method); 2 – Yes (included as a method)

C = CANDIDATE

APPENDIX 3B: MASTERS RESEARCH PROJECTS

METHOD	C14	C15	C16	C17	C18	C19	C20	C21	C22	C23	C24	C25	C26
Researcher's Visit To Relevant Sites	1	1	1	1	1	1	1	1	1	1	1	1	1
Participant's Visit To Relevant Sites	1	1	1	1	1	1	1	1	1	1	1	1	1
Reflexivity	1	1	1	1	1	1	1	2	2	1	2	1	1
Recording Non-Verbal Communication	1	1	1	1	1	1	1	2	1	1	1	1	2
Anal_OpnAxialSel	1	1	1	1	1	1	1	1	1	1	1	1	1
Assessment	1	1	1	1	1	1	1	1	1	1	1	1	1
Participant CndtIntrvws	1	1	1	1	1	1	1	1	1	1	1	1	1
Mind Mapp & FloCht	1	1	1	1	1	1	1	1	1	1	1	1	1
Root-Cause Analysis	1	1	1	1	1	1	1	1	1	1	1	1	1

1 – No (Not included as a method); 2 – Yes (included as a method)

C = CANDIDATE

APPENDIX 3C KEY RESEARCH TERMS

The following table provides definitions of key words used in describing research processes. The definitions will help inform consistent interpretation of key terms.

KEY RESEARCH TERMS	DEFINITIONS
Brainstorming	'..using the brain to storm a creative solution for a problem. Brainstorming is a method of generating ideas and solving problems' (Gogus 2012).
Case Study	..a research approach that is used to generate an in-depth, multi-faceted understanding of a complex issue in its real-life context. It is an established research design that is used extensively in a wide variety of disciplines, particularly in the social sciences. A case study can be defined in a variety of ways … the central tenet being the need to explore an event or phenomenon in depth and in its natural context. (Crowe et al 2011, p.1).
Chain of Evidence	…researchers need to show how the evidence at one stage of data collection, analysis, interpretation, and reporting is associated with the evidence at other stages. (Moss 2020).
Clustering	….cluster analysis is an exploratory tool to support the identification of associations within qualitative data. While not appropriate for all qualitative projects, cluster analysis can be helpful in identifying patterns where numerous cases are studied. (Macia 2015, p.1083).

KEY RESEARCH TERMS	DEFINITIONS
Discussion	…'a critical conversation about a particular topic, or perhaps a range of topics, conducted in a group of a size that allows participation by all members.'
Document Analysis	a systematic procedure for reviewing or evaluating documents— both printed and electronic (computer-based and Internet-transmitted) material. Like other analytical methods in qualitative research, document analysis requires that data be examined and interpreted in order to elicit meaning, gain understanding, and develop empirical knowledge (Corbin & Strauss, 2008; see also Rapley, 2007, cited in Bowen 2009, p. 27).
Document collection	'Collection of documents- in particular secondary sources of data. (also see operationalisation of document analysis)' (Taddeo, 2024).
Emancipatory	…it is collaborative, critical and self-critical inquiry by practitioners (e.g., teachers, managers) into a major problem or issue or concern in their own practice. They own the problem and feel responsible and accountable for solving it through teamwork and through following a cyclical process of: 1. Strategic planning; 2. Action i.e., implementing the plan; 3. Observation, evaluation and self-evaluation; 4. Critical and self-critical reflection on the results of points 1-3 making decisions for the next cycle of action research, i.e., revising the plan, followed by action, observation and reflection, etc. (Zuber-Skerritt 2003, p2).

KEY RESEARCH TERMS	DEFINITIONS
Evaluation	...the use of scientific principles and methods to assess the influence or effectiveness of social interventions and programs, including those related to mental health, education, and safety (e.g., crime prevention, automobile accident prevention). Evaluation research is thus a type of applied research. (Zedeck 2014, p118).
Focus Group	...a small set of people, typically 8 to 12 in number, who share common characteristics (e.g., working parents with 5- to 8-year-old children) that are relevant to the research question and who are selected to discuss a topic of which they have personal experience (e.g., their children's reading abilities and school performance). A leader conducts the discussion and keeps it on target while also encouraging free flowing, open-ended debate. Originally used in marketing to determine consumer response to particular products, focus groups are now used for determining typical reactions, adaptations, and solutions to any number of issues, events, or topics and are associated particularly with qualitative research. (Zedeck 2014, p140).

KEY RESEARCH TERMS	DEFINITIONS
Interpretivism	'According to the interpretivism paradigm, reality is not predefined but is the product of social constructions.' (Vitale, 2023). According to the interpretive philosophy, reality and human knowledge are social products, and, therefore, they are impossible to understand apart from the social actors (including researchers) who build and give meaning to that reality. (Orlikowski & Baroudi 1991, cited in Vitale 2023, p79). 'Ontologically speaking, in interpretivism, reality exists, but it is not objectively predetermined; rather it turns out to be the product of social constructions'. (Husserl 1965, cited in Vitale 2023).
Interview	...a directed conversation in which a researcher, therapist, clinician, employer, or the like (the interviewer) intends to elicit specific information from an individual (the interviewee) for purposes of research, diagnosis, treatment, or employment. Conducted face to face or by telephone, interviews may be either standardized, including set questions, or open ended, varying with material introduced in responses by the interviewee. Their reliability is of particular concern, and interviewers must be careful to minimize or eliminate personal judgment and biases in evaluating responses. (Zedeck 2014, p. 181).

KEY RESEARCH TERMS	DEFINITIONS
Meetings	….represent a mechanism of knowledge creation and transformation. Meetings are a fundamental part of a group decision-making process. Meetings become more complex, and new technologies expanded them from a face-to-face situation to an activity distributed in space and time. (Motta et al 2022, p.82).
Methodology	The science of method or orderly arrangement; specifically, the branch of logic concerned with the application of the principles of reasoning to scientific and philosophical inquiry. 2. the system of methods, principles, and rules of procedure used within a particular discipline. For example, in research and experimental design the term refers to the techniques used to collect information, and in statistics it refers to the procedures used to analyze such data. (Zedeck 2014, p.214).
Mixed methods research	…a study that combines aspects of both qualitative research and quantitative research so as to more fully understand the phenomenon of interest. For example, a researcher studying disease could conduct a focus group with a set of individuals who would share their experiences in dealing with the disease, and then supplement those qualitative findings by surveying a different set of individuals to obtain quantitative knowledge or risk factors for the disease. (Zedeck 2014, p.218).

KEY RESEARCH TERMS	DEFINITIONS
Naturalistic Setting	...'occurred in naturalistic settings, such as the workplace'. (see also operationalisation of the term Case Study) (Taddeo, 2024).
Open, Axial, Selective Coding	Aligned to grounded theory, open, axial and selective coding is a three step process of 1) open coding: identifying distinct initial themes in an organised systematic approach to enable categorisation of themes and concepts. 2) axial coding: where themes are further refined, aligned, integrated and categorised to enable core codes/themes, and the relationships between the codes/themes, to be identified 3) selective coding which occurs at a macro/overarching/high level to bring together categories/relationships identified in the previous steps to enable construction/ generation of the core/primary meaning or story from the data. (Simmons 2017; Williams & Moser 2019).
Paradigm	1. a model, pattern, or representative example, as of the functions and interrelationships of a process, a behavior under study, or the like.

2. an experimental design or plan of the various steps of an experiment.

3. a set of assumptions, attitudes, concepts, values, procedures, and techniques that constitutes a generally accepted theoretical framework within, or a general perspective of, discipline. (Zedeck 2014, p.251). |

KEY RESEARCH TERMS	DEFINITIONS
Participant's Observations	'Participants observing other participants'. (Also see operationalisation of Researcher Observations). (Taddeo, 2024).
Personal Diary	diary method a technique for compiling detailed data about an individual who is being observed or studied by having the individual record his or her daily behaviour and activities. Also called diary survey. (Zedeck 2014, p.92).
Positivism	...a family of philosophical positions holding that all meaningful propositions must be reducible to sensory experience and observation, and thus that all genuine knowledge is to be built on strict adherence to empirical methods of verification. Its effect is to establish science and the scientific method as the model for all forms of valid inquiry and to dismiss the truth claims of religion, metaphysics, and speculative philosophy. (Zedeck 2014, p.265).
Pragmatism	...a philosophical position holding that the truth value of a proposition or a theory is to be found in its practical consequences...Arguably, all forms of pragmatism. tend toward relativism, because they can provide no absolute grounds- only empirical grounds- for determining truth and no basis for judging whether the consequences in question are to be considered good or bad. (Zedeck 2014, p.268).

KEY RESEARCH TERMS	DEFINITIONS
Primary data source	1. Information cited in a study that was gathered directly by the researcher, from his or her own experiments or from first-hand observation. 2. Original experimental or observational data, that is, raw data. (Zedeck 2014, p.271).
Qualitative research	...a method of research that produces descriptive (non-numerical) data, such as observations of behaviour or personal accounts of experiences. The goal of gathering this qualitative data is to examine how individuals can perceive the world from different vantage points. A variety of techniques are subsumed under qualitative research, including content analysis of narratives, in-depth interviews, focus groups, participant observation, and case studies, often conducted in naturalistic settings. Also called qualitative design; qualitative inquiry; qualitative method; qualitative study. (Zedeck 2014, p.283).
Quantitative research	...a method of research that relies on measuring variables using a numerical system, analyzing these measurements using any of a variety of statistical models and reporting relationships and associations among the studied variables. For example, these variables may be test scores or measurements of reaction time. (Zedeck 2014, pp.284-285).

KEY RESEARCH TERMS	DEFINITIONS
Questionnaire	...a set of questions or other prompts used to obtain information from a respondent about a topic of interest, such as background characteristics, attitudes, behaviors, personality, ability, or other attributes. A questionnaire may be administered with pen and paper, in a face-to-face interview, or via interaction between the respondent and a computer or website. (Zedeck 2014, pp.286-287).
Reflection	Where the researcher is reflecting on any aspect of the process/research. Where the researcher is reflecting on any aspect of the process/research. Self-reflection or introspection means self-observation and report of one's thoughts, desires, and feelings. It is a conscious mental process relying on thinking, reasoning, and examining one's own thoughts, feelings, and, ideas. It is contrasted with extrospection, the observation of things external to one's self. (Gläser-Zikuda 2012, p.3012).
Reflexivity	...2. In qualitative research, the self-referential quality of a study in which the researcher reflects on the assumptions behind the study and especially the influence of his or her own motives, history, and biases on its conduct. (Zedeck 2014, p.300).

KEY RESEARCH TERMS	DEFINITIONS
Researcher/ participant Observations	...a quasi-experimental research method in which a trained investigator studies a preexisting group by entering it as a member, while avoiding a conspicuous role that would alter the group processes and bias the data. The researcher's role may be known or unknown to the other members of the group. Cultural anthropologists become participant observers when they enter the life of a given culture to study its structure and processes. A downside to the approach is that the researcher can become enmeshed with the group to the extent that he or she is no longer able to document it in an unbiased way. Also called participative research; participatory research. (Zedeck 2014, p.254).
Secondary data source	....information cited in a study that was not gathered directly by the current investigator but rather was obtained from an earlier study or source. The data may be archived or may be accessed through contact with the original researcher. When consulting or analysing this information, the investigator should be sensitive to the original research questions and the conditions under which the observations were gathered. (Zedeck 2014, p.329).

KEY RESEARCH TERMS	DEFINITIONS
Statistics	1. a number measuring some characteristics, construct, variable, or other item of interest… 2. Any function of the observations in a sample that may be used to estimate the unknown corresponding value in the population. Examples include measures of central tendency (e.g., the mean, median, mode), measures of dispersion (e.g., standard deviation, variance), and distributional attributes (e.g., skewness, kurtosis). (Zedeck 2014, p.353).
Survey	….a study in which a group of participants is selected from a population and some selected data about or opinions of those participants are collected, measured, and analyzed. Information typically is gathered by interview or self-report questionnaire, and the results thus obtained may then be extrapolated to the whole population. (Zedeck 2014, p.365).
Triangulation (Methodological)	The use of multiple quantitative and qualitative procedures to collect data so as to generate converging evidence on the topic of study. For example, a researcher studying alcohol consumption might employ methodological triangulation by measuring participants' blood alcohol levels, collecting self-reports on quantity of alcohol consumed, and obtaining input from peers on quantity of alcohol consumed. (Zedeck 2014, p.214).
Validation	…'the process of establishing the truth or logical cogency of something. An example is determining the accuracy of a research instrument in measuring what it is designed to measure'. (Zedeck 2014).

APPENDICES

APPENDIX 4:

As stated in chapter 4 of this book, this appendix sets out the research philosophy and research paradigm which were contained in the methodology chapter of the doctoral thesis of Lisa Mohammed.

RESEARCH PHILOSOPHY

Burns (1997) provides a succinct description of research as a systematic investigation utilising the collection, analysis and interpretation of data. Seale (1999) too emphasises that research allows researchers to have a more comprehensive understanding of the phenomenon under study. Mertens (2005, p. 2) suggests that the intent of this process is to "understand, describe, predict or control an educational or psychological phenomenon or to empower individuals in such contexts." Additionally, the primary intent of research, as noted by Bainbridge et al. (2015, p. 3), is the generation of new knowledge.

A key aspect of research is a clarification of the philosophy which primarily allows researchers to open their minds to many possibilities, resulting in confidence that the appropriate methodology is being used (Holden & Lynch 2004). The determination by researchers of 'what to research' will have an impact on the methodology to be used. The improper matching of the methodology to the research problem may compromise the quality and accuracy of the results, which will ultimately reflect negatively on the researcher's professionalism. Therefore, once the researchers have established their philosophical position they will then be able to match the methodology to philosophy and the research problem (Holden & Lynch 2004; Myers 1997).

Research Paradigms

Perry (2013, p. 103) points to four major categories of research paradigms namely, positivism, critical theory, constructivism and realism. Iofrida et al (2014) and Solomonidou (2015), highlight quantitative research approaches as being associated with a positivist-oriented paradigm, and qualitative research approaches associated with an interpretivist-oriented paradigm. Table 4A represents a comparison of these two paradigms. Additionally, Table 4B shows the relationship between the research paradigm, methods and tools (Mackenzie & Knipe 2006).

Table 4A – Comparison between Positivist-oriented and Interpretivist-oriented Paradigms

	Positivism-oriented		Interpretivism-oriented	
	Positivism	Post-positivism	Interpretivism	Constructivism
Ontology: What is reality?	Naïve realism Objective reality.	Critical realism Reality is imperfectly apprehendable.	Subject and object are dependent. The real essence of the object cannot be known. Reality is constructed.	
Epistemology: How do you know?	Dualism researcher research. Replicable findings are "true". Reality can be explained.	Dualism is not possible. Replicated findings are "probably" true. Impossible to fully explain reality.	Knowledge is interpreted Reality can be understood.	Knowledge is constructed Reality can be constructed.
Methodologies: How do we find it out?	Experimental, deductive Mainly quantitative Relationship cause-effect. Statistical analysis.	Experimental. Mainly quantitative methods, manipulative. Scientific Community plays an important role of validation. Statistical analysis Probability sampling.	Interpretation. Mainly qualitative methods. Purposive and multipurpose sampling.	Mainly qualitative methods Purposive and multipurpose sampling. Stakeholders involvement.
Goodness or quality criteria	Rigorous data production through scientific method.	Statistical confidence level and objectivity in data produced.	Intersubjective agreement and reasoning reached through dialogue, shared conversation and construction.	

Source: Iofrida et al. 2014, p. 45.

Table 4B – Relationship between paradigms, methods and tools

Paradigm	Methods (primarily)	Data collection tools (examples)
Positivist/Postpositivist	Quantitative. "Although quantitative methods can be used within this paradigm, quantitative methods tend to be predominant…"	Experiments Quasi-experiments Tests Scales
Interpretivist/ Constructivist	Qualitative methods predominate although quantitative methods may also be utilised.	Interviews Observations Document reviews Visual data analysis
Transformative	Qualitative methods with quantitative and mixed methods. Contextual and historical factors described, especially as they relate to oppression.	Diverse range of tools - particular need to avoid discrimination e.g. sexism, racism and homophobia.
Pragmatic	Qualitative and/or quantitative methods may be employed. Methods are matched to the specific questions and purpose of the research.	May include tools from both positivist and interpretivist paradigms e.g. interviews, observations and testing and experiments.

Source: Mackenzie and Knipe 2006, p. 199.

Positivism

One of the earliest proponents of positivism was the social philosopher August Comte. His view was that scientific methods could be applied to social phenomena as a prediction and realisation of causal variables (Danuwar 2014). The focus of positivism is on the effort to verify a priori hypotheses that are usually stated in a quantitative proposition (Orlikowski & Baroudi 1991; Guba & Lincoln 1994; McGrath & Johnson 2003). It analyses behaviour and makes considerations based on observations by looking at the actions associated with human experiences (Winkler 2016). Ponterotto (2005) also noted that the primary goal of a positivist inquiry is to derive an explanation that eventually leads to a prediction and the control of phenomena.

Other authors such as Myers (1997) and Amaratunga et al. (2002) confirm this goal of positivist inquiry. In order to achieve this goal, positivists rely on experiments where there is a quantifiable measure of variables and similar methods through observations. This translates into a research paradigm that is most commonly aligned with quantitative methods of research, inclusive of data collection and analysis bound by strict rules of logic (Amaratunga et al. 2002; Mackenzie & Knipe 2006; Danuwar 2014; Shahzad 2016).

Interpretivism
Unlike the belief in positivism that all things are measurable, interpretivism operates on the assumption "that we do not have direct relationship with a clearly definable, objective reality and that there is always a degree of interpretation due to the limitations of our senses" (Hepworth 2016, p.4). A comparison and summary of positivism and interpretivism principle research paradigms are presented in the following Table 4C (Russell 2014, p. 2) based on data sourced from Cleaver, Lintern and McLinden 2014.

Table 4C – Summary and comparison of positivism and interpretivism principle research paradigms

Question	Positivism	Interpretivism
How is knowledge defined and created?	Knowledge is truth as defined by testable hypotheses. It is not created, only discovered or identified. The objective researcher is key to this process and occupies an 'expert' position in relation to the subject of the research.	The construction of knowledge is a social process involving all who are involved in the research process. Knowledge is constructed from multiple perspective and subjective biases are expected, recognised and identified.
What role do theory, research questions or hypotheses play in the research process?	Theories are models that have been constructed out of a series of tested hypotheses. They are testable and can be used to make predictions and form the basis through which research design is predetermined. They are 'true' as long as the consensus of research supports them and will be disproved when a 'better' theory or model comes along.	Theories are ever developing 'understandings' of the world around us. They form an overarching explanatory framework for the social world and research questions are contextualised by these frameworks. Theories are not disproved; rather they emerge and develop from a dialogue between research and theory.

Table 4C – (Continued)

Question	Positivism	Interpretivism
What is the role and status of the 'researcher' and the 'researched?'	The researcher is an objective observer that ideally has no influence over the researched. They design the experiment, control all of the variables bar the one of interest and eliminate confounding factors so as to ensure only the object of interest can influence the outcomes. That way the results and outcomes can be directly attributed to the variable factor and its role in the system can be described.	The researcher recognises the multiple perceptive that come to play on any given social situation and recognises how they (and their respondents) form an artificially created research setting and may all be affected by this. Issues related to status and power are all deemed to be important in this process. Research subjects are given equal status in co-constructing understanding, knowledge and outcomes.
What actually exists or can be said to exist; what is reality?	Reality is objective, rational and exists independent of observation or form the perspective of the observer. It is 'out there' waiting to be discovered and observed.	Reality is socially and culturally constructed; it has many dimensions and its particular form will depend on the frame of reference within which it is being observed.

Table 4C – (Continued)

Question	Positivism	Interpretivism
What constitutes validity, reliability and credibility?	A valid theory must have no other plausible, simpler explanation and the chain of cause and effect should have no gaps or assumptions but be made of clear, logical, testable steps. Validity also refers to the means of measurement, whether they are accurate and whether they are measuring what they are intended to measure. A reliable theory must always give the same result under the same conditions. The replicability of results or observations is key and central to this process is the method of data collection and the objectivity of the researcher.	Validity involves the recognition that there is confidence in the accuracy of the data, due to the methods of gathering and analysis data. Reliability comes not from a predictability of result through replication, but from a recognition and awareness of the multiple sources and ways of creating knowledge in any given situation. Although reliability and validity are treated separately in positivism, these terms are not viewed separately in interpretivism. Instead, terminology that encompasses both, such as credibility, transferability and trustworthiness are often used.
How can we communicate our findings?	Research dissemination and communication techniques are rigorous and objective and present, using techniques which have been developed to ensure objectivity and a reliable representation of reality.	Research dissemination and communication techniques rely on the conventions and linguistic and explanatory frameworks available. As such, we are unlikely to represent 'reality' as it happened, but only our linguistic or written interpretation of it, often within particular predefined parameters.

Source: Russell 2014, p. 2.

Quantitative and Qualitative Research Methods

There has been a long-standing epistemological debate amongst philosophers of science and methodologists as to the best way to conduct research (Amaratunga et al. 2002; Basri 2014). Despite the fact that research methods can be classified in various ways, the division into quantitative and qualitative research methods remains one of the most common distinctions (Myers, 1997). Significant differences between them can be seen (Basri 2014). Qualitative research concentrates on words and observations with the intent on describing people in natural situations. It looks into human experiences at a deeper level with the aim of generating theoretically richer observations.

Some commonly used qualitative methods include participant observation, direct observation, unstructured interviews, semi-structured interviews, convergent interviews, focus groups among others. However, quantitative research is centred on the strong emphasis upon measurement that emphasises the use of numbers to represent opinions and concepts. It also emphasises findings that are generalised yet precise and objective (Amaratunga et al. 2002; Rubin & Babbie 2016).

Quantitative and qualitative research paradigms differ in various aspects including their epistemological foundations, and form two distinct clusters of research strategy (Bryman & Bell 2007; Donnellan, Murray & Holland 2014). Quantification in data collection and analysis is associated with quantitative research as compared to qualitative research that is usually associated with words in collection and analysis of data rather than quantification. Pietkiewicz and Smith (2014) highlighted that in quantitative research the phenomenon is reduced to numerical values so that it can be statistically analysed. In contrast, qualitative research looks at the meaning and experience of the event, as well as what meaning is attached to the phenomena from data collected in a naturalistic setting. The interpretation of both the participants and researcher, are taken into consideration during the analysis of data.

The quantitative paradigm is principally deductive, with epistemological and ontological orientations in positivism and objectivism respectively. The qualitative paradigm on the other hand is principally inductive, with epistemological and ontological orientations in interpretivism and objectivism constructionism respectively (Bryman & Bell 2007). Table 4D, adapted from Antwi and Hamza (2015) and Holloway and Galvin (2016), presents the differences between the quantitative and qualitative research approaches.

Table 4D – Differences between Qualitative and Quantitative Research

	Qualitative	Quantitative
Paradigm	• Interpretivism/Idealism	• Positivism/Realism
Aim	• Exploration, understanding and description of participants' experience and life world • Discovery • Generation of theory from data	• Search for causal explanations and precise prediction • Testing hypothesis, prediction, control, findings stated with a degree of statistical certainty
Research Purpose	• Subjective description • Empathetic understanding • Exploration	• Numerical Description • Causal explanation • Prediction
Approach	• Initially broadly focused • Process oriented • Context-bound, mostly natural setting • Getting close up to the topic under investigation and immersion in data	• Narrow focus • Outcome oriented • Context-stripped, extraneous variables controlled or removed altogether • Context-free, often in settings
Research Methods	• Ethnographies • Case studies • Narrative research • Interviews • Focus group discussion • Observations • Field notes • Recordings and filmings	• Empirical examination • Measurement • Hypothesis testing • Randomisation • Blinding • Structured protocols • Questionnaires

Table 4D – (Continued)

	Qualitative	Quantitative
Sampling	• Participants, informants • Purposive and theoretical sampling • Flexible sampling that can develop during the research as led by the data	• Respondents, participants (the term 'subjects' is now discouraged in the social sciences) • Population defined in advance • Controlled sampling methods • Randomised sampling • Sample frame fixed before the research starts
Data Collection	• In-depth non-standardised interviews • Semi-structured interviews • Participant observation/fieldwork • Discovery-oriented immersion • Documents, diaries, photographs, videos	• Scales, close-ended questionnaires, standardised interviews, outcome measures • Highly structured observation using predeveloped tools • Non-participant observation • Secondary data and documents • Randomised controlled trials • Surveys
Analysis	• Thematic or constant comparative analysis, latent content analysis ethnographic, narrative analysis, phenomenological meaning units, etc.	• Descriptive and inferential statistical analysis
Outcome	• A description, story, ethnography, a theory	• Measurable and testable results with prediction
Results	• Particularistic findings • Provision of insider view points	• Generalisable findings
Final report	• Informal narrative report	• Formal statistical report with correlations, comparisons of means and/or reporting of findings with significant statistical significance

Table 4D – (Continued)

	Qualitative	Quantitative
Relationships	• Direct involvement of researcher • Researcher relationship: close	• Limited involvement of researcher with participant • Researcher relationship: distant (controlled standardised conditions)
Rigour	• Trustworthiness, authenticity • Also validity • Typicality and transferability • Validity	• Internal/external validity, reliability • Generalisability • Replicability

Source: Antwi and Hamza 2015, p. 222 and Holloway and Galvin 2016, p. 11.

In an attempt to answer the 'why' and 'how' questions in qualitative research, the researcher strives to develop an in-depth understanding of human behaviour and why people behave in the manner that they do (Lester, Inman & Bishop 2014). This often is characterised by a cyclical approach to analysis, involving continual observation and interpretation of data by the researcher, who then makes a decision as to how to proceed based on what has been already discovered (Kemparaj & Chavan 2013).

Much of the choice of research method is dictated by the nature of the research question. Yin (2018) highlighted the significance of the research question, whether in the form of 'how', 'why' or 'what', and how it helps to determine the research method to adopt. For example, in terms of the case study method, a descriptive case study deals with 'how' questions and an explanatory case study deals with 'why' questions.

Research Paradigm in the Current Study

The selection of the methodology for this study is based on the site of the research and the dynamic nature of the implementation of the WAL-OHSMS in a petroleum based organisation and more specifically, a Well Workover company in T&T. Additionally, the type of data that is needed is taken into consideration. The following table highlights the main components of qualitative research in relation to the current study, as justification for the use of a qualitative approach.

Table 4E – Summary of the components of Qualitative Research as it relates to the current study

	Qualitative	Quantitative
Paradigm	• Interpretivism/Idealism	This study seeks to interpret the phenomena being studied and establish understandings
Aim	• Exploration, understanding and description of participants' experience and life world • Discovery • Generation of theory from data	The current study is exploratory in nature, where the participants' experiences are used as a source of data. Through the process there is discovery and generation of the WAL-OHSMS
Research Purpose	• Subjective description • Empathetic understanding • Exploration	Investigation of the development and implementation of an improved OHSMS (WAL-OHSMS) for a Well Workover company in T&T
Approach	• Initially broadly focused • Process oriented • Context-bound, mostly natural setting • Getting close up to the topic under investigation and immersion in data	The researcher functions in the role of observer, participant and facilitator. Although the researcher is an outsider to the research site, she is involved with the participants in their natural setting. The study is broadly focussed at the inception to determine what is required for the WAL-OHSMS and eventually, based on the data, the key components are identified.
Research Methods	• Ethnographies • Case studies • Narrative research • Interviews • Focus group discussion • Observations • Field notes • Recordings and filmings	This study takes the form of a case study, utilizing the AR method and AL process.

Table 4E – (Continued)

	Qualitative	Quantitative
Sampling	• Participants, informants • Purposive and theoretical sampling • Flexible sampling that can develop during the research as led by the data	Sampling in this study is driven by the data that emerges and the interaction with the participants who possess intimate knowledge of the operations and challenges at the research site.
Data Collection	• In-depth non-standardised interviews • Semi-structured interviews • Participant observation/ fieldwork • Discovery-oriented immersion • Documents, diaries, photographs, videos	Data collection takes many forms in this study, including: • In-depth interviews • Semi-structured interviews • Participant observation/ fieldwork • Discovery-oriented immersion • Documents, photographs, reports • Interviews • Focus group discussion • Observations • Field notes • Journals • Recordings
Analysis	• Thematic or constant comparative analysis, latent content analysis ethnographic, narrative analysis, phenomenological meaning units, etc.	All interactions and data are recorded to develop the chain of evidence. Clustering of data is also used which allows for the categorisation of data and analysis.
Outcome	• A description, story, ethnography, a theory	The development and implementation of a WAL-OHSMS for a Well Workover company in the oil industry in T&T. Further, hypotheses and suggestions for further studies will be developed.
Results	• Particularistic findings • Provision of insider view points	Specific results critical to the WAL-OHSMS both during development, implementation and evaluation, will be identified.

Table 4E – (Continued)

	Qualitative	Quantitative
Final report	• Informal narrative report	A narrative report giving account of the entire study.
Relationships	• Direct involvement of researcher • Researcher relationship: close	The researcher, participants and the management of the research site form close relationships and will be involved throughout the study.
Rigour	• Trustworthiness, authenticity • Validity • Typicality and transferability	Validation in this study is conducted using triangulation where data from the AR group, the Validation Committee and the researcher's reflections are used. Additionally, the researcher is sensitive to the fact that she is not to impose her will on the participants and/or influence the participants in any way to manipulate the outcome of the study.

Source: adapted from Antwi and Hamza 2015, p. 222 and Holloway and Galvin 2016, p. 11

In summary, this study is exploratory in nature to determine the impact of a WAL approach to the development and implementation of a WAL-OHSMS in a Well Workover company in the petroleum industry.

Since there is also the element of unknown as the research proceeds, qualitative research provides the advantage of flexibility (Ritchie et al. 2013, pp. 74-75) to respond to the subjects and processes of inquiry. The data that emerges then is used in the design and implementation of the WAL-OHSMS.

APPENDICES

APPENDIX 5A:

As stated in chapter 5 of this book, this Appendix sets out the research paradigm which was contained in the methodology chapter of the doctoral thesis of Paul Jurman.

RESEARCH PARADIGM

Having set the research context by examining its purpose, the main research question, and the corollary research questions to be answered, it is useful to examine the research paradigm to be used by the research project. The term 'paradigm' was first defined by Kuhn (1962, pp. viii) as "universally recognized scientific achievements that for a time provide model problems and solutions to a community of practitioners". Building on this definition, Collis and Hussey (2013 pp. 43) define a research paradigm as "a framework that guides how research should be conducted, based on people's philosophies and their assumptions about the world and the nature of knowledge". It is through the utilisation of a research paradigm that a researcher attempts to increase understanding of the phenomena to be studied. The application of a specific research paradigm is critical to ensure an accurate ontological (how reality is perceived) view of the phenomena and the underlying epistemological (knowledge) development of the ontological view (Creswell 2007, pp. 16-19; Wahyuni 2012 pp. 70-71, Weber 2004).

Traditional research paradigms can be viewed as a continuum, with the paradigms of positivism and interpretivism at opposing ends (Morgan & Smircich 1980). Positivism is based on logic and objectivity (Creswell 2009), while interpretivism is based on interpretation and subjectivity (Smith 1983; Creswell 2009).

Positivism

Positivism has its origin in the natural sciences. It contains a number of key characteristics as defined by Kleinberg-Levin (1988), Travers (2001), Babbie (2004), Hughes (1997) and Myers (1997). It has a philosophical basis in realism and sees social reality as being static, able to be objectively analysed and unaffected by the act of investigation (Creswell 2009). Positivism is based on deductive theorising to predict or explain social phenomena. This deductive theorising finds its basis in empirical research utilising logical or mathematical proof allowing for the explanation, anticipation, prediction and therefore control of the phenomena. As a result, positivism has historically been associated with quantitative research methods, in particular the statistical analysis of quantitative data (Collis & Hussey 2013, pp. 52).

Interpretivism

Interpretivism has its origin in the social sciences (Smith 1983) and has its philosophical basis in hermeneutics and phenomenology (Boland 1985). It is based on the principle that it is impossible to separate individuals from the social context in which they exist. This principle extends to the researcher, who is not independent of the research (as they bring their own values). It also holds that the very impact of investigating a phenomenon has an effect on it (Smith 1983; Creswell 2009). Furthermore, it asserts that social reality is highly subjective as it is based on perceptions. As a result, there exist multiple realities (Robson 2011) which, in turn, make measurement difficult when using traditional positivist techniques. Such a view is supported by Bryman and Bell (2015 pp. 17), who state:

> *The subject matter of the social sciences – people and their institutions – is fundamentally different from that of the natural sciences. The study of the social world therefore requires a different logic of research procedure.*

To address this, the interpretivist approach focuses on the collection of qualitative research data and its interpretation via qualitative methods of analysis. Such techniques allow the researcher to gain real-world understanding by studying social behaviours in the context in which they occur. This approach is summarised well by Van Maanen (1983, p. 9) in stating that interpretivists utilise techniques which 'describe, translate and otherwise come to terms with the meaning, not the frequency of certain more or less naturally occurring phenomena in the social world'. As a result, interpretivist research seeks to understand phenomena through the meanings assigned by study participants (Myers 1997). In this way, some authors (Collis & Hussey 2013; Smith 1983; Creswell 2009; Williams 2000) argue that the approach of interpretivism addressed many of the shortcomings of positivism, including:

- Positivism seeks to synthesise complex phenomena down to a single measure, increasing the likelihood of misleading results.
- Positivism ignores the issue of researcher bias and its impact.

- Positivism requires a highly structured design, which increases the risk of constraining results or excluding other relevant findings.
- Positivism ignores the impact of social contexts.

Principal Research Paradigms

There are six principal research paradigms: positivism, post-positivism, realism, social constructivism, advocate/participatory and critical theory (Creswell 2007, p. 19; Perry 2013, p. 103). These paradigms are aligned to four overarching research approaches: positivist, realist, interpretivist and pragmatist. Figure 5A illustrates the relationship between these four overarching research approaches and their associated paradigms.

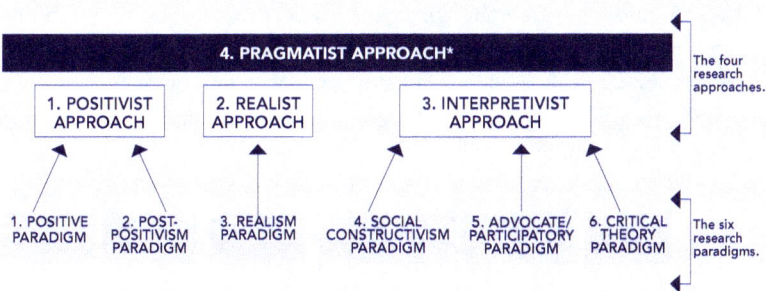

*The pragmatist approach is unique in that does not align to a particular approach rather it will use any approach necessary to understand the phenomena being studied.

Source: Developed for this research project.

Figure 5A – Relationship of research paradigms and approaches

The six principal research paradigms and four overarching approaches are set out in Table 5A, which summarises the characteristics of basic philosophy, ontology and epistemology, relationship of researcher with what is being researched, axiology (values), approach, reliability, validity, and sources in the literature.

Justification for Using an Interpretivist Approach in this Research Project

The interpretivist research approach was selected for this research project. This decision was based on an analysis of the characteristics of this research project, in accordance with the views of Collis and Hussey (2013, pp. 50), and the earlier work of Morgan and Smircich (1980), that the appropriate research approach can be determined by examining seven key characteristics of a study: sample size, location, use of theories and hypothesis, use of qualitative and quantitative data, reliability, validity and generalisability. The characteristics of this research project were compared with the characteristics of the positivist and interpretivist approaches as set out by Collis and Hussey (2013). The analysis of the seven characteristics is provided in Table 5B.

As illustrated in Table 5B, the research project was most closely aligned to the interpretivist research approach. This is because the research project involved a small sample over a period of time in a natural location and utilised a number of research methods to obtain perceptions. Furthermore, the primary importance of the research project was to ensure that interpretations made on different occasions by different observers were understood and findings were able to be generalised from one setting to another similar setting.

Table 5A – characteristics of the six research paradigms

	POSITIVIST		REALIST	PRAGMATIST	INTERPRETIVIST	
	POSITIVISM	POST-POSITIVISM	REALISM	SOCIAL CONSTRUCTIVISM	ADVOCATE/ PARTICIPATORY	CRITICAL THEORY
Basic Philosophy	Research that aims to uncover apprehensible objective reality.	Research that aims to uncover apprehensible objective reality while addressing human influences.	Attempts to describe the real world, but recognises that the real world is imperfectly and probabilistically apprehensible' (Sobh & Perry 2006).	Provides understanding of the world in which people "live and work" (Creswell 2007, p. 20).	Action based research which aims to understand communities and bring about change that emancipates them.	Empowers people who have constraints placed upon them, such as race, class, and gender.
Ontology & Epistemology	Reality is pure, universal, observable, measurable, and exists regardless of the human mind.	Reality exists regardless of the human mind as with positivism, but recognises that research is influenced by understanding of the human mind.	Current understanding of reality is an approximation of multiple views based on what is currently known, but each observation moves closer to reality.	Reality is a social construct from multiple perspectives, and therefore multiple realities, which are based on each individual's knowledge, values, and interactions with each other.	Reality is constructed collaboratively between the research participants and researcher, through their knowledge, values, and interaction with each other.	Perceptions of the group being studied is the reality in which reality, and reality and knowledge are altered over time.
Relationship of researcher with what is being researched	Researcher and research object are independent of each other with research being viewed through a "one way mirror" (Sobh & Perry 2006).	Researcher and research object are independent of each other but acknowledges that researcher's background can influence research.	Researcher views research subject through an "open window" Perry (2013), but more independent than with interpretative research.	Researcher is embedded in the group being researched and recognises that their own background influences how they interpret the data.	Researcher works collaboratively with the research object and provides direction and a voice, while recognising their background can affect interpretation and direction of research.	"[The] researcher is a "transformative intellect" who changes the social world within which participants live" (Sobh & Perry 2006).

Table 5A – (Continued)

	POSITIVIST		REALIST	PRAGMATIST	INTERPRETIVIST	
	POSITIVISM	POST-POSITIVISM	REALISM	SOCIAL CONSTRUCTIVISM	ADVOCATE/ PARTICIPATORY	CRITICAL THEORY
Axiology (values)	Free from values	Understanding that values can influence knowledge and reality.	Values provide insight into perceptions.	Values influence knowledge and reality that form the social construct.	Understanding that values influence knowledge and reality.	Understanding that values influence knowledge and reality.
Approach	"Mostly concerns with a testing of theory. Thus, mainly quantitative methods such as: survey, experiments, and verification of hypothesis" (Sobh & Perry 2006, p. 1195)	Usually quantitative.	"Mainly qualitative methods such as case studies and convergent interviews" (Sobh & Perry 2006, p. 1195).	"In-depth unstructured interviews, participant observation, action research, and grounded theory research" (Sobh & Perry 2006, p. 1195).	Usually Action Research.	"Action Research and participant observation" (Sobh & Perry 2006, p. 1195).
Reliability	"Replicability: research results can be reproduced" (Weber 2004, p. 4).		Replication can either be: "similar results for predictable reasons" or "contrary results for predictable reasons" (Sobh & Perry 2006, p. 1203).	"Interpretive awareness: researchers recognize and address implications of their subjectivity" (Weber 2004, p. 4).		

Table 5A – (Continued)

	POSITIVIST		REALIST	PRAGMATIST		INTERPRETIVIST	
	POSITIVISM	POST-POSITIVISM	REALISM	SOCIAL CONSTRUCTIVISM	ADVOCATE/ PARTICIPATORY		CRITICAL THEORY
Validity	"Certainty: data truly measures reality" Weber (2004, p. 4).		Predictable: data is an approximation of reality.		"Defensible knowledge claims" (Weber 2004, p. 4).		
Sources	Creswell (2007, p. 20), Marsden and Littler (1996, p. 648), Perry (2013, p. 103), Sobh and Perry (2006, p. 1195), Taneja et al. (2011, p. 349), Wahyuni (2012, p. 70), Weber (2004, p. 4)	Creswell (2007, p. 20), Henderson (2011), Wahyuni (2012, p. 70), Weber (2004, p. 4)	Maxwell (2012, pp. 3-13), Perry (2013, p. 106), Sobh and Perry (2006, p. 1195)	Creswell (2007, p. 20), Marsden and Littler (1996, p. 648), Perry (2013, p. 105), Sobh and Perry (2006, p. 1195)	Burns et al. (2014), Creswell (2007, p. 21), Ozanne and Saatcioglu (2008), Weber (2004, p. 4)		Creswell (2007, p. 27), Sobh and Perry (2006, p. 1195)

Source: Holyoake (2016, pp. 47–76).

Table 5B – Rationalisation of the research project's characteristics to determine the research approach

CHARACTERISTIC	POSITIVIST APPROACH	INTERPRETIVIST APPROACH	THIS RESEARCH PROJECT	RESEARCH APPROACH ALIGNMENT FOR RESEARCH PROJECT
Sample Size	Large samples	Small samples	• Small sample • Two cohorts with a maximum of 10 participants per cohort	Interpretivist
Location	Artificial location	Natural Location	Natural Location - Monash Health (a health service in Victoria)	Interpretivist
Theories & Hypothesis	Focused on hypothesis testing	Focused on development of theories	• Focused on development of theories. • This research project seeks to: 1) Explore the development and implementation of an action research-oriented Telemonitoring system to enable the home-based monitoring of diabetes patients in a Victorian Health Services Network. 2) Contribute to the literature of health care management globally of an action research-oriented Telemonitoring system for the home-based monitoring of diabetes patients in a Victorian Health Services Network. 3) Contribute to the policy and practice of health care management in Victoria, specifically an action research-oriented Telemonitoring system for the home-based monitoring of diabetes patients.	Interpretivist
Use of Quantitative and Qualitative Data	Data produced is precise, objective and quantitative	Data produced is "rich", subjective and qualitative	The data to be collected by the research will be "rich", subjective and qualitative derived from techniques such as participant observation, reflective practice, questionnaires, and focus groups in the form of Action Research group meetings. This will be supplemented by quantitative data analysis techniques such as triangulation to ensure data integrity as proposed by Gable (1994), Kaplan and Duchon (1988), Mingers (2001), Ragin (1987), Lee (1991), Myers and Avison (2002).	Combined: Interpretivist approach supplemented with quantitative data to ensure data integrity

Table 5B – (Continued)

CHARACTERISTIC	POSITIVIST APPROACH	INTERPRETIVIST APPROACH	THIS RESEARCH PROJECT	RESEARCH APPROACH ALIGNMENT FOR RESEARCH PROJECT
Reliability	Results have high reliability	Results have low reliability	• Reliability is of lower importance, with focus being the establishment of protocols that ensure the authenticity and dependability of the findings (Lincoln 1985). • Primary importance of the research is to ensure that interpretations made on different occasions by different observers are understood.	Interpretivist
Validity	Results have low validity	Results have high validity	High validity as the research design of the research project incorporates a number of methods to ensure that the measures taken by the researcher actually measure what they are meant to measure (Long and Johnson, 2000).	Interpretivist
Generalizability	Results able to be generalised from the sample to population	Findings able to be generalised from one setting to another similar setting	Findings will be able to be generalised from one setting to another similar setting. The research will utilise the approach outlined by Gummesson (2000) and Normann (1970), who argue that using an interpretivist approach with a small sample size will make it possible to generalise results if the research has captured the interactions and characteristics of the phenomena being examined.	Interpretivist

Source: Adapted from Collis and Hussey (2013, pp. 50).

Justification for Using the Advocate/Participatory Research Paradigm and the Action Research Method

Having identified that the interpretivist research approach is to be adopted, it is now appropriate to examine its associated research paradigms and determine which one will be used for the research project and why. As identified in Table 5A, within the interpretivist approach there are a number of research paradigms, including Social Constructivism, Advocate/Participatory and Critical Theory. Easterby-Smith (2012) suggests an approach to ensure the selection of the most appropriate research paradigm and associated research method for a specific study. This approach is based on the researcher having a full understanding of the underlying paradigm of the research and the relationship between theory and data collection. This deep understanding benefits the researcher in that it:

- Assists in the analysis of the data obtained to answer the main research question.
- Clarifies what data is required and how this data will be obtained.
- Assists the researcher in determining the specific methods to use.
- Aids the researcher in formation of wider research strategy or the adoption of an established methodology.

Based on the approach suggested by Easterby-Smith (2012) and others (Creswell 2007; Perry 2013; Henderson 2011; Wahyuni 2012), an analysis of the characteristics of the research project was undertaken in order to identify the research paradigm to be utilised.

In Table 5C, the three research paradigms within the interpretivist approach – Social Constructivism, Advocate/Participatory and Critical Theory – are examined. It reviews each of the seven characteristic (basic philosophy, ontology/epistemology, relationship of researcher with what is being researched, axiology, approach, reliability and validity) in the context of the research project to determine which paradigm is most closely aligned to the research project. This guides the choice of an Advocate/Participatory research paradigm for the current research project.

Table 5C – Analysis of the research project's characteristics to determine the research paradigm within the interpretivist approach

	INTERPRETIVIST				
	SOCIAL CONSTRUCTIVISM	ADVOCATE/ PARTICIPATORY	CRITICAL THEORY	THIS RESEARCH PROJECT	RESEARCH PARADIGM ALIGNMENT FOR RESEARCH PROJECT: PARTICIPATORY
Basic Philosophy	Provides understanding of the world in which people "live and work" (Creswell 2007, p.20).	Action based research which aims to understand communities and bring about change that emancipates them.	Empowers people who have constraints placed upon them such as race, class, and gender.	Researcher aims to understand the barriers to adoption and bring about change through the planning and implementation of a Telemonitoring system.	Advocate / Participatory
Ontology & Epistemology	Reality is a social construct form multiple perspectives, and therefore multiple realities, which are based on each individual's knowledge, values, and interaction with each other.	Reality is constructed collaboratively between the researcher participants and researcher, through their knowledge, values, and interaction with each other.	Reality is shaped by social values established over time. Researcher is transformative and changes the social world which participants inhabit.	The research project is based on collaboration between participants, the researcher, and clinical staff through interaction.	Advocate / Participatory
Relationship of researcher with what is being researched	Researcher is embedded in the group being researched and recognises that their own background influences how they interpret the data.	Researcher works collaboratively with the research object and provides direction and a voice, while recognising their background can affect interpretation and direction of research.	"[The] researcher is a "transformative intellect" who changes the social world within which participants live" (Sobh & Perry 2006).	The research project is based on the researcher working collaboratively, and providing guidance with awareness rather than acting as "transformative intellect." (Sobh & Perry 2006).	Advocate / Participatory

Table 5C – (Continued)

	SOCIAL CONSTRUCTIVISM	ADVOCATE/ PARTICIPATORY	CRITICAL THEORY	THIS RESEARCH PROJECT	RESEARCH PARADIGM ALIGNMENT FOR RESEARCH PROJECT/ PARTICIPATORY
		INTERPRETIVIST			
Axiology (values)	Values influence knowledge and reality that form the social construct.	Understanding that values influence knowledge and reality.	Understanding that values influence knowledge and reality.	The research project was based on the understanding that values influence knowledge and reality.	Advocate / Participatory or Critical Theory
Approach	"In-depth unstructured interviews, participant observation, action research, and grounded theory research" (Sobh & Perry 2005, p. 1195).	Usually Action Research.	"Action Research and participant observation" (Sobh & Perry 2005, p. 1195).	The research project approach most closely matched those of Action Research. See Table 5.6.	Advocate / Participatory
Reliability	"Interpretive awareness: researchers recognize and address implications of their subjectivity" (Weber 2004, p.4).			The research project recognises the implications of subjectivity and will implement techniques to minimise such as triangulation, validation, control groups, and independent review.	Advocate / Participatory
Validity	"Defensible knowledge claims" (Weber 2004, p .4).			The research aims to develop defensible knowledge in the area of Telemonitoring.	Advocate / Participatory

Source: Adapted from Holyoake (2016, pp. 74–76)

APPENDIX 5B: GENERAL ACTION RESEARCH CHARACTERISTICS

	CHARACTERISTIC Featured in the current review	CHARACTERISTIC Featured in Abraham's 1993 Study	SUMMARY DESCRIPTION of the characteristics featured in this book	DIFFERENCE BETWEEN THIS BOOK AND ABRAHAM'S 1993 STUDY
1	Problem Focus	Problem Focus	The action research method is problem-focussed in the context of real life situations. The solving of such problems in a research sense contributes to professional practice and the development of social science knowledge.	In this review the importance of problem focus contributing to personal as well as social reconstruction is an extension of the previous perspective.
2	Action Orientation	Action Orientation	The diagnosis of a problem and the development of a plan to solve the problem can both be considered to be evidence of the action-oriented nature of action research, particularly if there is action to implement the plan. This brings an action element to the solving of an immediate problem of the organisation which has strategic change implications for the said organisation.	The development of a plan as a definite action step, is more clearly identified in the current study.

CHARACTERISTIC Featured in the current review	CHARACTERISTIC Featured in Abraham's 1993 Study	SUMMARY DESCRIPTION of the characteristics featured in this book	DIFFERENCE BETWEEN THIS BOOK AND ABRAHAM'S 1993 STUDY
3 Cyclical and Reflective Process	Cyclical Process	The Action Research method involves cycles of planning, action, observation, and reflection (evaluation). Thus, the cycles of the Action Research method allow the group members to develop a plan, to act, to observe and to reflect on this plan, based on the needs of the group members and the requirements of the organisation and situation. A record of the processes of each cycle enables its strengths and weaknesses to be reviewed so that modifications and strategies can be developed for future cycles.	The view of the cyclical nature of Action Research which involves integral reflective aspects throughout the whole process, is an extension of the previous action research cycle formulation, where reflection was only identified in one stage, rather than throughout the whole process.

#	CHARACTERISTIC Featured in the current review	CHARACTERISTIC Featured in Abraham's 1993 Study	SUMMARY DESCRIPTION of the characteristics featured in this book	DIFFERENCE BETWEEN THIS BOOK AND ABRAHAM'S 1993 STUDY
4	Collaboration	Collaboration	Collaboration is a fundamental ingredient of the Action Research method, because, without a team effort to solve problems in an environment of participation, Action Research cannot exist. Collaboration of group problems using the Action Research method can be viewed as a continuum from total dependence on the facilitator, who acts as a leader directing the group problem-solving process, through to the total management of the problem by the group members with the facilitator acting as a resource person. The position of the facilitator and the group on this continuum depends on the situation and the needs of the group.	In considering collaboration in Action Research its value has generally been affirmed since 1993, but action research is now thought to also include first-person Action Research with minimal collaboration, and the importance of authentic and total involvement of all participants is more strongly emphasised in collaborative Action Research.

CHARACTERISTIC Featured in the current review	CHARACTERISTIC Featured in Abraham's 1993 Study	SUMMARY DESCRIPTION of the characteristics featured in this book	DIFFERENCE BETWEEN THIS BOOK AND ABRAHAM'S 1993 STUDY
5 Ethical Practice	Ethical	Community interests, improvements in the lives of the group members, justice, rationality, democracy and equality are some of the themes of 'ethical' behaviour. The ethical basis of Action Research is an important characteristic to consider, because the Action Research method involves, to a large extent, groups of people with limited power who are open to exploitation. It requires the researcher to concede their personal needs so that the needs of the group are given the highest priority.	The change in the characteristic term Ethical to Ethical Practice, emphasises the need to include ethics as a practice and not just viewed from a notional perspective.
6 Group Facilitation	Group Dynamics	The success of the Action Research method will depend on how well the group can operate as an effective team. An understanding of group dynamics, therefore, seems essential in facilitating this process and dealing with problems that arise during the Action Research cycles.	The change in the characteristic term Group Dynamics to Group Facilitation, acknowledges that the success of the AR Group relies on more than just a group of people working co-operatively, and must include professional and effective facilitation of the group dynamic process.

	CHARACTERISTIC Featured in the current review	CHARACTERISTIC Featured in Abraham's 1993 Study	SUMMARY DESCRIPTION of the characteristics featured in this book	DIFFERENCE BETWEEN THIS BOOK AND ABRAHAM'S 1993 STUDY
7	Creative Thinking	Not featured in Abraham's 1993 study.	The AR Group members will experience creative thinking as they go through stages of saturation, deliberation, incubation, and illumination where the group members look for different options and seek the opinions of different relevant parties to accommodate and validate those options.	Creative Thinking is a new and important characteristic identified and defined by Abraham (2015), which is very important for Action Research in the context of WAL and change.
8	Learning and Re-education	Re-educative	Action Research can be viewed as re-educative since it contributes to a change in the knowledge base of the organisation, a change in the skills, attitudes and knowledge of the individual group members, and a change in the skills and knowledge of the researcher. It also makes a contribution to several of the social sciences.	The change in the characteristic term Re-educative to Learning and Re-education, emphasises the importance of learning as a valuable outcome of Action Research.

APPENDIX 5C: DETAILS OF RESEARCH SITE

About us

- Monash Health is Victoria's leading integrated health service serving the south eastern suburbs of Melbourne, Victoria, Australia.

- We integrate uniquely in one organisation, primary, secondary and tertiary health services, as well as university affiliated international research and teaching facilities.

- We offer our community quality patient health care across the entire lifespan from pre-birth to palliative care, for all groups and stages of life.

- Extensive range of programs and disciplines are provided from prevention to early intervention and primary care; through to highly complex acute, aged residential and mental health services.

- We play wider specialist referral roles for many specialities serving greater Melbourne, Victoria and interstate.

- We are a member of the Monash Health Translation Precinct with Monash University and the Hudson Institute of Medical Research. We are also in partnership with other leading educational institutions such as Deakin and LaTrobe Universities.

- We are recognised by the World Health Organisation as a registered health promotion body.

- Our core community of more than one million people depends on us for all aspects of its public healthcare, with our services available to more than 1.5 million people.

- More than 16,000 staff work at more than 40 sites, admitting more than 260,000 hospital patients, handling more than 220,000 emergency presentations and delivering more than 10,000 babies.

Our organisation

Our staff — More than **16,000 employees**

Our investment — **$1.8 billion** spent delivering our health services

Our research — More than **900** research projects involving patients, either in clinical drug or device trials.

Our sites — More than **40 sites** including:

- **Six public hospitals**

    Monash Medical Centre (640 beds)
    Moorabbin Hospital (147 beds)
    Dandenong Hospital (573 beds)
    Casey Hospital (273 beds)
    Kingston Centre (213 beds)
    Cranbourne Centre (same-day acute and sub-acute)

- **One private hospital**

    Jessie McPherson Private Hospital (105 beds)

- **11 major community health sites**

    Cranbourne Centre, Mundaring Drive, Cockatoo, Doveton, Kingston, Berwick, Clayton, Pakenham, Parkdale, Springvale, and Dandenong

- **Hospital in The Home** (140 bed virtual acute ward)

- **Six aged care facilities** (249 beds)

    Chestnut Gardens, Yarraman, Mooraleigh, Eastwood, Allambee and Kingston Centre

- **Eight mental health facilities**

    Inpatient, residential, community care and drug and alcohol units.

Our care

Total episodes of care	**3.6 million** episodes of care provided across our services to the community
Hospital admissions	**260,786** people admitted to our hospitals
Emergency	**220,913** people came to our three emergency departments for treatment
Ambulance arrivals	**54,495** ambulance arrivals handled by our emergency departments
Surgical operations	**48,480** elective and emergency operations performed
Outpatient services	**1.2 million** people received care as outpatients at 375 clinics
Births	**10,162** babies delivered
Children	**40,206** children under age 19 were admitted to our Monash Children's Hospital wards and neonatal units
Mental health	**224,460** client contacts

Our care locations

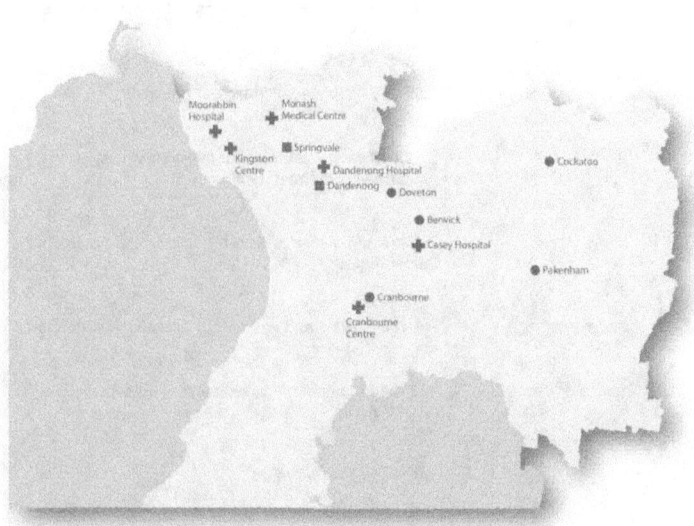

Monash Medical Centre

Monash Medical Centre is a 640-bed teaching and research hospital providing a comprehensive range of specialist surgical, medical, allied health and mental health services to our community. This tertiary site is a designated national provider of renal and pancreatic transplants, and state-wide provider of thalassemia, and children's cancer services. It is also the base for MonashHeart, a centre-of-excellence in cardiac assessment, treatment and research; and Monash Children's Hospital, the third largest provider of paediatric services in Australia. Uniquely offering maternity and newborn services including a Neonatal Intensive Care Unit and Special Care Unit integrated on one site, Monash Medical Centre provides one of Victoria's largest women's health services. It is also renowned for men's health services and ambulatory models of care. McCulloch House, located onsite, is a 16-bed facility providing palliative care for people within our catchment area with advanced progressive disease.

Moorabbin Hospital

Moorabbin Hospital is a 147-bed hospital incorporating Monash Cancer Centre, one of Victoria's leading cancer treatment centres, and operating in partnership with Peter MacCallum Cancer Centre. The hospital also offers elective surgery, short-stay care and dialysis. Home to Victoria's first Patient Simulation Centre, the hospital plays a major role in the education and training of undergraduate and postgraduate medical students, nurses and allied health professionals. The hospital hosts the Southern Melbourne Integrated Cancer Services and is a centre for research, and, in particular, a major contributor to cancer-related research.

Dandenong Hospital

Dandenong Hospital is a 573-bed acute hospital providing a wide range of health services to the people living and working in Dandenong and its surrounding areas. The hospital provides a number of general and specialist services. These services include general medical and surgical, an intensive care unit, MonashHeart cardiac care centre, rehabilitation and aged care services, pathology, radiology, maternity unit, special care nursery, children's services, outpatients, day chemotherapy, home haemodialysis, mental health services and allied health services. Dandenong Hospital also provides specialist services including orthopaedic, plastics, vascular, facio-maxillary, gynaecology, respiratory and infectious diseases.

Casey Hospital

Casey Hospital is a 273-bed hospital serving one of the fastest growing areas in Melbourne's south-east. Services include an emergency department, general medical, mental health, rehabilitation, surgical and ambulatory care services, maternity and a special care nursery. The hospital is a provider of paediatric services for Monash Children's Hospital and gives access to the leading cardiac services of MonashHeart.

Cranbourne Centre

Cranbourne Centre provides a range of same-day acute and sub-acute services including surgery, renal dialysis, specialist consulting services, regional ophthalmology services and mental health services. It also provides the local community with access to community health services and a community rehabilitation centre.

Kingston Centre

Kingston Centre is a 213-bed sub-acute facility specialising in high-quality rehabilitation, functional restoration, transitional care and aged mental health. The highly regarded rehabilitation program focuses on restoring function after illness or injury with the full range of allied health services provided to adults of all ages. The centre provides specialist services for older people including aged care assessment, cognitive dementia and memory services. It also offers a falls and balance clinic, pain clinic, clinical gait analysis and continence service. It is at the forefront of research into movement and gait disorders, aged mental health and geriatric medicine.

Our services

Aged residential care

Aged residential care is provided at: Allambee Nursing Home; AG Eastwood Hostel; the Kingston Centre (Cheltenham); Chestnut Gardens Aged Care (Doveton); Yarraman Nursing Home (Noble Park); and Mooraleigh Hostel (East Bentleigh), collectively providing 249 aged and aged mental health residential beds.

Mental health services

Mental health services are provided through hospital and community-based facilities. Our services for children, youth and adults experiencing mental health issues include: the Monash Health Drug and Alcohol Service; a telephone psychiatric triage service; community and inpatient perinatal, child and youth services; crisis assessment and treatment teams and enhanced crisis assessment and treatment teams; consultation liaison psychiatry; psychological medicine; mental health Hospital in the Home (HITH), community care teams; mobile support and treatment services; acute inpatient care; secure extended care services; perinatal infant service including an inpatient unit; eating disorders services; gender dysphoria services, prevention and recovery care services; and community residential and rehabilitation services.

Community rehabilitation services

Community rehabilitation services are provided from centres at Kingston, Clayton, Doveton, Springvale, Dandenong, Cranbourne and Pakenham and in clients' homes through the Rehabilitation in the Home services.

Hospital in the Home

Hospital in the Home operates a '140-bed' virtual acute ward from patients' homes or residential care facilities. In-home care is provided by medical and nurse practitioners to people who require acute care, but can safely receive it in their home environment.

Community services

Community services are provided across the catchment. Our staff are located across 11 major sites (Cranbourne Centre and Mundaring Drive, Cockatoo, Doveton, Kingston, Berwick, Clayton, Pakenham, Parkdale, Springvale, and Thomas Street, Dandenong). A range of services are provided at each site by multi-disciplinary teams of allied health workers including physiotherapists, podiatrists, occupational therapists, dieticians, counsellors, speech pathologists, nurses, health promotion practitioners, and exercise physiologists. Co-located services include dialysis, dental, pregnancy care clinics, and adult mental health. We also facilitate group programs to support respite, social inclusion and improved health.

Some of our services are targeted at specific populations in our community and are led by experienced staff in these fields. This includes aged care, Aboriginal health, refugee health, youth and other vulnerable groups. Self-management is central to our care - we aim to empower and prepare clients to manage their health and healthcare across all levels of the care continuum. Community Support Options provide personalised services to assist people who are aged or have a disability to remain in their own homes. Respite services are also provided to support carers.

APPENDIX 5D: PARTICIPANT INFORMATION SHEET

Information for Patients and Families

MonashHealth

Telemonitoring Pilot Study: the use of home based telemonitoring to improve glycaemic control for patients with diabetes mellitus

MONASH University
Medicine, Nursing and Health Sciences

What will happen to information about me?

The information obtained is the same as that obtained in standard care and is treated in the same way. It becomes part of your scanned medical record.

All electronic data will be kept secure during the trial and securely destroyed at its conclusion.

At the end of all data collection participants will be provided with results of the project. It is anticipated that this will be mid 2016.

Can I access research information kept about me?

In accordance with relevant Australian and/or Victorian privacy and other relevant laws, you have the right to access the information collected and stored by the researchers about you. Please contact one of the researchers named at the end of this document if you would like to access your information.

Further, in accordance with regulatory guidelines, the information collected in this research project will be kept indefinitely. You must be aware that the information may become de-identified at some point and access to information about you after this point will not be possible.

Is this research project approved?

The ethical aspects of this research project have been approved by the Human Research Ethics Committee of Monash Health.

This project will be carried out according to the National Statement on Ethical Conduct in Human Research (2007) produced by the National Health and Medical Research Council of Australia. This statement has been developed to protect the interests of people who agree to participate in human research studies.

Who can I contact?

If you require any further information concerning this project you can contact:

Paul Jurman
Principal Investigator
Phone: 03 9594 7745

Or

Lorraine Marom
Nurse Practitioner and Clinical Lead
Phone: 03 9554 8117

If you have any complaints about any aspect of the project, the way it is being conducted or any questions about being a research participant in general, then you may contact Deborah Dell, Manager Human Research Ethics Committee, on 9594 4611.

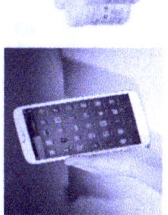

Telemonitoring Pilot Study

Full Project Title: Pilot of the use of home based telemonitoring to improve glycaemic control for patients with diabetes mellitus

Principal Investigator: Paul Jurman
Associate Investigator: Professor Helena Teede

Introduction

We are developing and piloting the use of home based telemonitoring to improve blood glucose levels for people with Diabetes Mellitus.

This explanatory statement is intended for you the patient, or your next of kin, and explains what is involved to help make a decision as to whether or not to take part in the study. We will be collecting data on blood glucose levels for patients who have Type 2 diabetes and are undergoing insulin therapy at Dandenong Diabetes Outpatient Unit.

This Participant Explanatory Statement tells you or your next of kin about the research project. It explains what is involved to help you decide if you want to take part in the study.

Please read this information carefully. Ask questions about anything that you don't understand or want to know more about. Before deciding whether or not to take part, you might want to talk about it with a relative, a friend or your local health worker.

What is the purpose of this research project?

The purpose of the study is to investigate:

1) The design and implementation of a Telemonitoring system for use by patients with diabetes in a Victorian Health Services Network using action research.

2) The results of the research will be used by the Study Investigator to investigate the use of Telemonitoring to better manage diabetes.

We will collect information on:

- Number of insulin adjustments made in a six week period;
- Number of contacts with health professional in stabilisation period;
- Time spent by health professional and patient with insulin stabilisation.

All patient information will be de-identified

What does participation in this research project involve?

The telemonitoring system utilises a smart phone application and does not require expensive hard wired systems to be installed. Monitoring occurs via the application which transmits information from Wi-Fi enabled monitoring devices to a clinician and patient website. Telstra will provide telemonitoring devices free of charge and these devices will be returned at the end of the study.

The telemonitoring system trial is being piloted at Dandenong Hospital diabetes outpatient clinic at Monash Health in Victoria. There will be 20 participants in total. 10 participants will be assigned to standard care insulin titration and 10 participants will be assigned to telemonitoring application.

We will then follow your progress over the next three months to assess your glycaemic control and HbA1c.

All information is standard care except for the time health professionals and patients spend with insulin stabilisation.

A personalised care plan will be developed in consultation with you by the Diabetes Clinical Nurse Consultant/ Nurse Practitioner and include:

1) Frequency of daily blood glucose monitoring.
2) Day/ time for communicating with clinician.
3) What to do if you need to speak with a clinician out of hours. You must be willing to communicate at least 1-2 times weekly to discuss insulin adjustment based on your blood glucose results over the previous several days.

What are the possible benefits?

You will receive no payment from contributing to this research study. You may receive a parking voucher for the initial set up consultation.

Planned benefits are:

1) Improved glycaemic control with reduction in adverse events and related complications.
2) Improved quality of care.

What are the possible risks?

You are already to be commenced on insulin in consultation with your Doctor. This project focuses on how to best assist you to stabilise your blood glucose levels and adjust your insulin doses. As such the risks relate to equipment failure, communication failure or failure in monitoring blood glucose levels.

Do I have to take part in this research project?

You do not have to take part in this research project. Participation in any research project is voluntary. Your decision whether to take part or not, or to take part and then withdraw, will not affect your relationship with Monash Health.

This is an opt-out research study. That means that your details will automatically be included in the study unless you let us know that you don't want to participate. You can opt out by contacting one of the research team before you withdraw.

If you do not contact us within two weeks, we will assume that you are happy for us to collect this information.

INDEX

A

Abraham, Selva, vii, viii, x, xiii, 1, 25, 55, 129, 149, 195, 207, 243, 244
action, meaning of, 4
action leadership, 8, 11–12, 18–22, 55
Action Learning (AL), 3, 25, 27, 33, 55, 243
   vs Action Research (AR), 146–147
   characteristics, 144–146
   formula, 36–37, 151
Action Research and Action Learning and Reflective Practice (ALRP), 42
Action Research (AR), 2, 5, 25, 31–32, 33, 55, 243
   vs Action Learning (AL), 146–147
   characteristics, 34–36, 184–187, 201–202, 206–207
   formula, 36–37, 151
   literature review, 131–144
Action Research Method and Action Learning process (ARAL), 5, 8, 9, 12, 21, 22, 27, 29, 31–32, 36, 37, 55, 129, 131, 144, 149, 151, 164, 169, 187
   current applications, 153
   formula, 37, 151
   in relation to WAL phases, 29
advocate/participatory, 320–322, 331–333
AR cycles, 11, 27, 32, 39, 42–44, 48, 50–52, 150, 154, 181, 210
   evaluation, 49
   phases in, 7, 44
   planning phase, 44–45
   validation, 49
AR group, 6–7, 49, 91, 159, 162–163, 164–166, 164–169
   meetings, 44–45, 50–52, 63, 154, 161, 174, 212, 223, 225, 231, 235, 236
   selection of, 101–106
artificial intelligence, 248–249
Australian Institute of Business (AIB), 4, 21

B

Barnes, Alan, xvi, xvii, 243
brainstorming, 122, 123
   definition, 301

C

case study. *see also* Kuju CDEP; Monash Health; Well Workover company (WWC)

definition, 301
methodology, 3
chain of evidence, 101, 113, 114, 161, 177, 181, 188, 192, 201, 211–213, 222, 231–232, 246, 295, 297, 299
   definition, 301
change leader, x, 25, 27, 33, 38, 39, 41–42, 44, 44–45, 50–51
cluster analysis, 121, 177–178, 181, 188
   definition, 301
constructivism, 313–314, 320–322, 329, 331–333, 337–338
content analysis, 56, 113, 114, 192, 211–213, 222, 230–231
control groups, 192, 193, 199, 210, 222, 226, 233, 235, 237–240, 246
Covid pandemic, 248
creative thinking and learning process, 25, 35, 38, 142, 185, 201, 204, 244
   stages of, 40–41
critical theory, 4, 17–18, 19, 313, 320–322, 331–333

D

data analysis, 17, 56, 83, 96, 112, 113–114, 121, 128, 154, 175, 176–177, 188, 192, 211–213, 230, 245
data collection and validation, 120–122, 128, 154, 170–171, 192, 222, 245
discussion, 37, 63, 96, 99, 114, 122, 124, 157, 158, 164, 167, 171, 172–173, 176, 187, 192, 194, 205, 209, 223, 234–236, 240, 246, 299, 320, 324
   definition, 302
document analysis, 113, 128, 177, 178, 181, 188, 302
document analysis, definition, 302
document collection, definition, 302
document review, 128, 170, 171, 174, 188, 315

E

emancipatory approach, 2, 36, 76–77, 115, 117–118, 120, 122, 141–142, 186, 201, 205, 243, 249
   definition, 302
ethical issues, 35, 108–112, 175, 181–183, 187, 188, 192, 204, 210, 216, 218–219, 239, 241, 249
evaluation, definition, 303
experiential learning theory, 4, 15, 19

F

field notes, 128, 171, 174–175, 188, 222, 320, 323
focus groups, 128, 171, 172–173, 177, 188, 222, 319
   definition, 303

G

Global Centre for Work-Applied Learning (GCWAL), 4, 21
Global University for Lifelong Learning (GULL)., 21
grounded theory, 4, 16–17, 19

I

interpretivism, 316–318, 320–322, 328, 331–333
  definition, 304
interviews, 171–172, 188, 215, 222, 319
  definition, 304

J

Jurman, Paul, xv, xvii, 189, 246, 327

K

knowing and learning theories
  critical theory, 17–18
  critical theory and critical realism, 19
  experiential learning theory, 15, 19
  grounded theory, 16–17, 19
  phenomenology, 14–15, 19
  strengths-based theory, 15–16, 19
Kuju CDEP
  definition of terms, 92–93
  effectiveness, 246–247
  ethical issues, 110
  justification of research site, 97–98
  limitations, 88–90
  literature review process, 75
  organisational thematic concern, 64–67
  purpose and research questions, 78–79
  research methods, 113–114
  research problem, 64–65
  selection of AR group, 102–103
  significance of project, 85
  unit of analysis, 84
  WAL program for, 30–31

L

learning, individual, 27, 28
learning, team, 27, 28
lifelong learning, 8, 10–11, 243
literature review, 56, 58, 59, 61–62, 73–75, 128–131, 192, 193, 195–199

M

meetings, 115, 122, 154, 174, 181, 214–215

definition, 305
methodology, 3, 112, 114, 122, 125, 133, 187, 241, 245, 246, 313, 322, 327, 336
  definition, 305
mixed methods research,
  definition, 305
Mohammed, Lisa, xv, xvii, 215, 245, 313
Monash Health
  Action Research (AR), 203–205
  AR cycles, 208–209
  AR design, 210–242
  chain of evidence, 231–232
  conceptual stage, 193
  content analysis, 231
  control groups, 237–238, 240–241
  ethical issues, 111–112, 218–219
  justification of research site, 100–101, 216–217
  limitations, 91
  literature review, 73–75, 192, 193, 195–199
  Major Cycle 1, 210, 211, 214
  Major Cycle 2, 210, 212, 215
  Major Cycle 3, 210, 213, 215
  organisational thematic concern, 72
  peer review, 235–236
  purpose and research questions, 81–83, 189–191
  quantitative data, 225–226
  questionnaires, 228–230
  reflective practice, 224–225
  research design, 192–193
  research methods, 113–114
  research problem, 70–72
  research protocol, 241–242
  researcher's interest, 194–195
  selection of AR group, 106–107
  significance of project, 87
  statistical calculations, 227–228
  summary, 246
  telemonitoring programme, 214
  triangulation, 236
  unit of analysis, 84, 216–217
  validity and reliability, 232–242

N

naturalistic setting, 35, 118, 142, 185, 201, 205, 223, 239, 298, 319, 396
  definition, 306

O

observation, 14, 90, 119, 138, 173–174, 188, 315, 319, 322, 331
observation and reflection, 7, 11, 22, 44, 48, 79, 120, 154, 161, 184, 206, 308
open, axial, selective coding, 115, 296, 298, 300
  definition, 306
organisational change, 2, 5, 27, 30, 42, 55, 155, 164, 243, 246, 249, 250
organisational learning, 6, 8, 10, 21, 27–32, 28, 36, 50, 146, 150–151

P

paradigm, definition, 306
participant observation, 56, 113, 115–116, 120, 128, 158, 170, 171, 173–175, 192, 205, 212, 213, 222–223, 295, 297, 299, 310, 319, 321, 324, 332, 334, 338
   definition, 307
Participatory Action Learning and Action Research (PALAR), 6, 13
peer review, 233, 235–236, 246
personal diary, 15, 113, 115–116
   definition, 246
personal diary, definition, 307
persuasion, stages of, 40–41
phenomenology, 4, 14–15, 191–183
positivism, 313, 314–316, 320–322, 327–329, 331–333
   definition, 307
practitioner researcher, ix, xix–xx, 2–3, 3, 5, 12, 14–15, 18–21, 25, 53, 55, 57–58, 96, 117, 119, 121, 123–124, 182
pragmatic, 315
pragmatism, 146
   definition, 307
primary data source, definition, 308
programme advisor, 44

Q

qualitative research, 319–322
   definition, 308

quantitative research, 319–322
   definition, 308
questionnaire, 113, 115, 192, 209, 215, 222, 233, 235ß236, 246
   definition, 309

R

realism, 14, 17–18, 313, 320–322, 331–333
reflection, definition, 309
reflective practice, 3, 8, 9–10, 25, 27, 33, 55, 164, 187, 222, 223–225, 243, 246
literature review, 147–149
reflexive journals, 128, 175–176, 188
reflexivity, definition, 309
reliability. see validity and reliability
research methods, 112–124, 192, 295–300, 319, 322, 331
   brainstorming, 122, 123
   chain of evidence, 101, 113, 114, 161, 177, 181, 188, 192, 201, 211–213, 222, 231–232, 246, 295, 297, 299
   cluster analysis, 121, 177–178, 181, 188, 301
   content analysis, 56, 113, 114, 192, 211–213, 215, 222, 230-231
   control groups, 192, 193, 199, 210, 222, 226, 233, 235, 237 238, 238–240, 246
   data analysis, 17, 56, 83, 96, 112, 113–114, 121, 128, 154,

175, 176–177, 188, 192, 211-213, 230, 245
data collection and validation, 120–122, 128, 154, 170–171, 192, 222, 245
document analysis, 113, 128, 177, 178, 181, 188, 302
document review, 128, 170, 171, 174, 188, 315
emancipatory approach, 36, 76–77, 115, 117–118, 120, 122, 141–142, 186, 201, 205, 243, 249
field notes, 188, 222, 320, 323
focus groups, 128, 171, 172–173, 177, 188, 222, 319
interviews, 171–172, 188, 215, 222, 319
observation, 14, 90, 119, 138, 173–174, 188, 315
participant observation, 56, 113, 115–116, 128, 170, 171, 173, 174–175, 192, 212, 213, 222, 222–223, 295, 297, 299, 310, 319, 332, 334, 338
peer review, 233, 235–236, 246
quantitative vs qualitative, 319–322
questionnaire, 113, 115, 192, 209, 215, 222, 228–230, 246, 295, 297, 299, 320, 334
reflective practice, 3, 8, 9–10, 25, 27, 33, 55, 164, 187, 222, 223–225, 243, 246
reflexive journals, 128, 175–176, 188
statistical calculations, 227–228
triangulation, 56, 128, 179–180, 181, 188, 215, 222, 233, 235–236, 246
used in theses, 114–118, 295–300

research paradigms, 2, 7, 13, 136, 187, 189, 242, 249–250, 313–320, 322–323, 327, 329, 336–337
constructivism, 320–322, 331–333
critical theory, 4, 17–18, 19, 313, 320–322, 331–333
interpretivism, 314–318, 320–322, 331–333
participatory, 13, 16, 18, 55, 249, 250, 329
positivism, 314–318, 320–322, 331–333
realism, 14, 17–18, 320–322, 331–333

research philosophy, 313
research terms, definitions of, 301–311
researcher/participant observations, definition, 310

S

secondary data source, definition, 310
statistics, definition, 311
strengths-based theory, 4, 15–16, 19
survey, definition, 311

T

Taddeo, Carmel, xvii, 116, 117
theses and dissertations, 61, 247, 313, 327
   methods used, 114–118, 295–300
triangulation, 56, 128, 179–180, 181, 188, 215, 222, 233, 235–236, 246
   definition, 311

U

unit of analysis, 58, 59–62, 77, 83–84, 192, 210, 216–217

V

validation, definition, 311
validation committee, 44
   meetings, 188, 209, 222–223, 225, 231, 235
validity, 56, 88, 143–144, 171, 178, 179, 219, 234, 236, 333, 335, 338
validity and reliability, 121, 125, 180–181, 187, 192, 209, 216, 222, 230, 232–233, 245, 318, 322
   definition of terms, 232–233
   strategies, 234–235

W

WAL change process and practice, 42
   AR cycles, 42–44, 50–52
   flow chart, 50
   participants, 44
   template, 47
WAL paradigm, 13–14
WAL Research Plan, 55, 58
   action research method stage, 56, 96
   case studies, 64
   conceptual stage, 56
   definition of terms, 92
   ethical issues, 108–112
   justification of research site, 97–101, 154–157
   limitations, 88–91
   literature review process, 73–75
   organisational thematic concern, 63
   phases in conceptual stage, 59–62
   purpose and research questions, 76–83
   research methods, 112
   research problem, 63
   selection of AR group, 101–106
   significance of project, 84–87
   unit of analysis, 83–84
Well Workover company (WWC)
   AR design, 159–169
   conceptual stage, 128
   definition of terms, 93–94
   ethical issues, 110–111
   justification of research site, 99, 154–157

limitations, 90–91
literature review, 75, 128–131
Major Cycle 1, 164–166
Major Cycle 2, 166–169
organisational thematic concern, 69–70
purpose and research questions, 80–81, 125–127
qualitative research, 323–325
research design, 127–128
research methods, 113–114
research problem, 67–69
researcher's interest, 129
selection of AR group, 103–105
significance of project, 86
summary, 245
unit of analysis, 84

word formulae, 36, 36–37, 41, 145, 146, 151, 154
symbols used, 37, 39, 152

Work-Applied Learning (WAL), 5
body of case studies, 250
change process, 28
comparison with WBL, 27
conceptual framework, 2, 13, 20, 243–244
cyclical nature, 6, 38–41
definition, 8–9
designing research plan, 244–245
effectiveness across diverse settings, 246, 247–248
emancipatory approach, 249
as emerging concept, 21–22
as extension of WBL, 25–26
formula, 38–39
for future developments, 248–249
future directions, 250–251

key concepts, 8, 25
learning model, 244
use of artifical intelligence, 250

Work-Based Learning (WBL), 3, 25, 42
comparison with WAL, 27
evaluation, 48
features of, 26, 149–151
formula, 154
joint observation and reflection, 48
phases in, 46–47
symbols used, 152
validation, 48

Z

Zuber-Skerritt, Ortrun, x, xv, xvii, xx, 1, 243

www.ingramcontent.com/pod-product-compliance
Lightning Source LLC
Chambersburg PA
CBHW051348290426
44108CB00015B/1924